Voltaire's history of Charles XII, king of Sweden

Voltaire

(Translator: Winifred Todhunter)

Alpha Editions

This edition published in 2024

ISBN : 9789364735803

Design and Setting By
Alpha Editions
www.alphaedis.com
Email - info@alphaedis.com

As per information held with us this book is in Public Domain.
This book is a reproduction of an important historical work. Alpha Editions uses the best technology to reproduce historical work in the same manner it was first published to preserve its original nature. Any marks or number seen are left intentionally to preserve its true form.

Contents

PREFATORY NOTE..- 1 -
INTRODUCTION ....- 2 -
TRANSLATOR'S NOTE ....- 9 -
BOOK I ....- 11 -
BOOK II ....- 26 -
BOOK III ....- 54 -
BOOK IV ....- 77 -
BOOK V ....- 95 -
BOOK VI ....- 115 -
BOOK VII ....- 133 -
BOOK VIII ....- 149 -

PREFATORY NOTE

"*To Charles the Twelfth of Sweden I owe much of what has stood me in best stead all my life. It was nearly thirty years ago, when but a boy, that I bought his Life for a penny in the New Cut. I took it home and devoured it. It made a great impression on me. Not his wars, but the Spartan heroism of his character. He inspired me with the idea of triumphing over physical weakness, weariness and pain. To inure his body to bear all manner of hardships indifferently, to bathe in ice, or face the torrid rays of the sun, to discipline his physical powers by gymnastics, to despise the niceties of food and drink, to make his body an instrument as of tempered steel, and at the same time to have that body absolutely at the disposition of the mind, that seemed to me conduct worthy of a hero. And so, boylike, I tried to imitate him, and succeeded at least so far as to be happily indifferent to the circumstances of my personal environment.*"

JOHN BURNS.

"Och än är det likt det slägte som bor

Bland Nordiska fjellar och dalar,

Och ännu på Gud och på Stålet det tror,

An fädernas kärnspråk det talar."

"And still as of old are the folk that abide

'Mid northerly mountain and valley;

In God and their weapons they ever confide,

To voice of their fathers they rally."

INTRODUCTION

THE "Life of Charles XII" that Mr. John Burns once bought for a penny in the New Cut—an incident in itself historical if one looks at it in the right way—was, he writes to say, an English version of Voltaire's book. The "Histoire de Charles XII, Roi de Suède," was first published at Rouen in 1731, first freely translated into English by Alexander Henderson in 1734, and soon afterwards reduced into a chap-book, which made the King a proverbial hero in English fairs and market-places. There have been other translations since Henderson's, and it is now retranslated by Miss Todhunter with a closer correspondence than his to Voltaire's original.

The book may claim a particular right to an English hearing, apart from the main interest of its subject. It was in England that the life of Charles XII was written by Voltaire, when he was on a visit of exigency there after the Rohan escapade and his second Bastille imprisonment. The effect of this stay in England was that of a determining event in his career. "Voltairism," writes Mr. John Morley, "may be said to have begun from the flight of its founder from Paris to London. This, to borrow a name from the most memorable instance of outward change marking inward revolution, was the decisive 'hegira,' from which the philosophy of destruction in a formal shape may be held seriously to date." We may supplement this passage from the criticism of a French critic of another school, who says, "England at this time was worked by a spirit of dogmatic irreligion which based itself on a false erudition, a bold criticism and an insidious metaphysic. It was the time of Woolston, of Toland, of Tindal, of Chubb, of Collins, of Bolingbroke. Until then, an *insouciant* disciple and imitator of the epicureans of the Temple and the *roués* of the Regency, Voltaire had only ventured on impiety by sallies; dogmas and mysteries had so far only inspired him with *bon mots*. In the school of the English philosophers he learnt to reason out his incredulity."

Voltaire had had time by this to mend his youth and find his intellectual stature. Born in 1694, he was now a man approaching thirty-three. He had written plays, for his love for the theatre, as it lasted late in him, began early; he had completed his epic, "la Henriade"; he had used his wit irresponsibly, and, thanks to it, had twice been in the Bastille. In England he learnt, if one may say so, to take his wit seriously, that is, to realize it as a decisive weapon in his inevitable revolt and warfare. Similarly he was to use some of his other faculties in their most adroit perfection. If in the "Henriade" the epic method had failed him, considered by the side of other poems as ambitious and as long, he was able to sit down on his return from his English exile and complete this rapid piece of biography, in effect a short prose epic, which shows us the narrative art used by a consummate master in that art.

More than this we need not claim for him. If we admit Carlyle's stigma of "persifleur" as applying to his first period, we need not go on to write him down now philosopher, by way of compensation, because he had studied for a brief period under certain notorious English philosophers. He was neither a persifleur nor a philosopher: he was a militant scribe and hyper-critic with a master bias, anti-religious or anti-Catholic, and an inimitable gift of expression. We see his gift in a very luminous special form in his "Charles XII," which luckily need offend no man's susceptibilities.

We do not know whether that extraordinarily long indicative nose of his was at this time as telling a sign of his character, backed by his keen twinkling black eyes, as it became later? The two best pen-portraits of Voltaire we have belong to a later day than 1728, when "Charles XII" was written. The first takes us to the year when his "Sémiramis" was produced, when he appears in a strange disguise among the casual nightly apparitions of the Café de Procope.

"M. de Voltaire, who always loved to correct his works, and perfect them, became desirous to learn, more specially and at first hand, what good or ill the public were saying of his Tragedy; and it appeared to him that he could nowhere learn it better than in the Café de Procope, which was also called the Antre (Cavern) de Procope, because it was very dark even in full day, and ill-lighted in the evenings; and because you often saw there a set of lank, sallow poets, who had somewhat the air of apparitions. In this café, which fronts the Comédie Française, had been held, for more than sixty years, the tribunal of those self-called Aristarchs, who fancied they could pass sentence without appeal, on plays, authors and actors. M. de Voltaire wished to compear there, but in disguise and altogether incognito. It was on coming out from the playhouse that the judges usually proceeded thither, to open what they called their great sessions. On the second night of 'Sémiramis' he borrowed a clergyman's clothes; dressed himself in cassock and long cloak; black stockings, girdle, bands, breviary itself; nothing was forgotten. He clapt on a large peruke, unpowdered, very ill combed, which covered more than the half of his cheeks, and left nothing to be seen but the end of a long nose. The peruke was surmounted by a large three-cornered hat, corners half bruised-in. In this equipment, then, the author of 'Sémiramis' proceeded on foot to the Café de Procope, where he squatted himself in a corner; and waiting for the end of the play, called for a *bavaroise*, a small roll of bread, and the Gazette. It was not long till those familiars of the Parterre and tenants of the café stept in. They instantly began discussing the new Tragedy. Its partisans and its adversaries pleaded their cause with warmth; each giving his reasons. Impartial persons also spoke their sentiment; and repeated some fine verses of the piece. During all this time, M. de Voltaire, with spectacles on nose, head stooping over the Gazette which he pretended to be reading, was listening to the debate; profiting by reasonable observations, suffering much to hear very absurd ones and not answer them, which irritated him. Thus, during an hour and a half, had he the courage and patience to hear 'Sémiramis' talked of and babbled of, without speaking a word. At last, all these pretended judges of the fame of authors having gone their ways, without converting one another, M. de Voltaire also went off; took a coach in the Rue Mazarine, and returned home about eleven o'clock. Though I knew of his disguise, I confess I was struck and almost frightened to see him accoutred so. I took him for a spectre, or shade of Ninus, that was appearing to me; or, at least, for one of those ancient Irish debaters, arrived at the end of their career, after wearing themselves out in school-syllogisms. I helped him to doff all that apparatus, which I carried next morning to its true owner—a Doctor of the Sorbonne."

Another cartoon, still better known, is that of the familiar scene of his apotheosis at the Comédie Française. A briefer sketch of that same year of his death, 1778, may be given, because it contrasts with his sharp sketch of Charles XII at Adrianople, carried on a sofa from his carriage, when, to avoid been seen, the King covered his face with a cushion—

"M. de Voltaire appeared in full dress on Tuesday, for the first time since his arrival in Paris. He had on a red coat lined with ermine; a large peruke, in the fashion of Louis XIV, black, unpowdered; and in which his withered visage was so buried that you saw only his two eyes shining like carbuncles. His head was surmounted by a square red cap in the form of a crown, which seemed only laid on. He had in his hand a small nibbed cane; and the public of Paris, not accustomed to see him in this accoutrement, laughed a good deal."

One interesting point about Voltaire's English associations, in so far as they prepare the way for the writing of his "Charles XII," has not hitherto been pointed out. It is this: that a history of the "Wars of Sweden," written by no less a hand than Defoe's, was in existence when Voltaire was studying English literature in London. The work, or at any rate its first part, was anonymously published, like Voltaire's, in 1715; a continuation was added, and the two parts were then issued together in 1720. Between these two dates, let us note, or in 1719, "Robinson Crusoe" had appeared. Defoe's career has some incidents of prison and persecution that are like enough to Voltaire's to warrant a fanciful apposition of the two rebel authors. He was in severe straits when he wrote the first part of his Wars of Charles XII; deeply involved in political intrigues. He had had, too, a severe illness—a violent fit of apoplexy—at the end of the previous year; and his trial for libelling Lord Annesley in the whig "Flying Post" was impending. His sentence, and curious escape from being imprisoned, and his "Hymn to the Mob," have at best a remote bearing on the present book. But one notes these ironical lines to the Mob as having an added irony, when read in the light of his "Charles XII" and Voltaire's interest in his writings—

"Thou art the Essence of the War;

Without thee who wou'd in the Field appear?

'Tis all thy own, whoever gets the Praise—

Thy Hands that fight, and 'tis thy purse that pays.

How partial is the common state of things,

And how unjust the Fame of Emperors and Kings!"

Defoe's "History of the Wars" is written as "by a Scots gentleman in the Swedish service." It is a more documentary book than Voltaire's, to all outward appearance; and in it he has written with characteristic fidelity to the make-believe of his literary double the pseudo "Scots gentleman." It has much the air of the off-hand, matter-of-fact military narrator, who does not look for rhetorical openings, or greatly trouble himself to make the most of his subject.

In his preface he says of Charles XII: "He has done Actions that Posterity will have room to Fable upon, till they make his History Incredible, and turn it into Romance." The romance is already in process in Defoe's pages. The following passage in the text may be quoted to give an idea of his Scots gentleman's estimate of the King—

"And such as these were his Discourses to us, who were his Servants, which so effectually convinc'd us, that his Cause was just, and his Foundations right, that however black the Prospect was, which we had before us; for we could see nothing attending us in the Process of the War, but Death, or being made Prisoners of War, which among Northern Princes especially, is but one Degree less in its Nature to a Soldier; and yet it must be said, in Honour of his *Swedish* Majesty's Service, and of his Servants too; that not an Officer of Note deserted him to the Day of his Death, or quitted his Service, tho' always unfortunate; nay, even the foreign Officers did not desert him; for we all thought, so much Virtue, such personal Bravery, such gallant Principles, such immoveable Steadiness, could not fail, but *one Time or other* must necessarily have a Turn of Fortune in the World, must *some Time or other* find Friends to support it: For who could imagine, that so gallant a Prince should at once be abandon'd of all the Princes of the Earth, from whom any Assistance could be expected; and that he, whose Ancestors had been the Refuge and Sanctuary of all the Protestant Powers and Princes in *Germany*, in their Distress, should at last receive Help from none of the Successors of those very Princes, who were establish'd by the Blood and Power of *Sweden*; nay, to apply it nearer, should at last be driven out of his Possessions by those very Powers, whose Ancestors ow'd the Being of their Government, to the Gallantry and Friendship of the King of *Sweden's* Predecessors."

Other extracts might be made which would show that Defoe was writing at his utmost stretch of speed when he wrote the "History." This, too, is proved by the occasional gaps, dates left blank, and uncorrected errors of fact, or of the press.

Voltaire's book, on the other hand, though it repeats some of Defoe's errors, is an admirably adroit, and a well-poised and considered biography: one of the best biographies of great soldiers ever given to the world. We may conclude, if we will, that Voltaire's English experiences in the decisive years of the writing of the book, which undoubtedly gave a new force and impulse to his genius, helped him also to his particular mastery in this vein. His tribute to England in his "Lettres Philosophiques sur les Anglais" is an indirect testimony to his intellectual expatriation; and with these two books and his tragedy, "Zaïre," which followed in 1732, Voltaire may be said to have attained his brilliant majority.

The students of history who wish to collate Voltaire's book with later authorities may be recommended to turn to Mr. Nisbet Bain's volume on Charles XII, in the "Heroes of the Nations" series, Mr. Oscar Browning's monograph, and Schuyler's "History of Peter the Great."

E. R.

The following are the works of Voltaire—

Dramatic Works:—Œdipe, 1718; Artémire, 1720; Mariamne, 1724; Zaïre, 1732; Samson (opera), 1732; L'Enfant Prodigue, 1736; Mahomet, ou le Fanatisme, 1742; Mérope, 1743; Sémiramis, 1748; Nanine, 1749; Oreste, 1750; L'Orpheline de la Chine, 1755; Tancrède, 1760; L'Ecossaise, 1760; Le Dépositaire, 1772; Irène, 1778; Agathoclès, 1779 (performed on the anniversary of the poet's death). Other dramas and operas.

Poems:—La Bastille, 1717; La Henriade (fraudulently published as La Ligue, 1723-4) 1728; Mort de Mlle. Lecouvreur, 1730; Temple du Goût, 1733 (prose and verse); Le Mondain, 1736; Discours sur l'homme (Épîtres sur le Bonheur, 1738-9); Sur les Événements de 1744; Fontenoi, 1745; Temple de la Gloire, 1745; La Pucelle d'Orléans, 1755 (some of the "Chants" had been in circulation since 1735), in twenty Chants, 1762; a supplemental one, "La Capilotade," appeared separately in 1760; Sur le désastre de Lisbonne, 1756; Sur la Loi Naturelle, 1756; La Vanité, Le Pauvre Diable, Le Russe à Paris, 1760; Contes de Guillaume Vadé (with prose, 1764); La Guerre Civile de Génève (burlesque poem), 1768; Les Trois Empereurs en Sorbonne, 1768;

Épître à Boileau, 1769; Les Systèmes, Les Cabales, 1772; La Tactique, 1773; and others.

Prose Tales:—Le Monde comme il va (or Babouc), 1746; Zadig, 1748 (published in 1747 as "Memnon, Histoire Orientale"); Memnon, ou la Sagesse Humaine, 1749; Micromégas, 1750; L'Histoire d'un Bon Bramin, 1759; Candide, 1759; Le Blanc et Le Noir, 1764; Jeannot et Colin, 1764; L'Homme aux Quarante Écus, 1767; L'Ingénu, 1767; La Princesse de Babylone, 1768; Histoire de Jenny, 1769; Lettres d'Amabed, 1769; Le Taureau Blanc, 1774; Les Oreilles du Comte de Chesterfield, 1774; and others.

Historical Works:—Histoire de Charles XII, 1731; Siècle de Louis XIV, 1751; enlarged edition 1753 (two chapters had been printed and suppressed in 1739); Abrégé de l'Histoire Universelle, vols. i and ii, 1753; vol. iii, 1754; complete edition, 1756 (fragments had appeared in 1745); Annales de l'Empire, 1753; Précis du Siècle de Louis XV, published in part 1755 and 1763, with additional chapters, 1769; Essai sur l'Histoire Générale et sur les Mœurs et l'Esprit des Nations depuis Charlemagne jusqu'à nos jours, five vols, 1756, given in vol. vii of Siècle de Louis XIV (some chapters had appeared in the "Mercure" in 1745-6); Histoire de Russie sous Pierre le Grand: first part, 1759; second part, 1763; La Philosophie de l'Histoire, 1765 (later the "Discours préliminaire" to "Essai sur les Mœurs"); La Défense de mon Oncle (in reply to an adverse criticism on the above work), 1767; Le Pyrrhonisme de l'Histoire, 1768; Fragments sur l'Histoire Générale (Pyrrhonism and Tolerance), 1773.

Works on Philosophy and Religion:—Épître philosophique à Uranie, 1732; Lettres sur les Anglaises (twenty-four letters), 1733, 1734 (also published as "Lettres Philosophiques"); Traité de Métaphysique, 1734; Éléments de la Philosophie de Newton, 1738; Métaphysique de Newton, 1740; Articles for the Encyclopédie, 1757; Dictionnaire Philosophique Portatif, 1764; Catéchisme de l'Honnête Homme, 1763; Le Philosophe Ignorant, 1766; La Raison par Alphabet (new edition of the Dictionnaire Philosophique), 1769; Lettres de Memmius, 1771; Questions sur l'Encyclopédie par des Amateurs, 1770-2; Lettres Chinoises, Indiennes, et Tartares par un Bénédictin, 1776; Mémoires pour servir à la vie de M. Voltaire (printed 1784); and others.

Critical Works:—Essai sur la Poésie, 1726; Utile Examen des Épîtres de J. J. Rousseau, 1736; Lettres sur la "Nouvelle Héloïse," 1761; Appel à toutes les Nations de l'Europe des Jugements d'un écrivain Anglais (later known as "Du Théâtre Anglais"), 1761; Éloge de M. de Crébillon, 1762; Idées Républicaines (in the "Contrat Social"), 1762; Théâtre de Corneille (with translation of Shakespeare's "Julius Cæsar"), 1764; Examen Important de Milord Bolingbroke, 1767; Commentaire Historique sur les Œuvres de l'auteur de la Henriade, 1776; Éloge et Pensées de Pascal (corrected and enlarged edition), 1776; Commentaire sur l'Esprit des Lois de Montesquieu, 1777; and others.

Miscellaneous Writings:—Épîtres aux Manes de Genonville, 1729; Épître des Vous et des Tu, 1732; Sur la Calomnie, 1733; Anecdotes sur Pierre le Grand, 1748; Mensonges Imprimés (on Richelieu's Will), 1749; Des Embellissements de Paris, 1750; Remerciement sincère à un Homme Charitable, 1750; Diatribe du Doctor Akakia, 1752; Les Quand, 1760; Writings for the rehabilitation of Jean Calas, who had been unjustly executed, 1762; Traité sur la Tolérance à l'occasion de la Mort de Jean Calas, 1763; Le Sentiment des Citoyens (attack on Rousseau), 1764; Discours aux Welches, 1764; Les Anciens et les Modernes, ou la Toilette de Mme. de Pompadour, 1765; Commentaires sur le livre des délits et des peines, 1766; Le Cri des Nations (against Papal domination), 1769; De la Paix Perpétuelle (on fanaticism and tolerance), 1769; La Méprise d'Arras (on another judicial mistake), 1771; Éloge de Louis XV; de la Mort de Louis XV et de la Fatalité, 1774; and other works.

Editions of Voltaire's works include a few works on physics and an enormous correspondence.

Chief General Editions of Works:—Ed. Beaumarchais, etc., 70 vols. 8°, 1784; 92 vols. 12°, 1785-90; Beuchot, 70 vols., 1828, etc.; Ed. du Siècle, 8 vols., 1867-70; Moland, 50 vols., 1877-83; with "Table Générale et Analytique," by Charles Pierrot, 1885; Selections have been published, and separate volumes of letters.

Bibliography:—G. Bengesco, 1882-90.

Life, etc.:—Condorcet, 1787; G. Desnoireterres, "Voltaire et la Société Française au XVIIIme Siècle," 1871-76; Longchamp et Wagnière, "Mémoires sur Voltaire, et ses ouvrages," 1825; Bersot, Études sur le XVIIIme Siècle, 1855; A. Pierron, "Voltaire et ses Maîtres," 1866; Maynard, "Voltaire; sa vie et ses œuvres," 1867; D. F. Strauss, 1870; J. Morley, 1872, 1886; James Paston, 2 vols., 1881; G. Maugras, "Voltaire et Jean Jacques Rousseau," 1886; E. Faguet, 1895; E. Champion, "Voltaire: Études Critiques," 1897; L. Cronslé, 1899; G. Lanson, 1907; and in Sainte-Beuve, "Causeries du Lundi," vol. ii; Brunetière, "Études Critiques," vols. i, iii, iv.

TRANSLATOR'S NOTE

"CHARLES XII" was written during the years 1727 and 1728. It is more than 170 years since it was first translated into English. Opinions of its merits differ widely. Macaulay, classing it with Boswell's "Johnson" and Marmontel's "Mémoires," says that it "may be perused with delight by the most frivolous and the most indifferent." Carlyle goes even further: "'Charles XII,'" he writes, "may still pass for a model in that oft-attempted species of biography; the clearest details are given in the fewest words; we have sketches of strange men and strange countries, of wars, adventures, negotiations, in a style which for graphic brevity rivals Sallust. It is a line engraving on a reduced scale of that Swede and his mad life, without colours, yet not without the foreshortenings and perspectives of a true picture. In respect of composition, whatever may be said of its accuracy and worth otherwise, we cannot but reckon it as greatly the best of Voltaire's histories."

Adverse criticism, on the other hand, began as early as 1732, when La Mottraye, who had lived on terms of intimacy with the King, wrote a scathing criticism of Voltaire's work. Voltaire succeeded in making a laughing-stock of this gentleman, but the publication of the works of Nordberg, the King's chaplain, and of Adlerfelt, his chamberlain, shortly afterwards, did bring discredit on some of Voltaire's details. Of the modern school of critics, Mr. Nisbet Bain, who has made a special study of original authorities, does not hesitate to call the book a "romance."

Underlying this difference of opinion is the time-honoured question of the "scientific" as opposed to the "epical" treatment of the lives of the great. The history of any great man's career is a kind of epic poem, and, to borrow Mr. Birrell's words, "I do not see why we children of a larger growth may not be interested in the annals of mankind simply as a story."

It must, indeed, be admitted that Voltaire is no precise or scientific historian; but, in the portrayal of the life of a man of action, rapidity and charm of style is surely as important as the careful tracing of cause and effect.

Voltaire's literary style is famous; but work of high literary merit always suffers in translation; so that any roughness in the present rendering must be attributed to the translator and not to the author.

"Ett vet jag som aldrig dör—

Det är dom öfver död man."

One thing I know that never dies—

The verdict passed upon the dead.

"The history of Sweden is the history of her kings," and of those kings the most striking is undoubtedly Charles XII, the Lion of the North. One of the few heroic figures in a prosaic age, he seems to belong rather to the times of Alfred the Great and Charlemagne than to those of Richelieu and Louis XIII. He has well been called "the last of the Vikings," for the extraordinary nature of his adventures no less than his dauntlessness and endurance make him a kind of Saga-hero. The stories told of his childhood show the beginnings of those Spartan powers of enduring hardship which made him the idol of his "brave blue boys" in later life.

It is said that at the age of six he almost killed himself by leaving his bed in a Swedish mid-winter to "harden himself" by sleeping on the bare boards. The obstinacy which was the most marked characteristic of his boyhood developed in after years into the resolution with which as a mere youth he faced the treachery of his neighbours. "I am resolved," he said in his first speech to his Parliament, "never to begin an unrighteous war, but I am also resolved never to finish a righteous war until I have completely humbled my enemies."

In all matters of convention he was "in his simplicity sublime." He cared nothing for the pomp of sovereignty, and always wore a soldier's plain buff coat; he took his meals standing, spreading the bread and butter, which was his usual fare, with his thumbs. His letters to his sister (whom he addresses as "mon cœur") are full of real affection, and a glance at them dispels the popular illusion that he was cold and heartless, just because he could resist the blandishments of Anna von Königsmarck!

Apart from occasional lapses into the fatalism characteristic of his race, he seems to have been devout. Shortly after his accession he ordered the titles "Our Most Gracious Majesty" to be removed from the liturgy, on the ground that "Almighty God is not appeased by high-sounding titles but by the prayers of humble and faithful hearts."

He was the last to lose heart in adversity; he lost his Empire with as good a grace as he won it. "It is only requisite," he wrote after Pultawa, where all was lost but honour, "not to lose courage, or let go the conduct of affairs."

His early death was a disaster not only for Sweden but for the whole of Europe, for he was the first to realize and check the growing power of Russia.

BOOK I

Outline of Swedish history up to the time of Charles XI—Charles's education—His enemies—Character-sketch of the Czar, Peter Alexiowitz—His peculiarities—Alliance of Russia, Poland, Denmark against Charles XII.

THE kingdom which is made up of Sweden and Finland is, according to our measurement, about 200 leagues broad and 300 long, and stretches from south to north as far as the 55th degree or thereabouts. The climate is severe; there is scarcely any spring or autumn, but there are nine months of winter in the year, and the heat of summer follows hard upon the excessive cold of winter. Frost from the month of October onwards is continuous, nor are there any of those imperceptible gradations between the seasons which, in other countries, render changes less trying. In compensation Nature has endowed the Swedes with clear sky and pure air. The summer sunshine, which is almost continuous, ripens fruit and flowers very rapidly. The long winter nights are shortened by the twilight evenings and dawns, which last in proportion to the sun's distance from Sweden; and the light of the moon, unveiled by any clouds, and intensified by reflection from the snow-clad ground, and often, too, by lights like the Aurora Borealis, makes travelling in Sweden as easy by night as by day.

The fauna are smaller than in the more central parts of Europe, on account of the poor pastures. The people are well developed; the purity of the air makes them healthy, and the severity of the climate hardens them. They live to a good old age when they do not undermine their constitutions by the abuse of strong drink, which Northern nations seem to crave the more because they have been denied them by Nature.

The Swedes are well built, strong and active, and capable of undergoing the most arduous labours, hunger and want; they are born fighters, high spirited and daring rather than industrious. They have long neglected commerce and are still poor business men, though commerce alone can supply their country's wants.

Tradition says that it was chiefly from Sweden (a part of which is still called Gothland) that there poured those hordes of Goths who overran Europe and wrested it from the sway of Rome, who for the past 500 years had played the rôle of tyrant, usurper and lawgiver in that country. The Northern countries were at that time far more populous than they are to-day; there was no religious restraint preventing the citizens from polygamy; the only reproach known to the womenfolk was that of sterility or of idleness, and as they were both as industrious and as strong as the men, the period of maternity was of longer duration.

In spite of this, Sweden, together with what remains to it of Finland, has not above 4,000,000 inhabitants. The soil is sterile and poor, and Scania is the only district which produces barley. There is not more than four millions current money in the whole land. The public bank, the oldest in Europe, was established to meet a want, because, as payments are made in brass and iron coin, difficulties of transport arose.

Sweden enjoyed freedom until the middle of the fourteenth century; during this long period several revolutions occurred, but all innovations were in the direction of liberty.

The chief magistrate had the title King, which in different countries involves very different degrees of power. Thus in France and Spain it implies an absolute monarchy, while in Poland, Sweden and Finland it stands for a representative or limited monarchy. In Sweden the King was powerless without the Council, and the Council in turn derived its powers from the Parliament, which was frequently convened. In these great Assemblies the nation was represented by the nobility, the bishops, and deputies from the towns. In course of time even the peasantry, that section of the community which had been unjustly despised and enslaved throughout almost the whole of North Europe, was admitted to the Parliament.

In about 1492 this nation, essentially liberty-loving, and never forgetful of the fact that she had conquered Rome thirteen centuries before, was brought into subjection by a woman and a nation weaker than the Swedes. Margaret of Valdemar, the Sémiramis of the North, Queen of Denmark and Norway, conquered Sweden partly by force of arms and partly by means of diplomacy, and united her vast estates into one kingdom.

After her death Sweden was rent by civil war; she alternately shook off and submitted to the Danish yoke, and was ruled by kings and ministers alternately. In about 1520 she passed through a period of cruel oppression at the hands of two tyrants: one was Christian II, King of Denmark, a monarch with all the vices, and no one redeeming feature; the other, Archbishop of Upsala, and Primate of the kingdom, was as cruel as the former. One day these two, acting in concert, had the consuls, the magistrates of Stockholm and ninety-four senators seized and massacred by the executioners, on the ground that they had been excommunicated by the Pope for having defended the State against the Archbishop. Whilst these two men, united in oppression, but opposed when it was a question of dividing the spoil, were exercising the utmost tyranny and the cruelest vengeance, a new event changed the whole aspect of affairs in the North.

Gustavus Vasa, a youth descended from the old line of kings, issued from the depths of the forest of Delecarlia, where he had been in hiding, and appeared as the deliverer of Sweden. He was one of those rare products of

Nature, a great genius with all the qualities of a commander of men. His noble stature and an air of distinction brought him adherents the moment he appeared. His eloquence, reinforced by his good looks, was all the more persuasive because it was unassumed. His genius led to the conception of great undertakings, which ordinary people deemed foolhardy, but which, in the eyes of the great, were simply brave. His never-failing courage carried him through all difficulties. He combined valour with discretion, was essentially gentle in an age of savagery, and had a reputation for uprightness, as far as that is possible for a party leader.

Gustavus Vasa had been a hostage of Christian, and kept prisoner contrary to the laws of nations. Having escaped from prison he had wandered, disguised as a peasant, in the mountains and woods of Delecarlia; there, to provide himself both with a livelihood and with a hiding-place, he found himself forced to work in the copper-mines. While buried in these vaults he dared to form the project of dethroning the tyrant. He revealed himself to the peasants, and impressed them as a man of extraordinary gifts, whom ordinary men instinctively obey. In a short time he turned these barbarians into veterans. He attacked Christian and the Archbishop, gained several victories over them, and drove them both from Sweden. Then the States duly elected him King of the country which he had liberated.

Scarcely was he firmly seated on the throne before he embarked on an enterprise of greater difficulty than his conquests. The real tyrants of the State were the bishops, who, possessing nearly all the wealth of Sweden, employed it to oppress the people and to make war on the kings. This power was all the more terrible because, in their ignorance, the people regarded it as sacred. Gustavus punished the Catholic Church for the crimes of her priests. In less than two years he introduced Lutheranism into Sweden, using as a means diplomacy rather than force. Having thus, as he put it, wrested the kingdom from the Danes and the clergy, he reigned in prosperity and absolutism, and died at the age of seventy, leaving his dynasty securely seated on the throne, and his form of faith firmly established.

One of his descendants was that Gustavus Adolphus who is called the Great. This king conquered Livonia, Ingria, Bremen, Verden, Vismar, Pomerania, besides more than a hundred towns in Germany, given up by Sweden after his death. He shook the throne of Ferdinand II, and protected the Lutherans in Germany, his efforts in that direction being furthered by the intrigues of Rome herself, who stood more in awe of the power of the Emperor than of heresy itself. He it was who, by his victories, contributed to the downfall of the House of Austria, an undertaking accredited to Cardinal Richelieu, who was past master in the art of gaining a reputation for himself, while Gustavus contented himself with great deeds. He was on the point of carrying war across the Danube, with the possibility of dethroning the Emperor, when, at the age of thirty-seven, he was killed in the battle of Lutzen, where he defeated Valstein. He carried with him to the grave the title of "Great," the regrets of the North, and the esteem of his enemies.

His daughter Christine, an extremely gifted woman, preferred disputations with savants to the government of a people whose knowledge was confined to the art of war.

She won as great a reputation for resigning the throne as her ancestors had gained in winning and securing it. The Protestants have defamed her, as if Lutherans have the monopoly of all the virtues; and the Papists exulted too much in the conversion of a woman who was a mere philosopher. She retired to Rome, where she passed the rest of her life surrounded by the arts which she loved, and for the sake of which she had renounced an empire at the age of twenty-seven. After her abdication she induced the States of Sweden to elect as her successor her cousin Charles Gustavus, the tenth of that name, son of the Count Palatinate, Duke of Deux Ponts. This king added new conquests to those of Gustavus Adolphus. First he invaded Poland, where he gained the celebrated three days' battle of Warsaw; for some time he waged war successfully against the Danes, besieged their capital, re-united Scania to Sweden, and secured the tenure of Sleswick to the Duke of Holstein. Then, having met with reverses, and made peace with his enemies, his ambition turned against his own subjects.

He conceived the idea of establishing absolutism in Sweden, but, like Gustavus the Great, died at the age of thirty-seven, before having achieved the establishment of that despotism which his son, Charles XI, completed. The latter, a warrior, like all his ancestors, was more absolute than them all. He abolished the authority of the Senate, which was declared to be a royal and not a national assembly. He was economical, vigilant, and hard-working—in fact, such a king as would have been popular had not fear dominated all other sentiments in the hearts of his subjects. He married, in 1680, Ulrica Eleanora, daughter of Ferdinand, King of Denmark, a virtuous princess worthy of more confidence than her husband gave her; the offspring of this marriage was Charles XII, perhaps the most extraordinary man ever born—a hero who summed up in his personality all the great qualities of his ancestors, and whose only fault and only misfortune was that he carried them all to excess. It is of him, and all that is related of his actions and person, that we now purpose writing.

The first book they gave him to read was *Samuel Puffendorf*, in order that he might become early acquainted with his own and neighbouring States. He then learned German, which he henceforward spoke as fluently as his mother tongue. At seven years old he could manage a horse. Violent exercise, in which he delighted and which revealed his martial inclinations, early laid the foundation of a strong constitution equal to the privations to which his disposition prompted him.

Though gentle enough in early childhood he was unconquerably obstinate; the only way to manage him was to appeal to his honour—he could be induced to do anything in the name of honour. He had an aversion to Latin, but when he was told that the Kings of Poland and Denmark understood it, he learned it quickly, and for the rest of his days remembered enough to speak it. Recourse was had to the same means to induce him to learn French, but he was so obstinately determined against it that he could not be prevailed upon to use it even with French ambassadors who knew no other language. As soon as he had some knowledge of Latin they made him translate Quintus Curtius; he took a liking to the book rather for the subject than the style. The tutor who explained this author to him asked him what he thought of Alexander. "I think," said the Prince, "that I would like to be like him." "But," was the answer, "he only lived thirty-two years." "Ah!" replied the Prince, "and is not that long enough when one has subdued kingdoms?" These answers were reported to the King his father, who exclaimed, "That child will excel me and he will even excel Gustavus the Great."

One day he was amusing himself in the King's room by looking over some geographical plans, one of a town in Hungary taken by the Turks from the Emperor, and the other of Riga, capital of Livonia, a province conquered by the Swedes a century earlier. At the foot of the map of the Hungarian town was this quotation from the Book of Job, "The Lord gave, and the Lord hath taken away; blessed be the name of the Lord." The young Prince read these words, then took a pencil and wrote beneath the map of Riga, "The Lord gave thee to me, and the devil shall not take thee from me." Thus, in the most insignificant acts of his childhood, his resolute disposition revealed traits characteristic of greatness, showing what he was one day to be.

He was eleven years old when he lost his mother; she died from an illness brought on by the anxiety caused her by her husband and by her own efforts to conceal it. By means of a kind of court called the Chamber of Liquidation, Charles XI had robbed many of his subjects of their property. A crowd of citizens ruined by this court—merchants, farmers, widows and orphans—filled the streets of Stockholm, and daily poured forth their useless lamentations at the gate of the Palace. The Queen gave all her substance to help these poor wretches: her money, jewels, furniture and even her clothes. When she had nothing left to give them she threw herself weeping at her husband's feet, praying him to have compassion on his subjects. The King answered sternly, "Madam, we have taken you that you may give us children, not advice." Henceforward he is reported to have treated her with such severity that he shortened her life. He died four years after her, in the fifty-second year of his age and the thirty-seventh of his reign, just as the Empire, Spain and Holland on the one hand, and France on the other, had referred the decision of their quarrels to his arbitration, and when he had already begun the work of peace-making between these powers.

To his son of fifteen he left a kingdom secure at home and respected abroad. His subjects were poor, but brave and loyal; the treasury in good order and managed by able ministers. Charles XII, on his accession, not only found himself absolute and undisturbed master of Sweden and Finland, but also of Livonia, Carelia and Ingria; he possessed Wismar, Wibourg, the Isles of Rügen, Oesel, and the most beautiful part of Pomerania and the Duchy of Bremen and Verden, all conquests of his ancestors, assured to the crown by long tenure and by the solemn treaties of Munster and Oliva, strengthened by the prestige of Swedish arms. The peace of Ryswick, begun under the auspices of the father, was completed by the son; who was thus arbiter of Europe from the beginning of his reign.

Swedish law fixes the age of the King's majority at fifteen years; but Charles XI, who exercised absolute power in all points, deferred that of his son, by will, to the age of eighteen. By this will he favoured the ambitious views of his mother, Edwiga Eleanora of Holstein, widow of Charles X.

This Princess was nominated by Charles XI guardian of her grandson and, in conjunction with a Council of six persons, regent of the kingdom. The regent had taken part in politics during the reign of the King her son. She was old, but her ambition, greater than her strength and ability, made her hope to enjoy the sweets of authority long during the minority of the King, her grandson. She kept him away from public business as far as possible; the young Prince passed his time hunting, or busied himself with reviewing his troops. Sometimes he even went through their exercises with them. These pursuits seemed the natural outcome of the vivacity of youth, and there was nothing in his conduct to alarm the regent. Then, too, she flattered herself that the dissipation of these exercises made him unable to apply himself, and so gave her the opportunity of a longer regency. One November day, the very year of his father's death, after he had reviewed several regiments accompanied by the State-councillor Piper, he was standing plunged apparently in deep thought. "May I take the liberty," said the latter to him, "of asking your Majesty of what you are thinking so seriously?" "I am thinking," answered the Prince, "that I feel worthy of the command of those fine fellows, and that it is not my will that either they or I should receive our orders from a woman." Piper at once seized the chance of making his fortune, and realizing that his own influence was not strong enough for him to venture on so dangerous an enterprise as depriving the Queen of the regency, and declaring the King of age, he proposed the matter to the Count

Axel Sparre, an ambitious and aspiring man, pointing to the King's confidence as a likely reward. Sparre was credulous, undertook the business, and worked hard in Piper's interests. The Councillors of the Regency were drawn into the scheme, and vied with one another in hastening the execution of it in order to gain the King's favour. They went in a body to propose it to the Queen, who did not in the least expect such a declaration.

The States-General were then assembled, the Councillors of the Regency laid the matter before them, and they voted unanimously for it. The affair was hastened on with a rapidity which nothing could check; so that Charles XII merely expressed a wish to rule, and within three days the States handed over the government to him. The power and influence of the Queen melted away at once. Henceforth she lived in private, a life more suited to her age, but less to her taste.

The King was crowned on the following 24th of December. He made his entry into Stockholm on a sorrel horse, shod with silver, with a sceptre in his hand, and amid the acclamations of a whole nation—a nation always extravagantly fond of novelty and full of great expectations of a young Prince.

The right of consecrating and crowning the King belongs to the Archbishop of Upsala, and is almost the only privilege remaining to him from among a number claimed by his predecessors. After having anointed the Prince according to custom, he was holding the crown ready to put on his head, when Charles seized it from his hands, and, with a proud glance at the Prelate, crowned himself. The mob, always impressed by a touch of majesty, applauded the King's action; even those who had suffered most from the tyranny of the father could not refrain from praising the pride which was the inauguration of their servitude.

As soon as Charles was master, he took Councillor Piper into his confidence, and handed over the direction of affairs to him, so that he was soon Premier in all but name. A few days later he made him Count, a title of distinction in Sweden, and not, as in France, an empty title to be assumed at will. The first period of the King's rule did not give people a good impression of him; it looked as if he had been rather impatient of rule than deserving of it. As a matter of fact, he indulged no dangerous passions, and the only remarkable thing about him seemed to be youthful fits of rage and a settled obstinacy. He seemed proud and unable to apply himself. Even the ambassadors to his court took him for a second-rate genius, and so described him to their masters. The Swedish people had the same opinion of him; no one understood his character; he himself had not realized it, when storms arising in the North suddenly gave his hidden talents an opportunity of displaying themselves.

Three strong princes, taking advantage of his extreme youth, made simultaneous plans for his ruin. The first was Ferdinand IV, King of Denmark, his cousin; the second Augustus, Elector of Saxony and King of Poland; the third, and most dangerous, was Peter the Great, Czar of Russia. It is necessary to explain the beginning of these wars, which had such great results. We will begin with Denmark.

Of the two sisters of Charles XII, the elder had married the Duke of Holstein, a young prince of great courage and kindliness. The Duke, oppressed by the King of Denmark, came to Stockholm with his consort, in order to put himself under the King's protection, and ask his help, not only as a brother-in-law, but also as King of a people which nourishes an undying hatred for the Danes.

The ancient house of Holstein, merged with that of Oldenburg, was elected to the throne of Denmark in 1449. All the Northern kingdoms were at that time elective, but that of Denmark shortly after became hereditary. One of its kings, Christian III, had an affection for his brother Adolphus for which there are few parallels in history. He neither wished to leave him powerless, nor could he dismember his own States. By an extraordinary arrangement he shared with him the duchies of Holstein-Gottorp and Sleswick. The descendants of Adolphus should, in future, rule Holstein in conjunction with the kings of Denmark, so that the two duchies should be common property, and the King could do nothing in Holstein without the sanction of the Duke, and *vice versa*. This extraordinary union, of which there had, however, been a parallel instance a few years previously, was, for more than eighty years, a source of quarrels between the Denmark and Holstein branches of the dynasty, since the kings always made it their policy to oppress the dukes, and the dukes were equally determined on independence. The struggle had cost the last Duke his liberty and his supremacy. He had regained both at the Conference of Altena in 1689, through the mediation of Sweden, Holland and England, the guarantors of the treaty.

But as a treaty between princes is often only a temporary makeshift, until the stronger is able to oppress the weaker, the quarrel between the new Danish King and the young Duke began again more violently than ever. While the Duke was at Stockholm, the Danes had already begun hostilities in the district of Holstein, and had made a secret alliance with the King of Sweden himself.

Frederic Augustus, Elector of Saxony, whom neither the eloquence and schemes of the Abbé de Polignac, nor the great qualifications of the Prince of Conti, his competitor for the throne, had been able to deprive of election as King of Poland, was a prince still more famed for his courage and chivalrous ideals, than for his incredible physical strength. His court, after that of Louis XII, was second to none in Europe in distinction. There was never a prince more generous or liberal, nor one who gave with so good a grace.

He had bought half the votes of the Polish nobility, and gained the other half by force on the approach of a Saxon army. He considered it better to keep a standing army to strengthen himself on the throne; but he wanted a pretext for keeping it in Poland. He had, in fact, planned to send it against the King of Sweden, on the occasion we are now going to relate.

Livonia, the most beautiful and fertile province of the North, had once belonged to the Knights of the Teutonic order. The Russians, Poles, and Swedes had since severally disputed their claim to it. Sweden had enjoyed it for nearly one hundred years, and was solemnly confirmed in possession of it by the Peace of Oliva.

The late King Charles XI, in his severity to his subjects, had not spared the Livonians. He robbed them of their privileges and part of their estates. Patkul, who from his unhappy death has since gained the notoriety of misfortune, was deputed by the nobility of Livonia to lay their grievances before the King. His speech to his master was respectful, but strong and full of the rugged eloquence begotten of calamity and courage. But kings too often regard public speeches as vain ceremonies, which they must endure without paying attention to. But Charles XI, who, when he did not give way to transports of rage, knew how to act a part, patted Patkul gently on the shoulder and said, "You have spoken for your country like a brave man; I honour you for it. Proceed." But a few days after he had Patkul declared guilty of high treason and condemned to death.

Patkul, who had hidden, took to flight, and carried his resentment to Poland. Some time after he was admitted to the court of King Augustus. Charles XI was dead, but the sentence of Patkul was not annulled, and he was still most resentful. He pointed out to the King of Poland how easily Livonia could be conquered; the people were in despair, and eager to shake off the Swedish yoke; the King was only a child, and unable to defend himself. These proposals were well received by a prince who had long meditated this conquest. Preparations were immediately made for a sudden invasion of Sweden, empty formalities of ultimata and manifestoes being dispensed with.

At the same time the storm darkened on the Russian frontier. Peter Alexiowitz, Czar of Russia, had already made his name feared by the battle in which he defeated the Turks in 1697, and by the conquest of Azov, which gave him the control of the Black Sea. But the actions which won him the title of "The Great" were far more glorious than conquests.

Russia occupies the whole of Northern Asia and Europe, and from the frontiers of China extends 1,500 leagues to the borders of Poland and Sweden. Yet the existence of this immense country was not even realized by Europe before the time of the Czar Peter. The Russians were less civilized than the Mexicans at the time of their discovery by Cortez; born the slaves of masters as barbarous as themselves, they were sunk deep in ignorance, and unacquainted with the arts and sciences, and so insensible of their use that they had no industry. An old law, held sacred among them, forbade them, on pain of death, to leave their own country without the permission of their Patriarch. Yet this law, avowedly enacted to prevent them from realizing their state of bondage, was agreeable to a people who, in the depths of their ignorance and misery, disdained all commerce with foreign nations.

The era of the Russians began with the creation of the world; they reckoned up 7,207 years at the beginning of the last century, without being able to give any reason why they did so. The first day of the year corresponded to our 13th of September. The reason they gave for this was that it was probable that God created the world in autumn, in a season when the fruits of the earth are in full maturity!

Thus the only traces of knowledge found among them were founded on gross mistakes; not one of them suspected that autumn in Russia might be spring in another country in the antipodes. Not long before, the people were for burning the secretary of the Persian ambassador, because he had foretold an eclipse of the sun. They did not even know the use of figures, but in all their calculations made use of little beads strung on wire; and this was their method of reckoning in all their counting-houses, and even in the treasury of the Czar.

Their religion was, and still is, that of the Greek Church, but intermingled with superstitions, to which they firmly adhered in proportion to their absurdity and their exacting nature. Few Russians dare eat a pigeon, because the Holy Ghost is portrayed in form of a dove. They regularly kept four Lents a year, and during that time might eat neither eggs nor milk. God and St. Nicholas were the objects of their worship, and next to them the Czar and the Patriarch. The authority of the latter was as boundless as the people's ignorance. He had power of life and death, and inflicted the cruelest punishments, from which there was no appeal. Twice a year he rode in solemn procession, ceremoniously attended by all the clergy; and the people prostrated themselves in the streets before him, like the Tartars before their Grand Lama.

They practised confession, but only in the case of the greatest crimes; and then absolution was held necessary, but not repentance; they believed themselves purified in God's sight as soon as they received the priest's benediction. Thus they passed without remorse straight from confession to theft or murder; so that a practice which, in the case of other Christians, acts as a deterrent, was, in their case, only an incentive to crime. They scrupled to drink milk on a fast-day, but on festivals fathers of families, priests, matrons and maids got inebriated with brandy. As in other countries they had religious differences among themselves, but the most important cause of dispute was whether laymen should make the sign of the cross with two fingers or with three, and a certain Jacob Nursoff had, during a previous reign, raised a rebellion on this question.

The Czar, in his vast kingdom, had many subjects who were not Christians; the Tartars, on the west coast of the Caspian, and the Palus Mæotis were Mahometans; while the Siberians, Ostiacs and Samoides, who live near the Baltic, were pagans. Some of these were idolators, and some were without God in the world; still, in spite of that, the Swedes, who were sent as prisoners among them, report more favourably of their manners than those of the ancient Russians.

Peter Alexiowitz had received an education which tended to increase the barbarity of his part of the world. His disposition led him to like strangers before he knew they could be useful to him. Le Fort was the first instrument that he made use of to change the face of Russia. Peter's mighty genius, checked but not destroyed by a barbarous education, suddenly broke out; he resolved to act a man's part, to hold command of men and to create a new nation. Several princes before him had renounced their thrones, from distaste for public business, but there was no instance of a prince resigning that he might learn to rule better, as Peter the Great did. He left Russia in 1698, before the completion of the second year of his reign, and took a journey into Holland, under an ordinary name, as if he were the domestic servant of M. le Fort, whom he appointed ambassador-extraordinary to the States-General. When he reached Amsterdam he entered his name on the list of ships'-carpenters to the Indian Admiralty, and worked in the dockyard like other carpenters. In his leisure time he learned those branches of mathematics which might prove useful to a prince, *e. g.* such as related to fortifications, navigation, and the making of plans. He went into the workmen's shops, examined all their manufactures, and let nothing escape his notice. Thence he passed to England, where he perfected himself in the science of ship-building, and, returning to Holland, carefully investigated everything which might be of use in his own country.

At last, after two years of travel and labour which nobody else would have willingly undergone, he reappeared in Russia, bringing thither with him the arts of Europe. A band of artists of all kinds followed him, and then for the first time great Russian vessels were to be seen on the Black Sea, the Baltic, and even on the ocean. Imposing buildings of architectural merit were set up amidst the Russian huts. He founded colleges, academies, printing-houses and libraries. The great towns were civilized; and gradually, though not without difficulty, the dress and customs of the people were changed, so that the Russians learned by degrees what social life really is. Even their superstitions were abolished, the Czar declared head of the Church, and the influence of the Patriarch suppressed. This last undertaking would have cost a less absolute Prince his throne and his life, but in the case of Peter not only succeeded, but assured his success in all his other innovations.

Peter, having subdued the ignorant and barbarous clerical orders, dared to venture to educate them, and so ran the risk of making them a power in the State—but he believed that he was strong enough to take this risk.

In the few monasteries which remained he had philosophy and theology taught; though this theology was only a survival of the age of barbarity from which Peter had rescued his country. A credible witness assured the writer that he had been present at a public debate, where the question was whether the use of tobacco was a sin; the proposer argued that it was lawful to intoxicate oneself with brandy, but not to smoke, because the Holy Scriptures say that, "Not that which goeth into the mouth defileth a man; but that which cometh out of the mouth, this defileth a man."

The monks were not content with the reform. Scarcely had the Czar set up printing-presses than they made use of them to abuse him. They called him Antichrist, because he had the men's beards cut off, and because post-mortem dissection was practised in his academy. But another monk, who wanted to make his fortune, wrote refuting this argument, and proving that Peter was not Antichrist because the number 666 was not included in his name! The author of the libel was broken on the wheel, and his opponent made Bishop of Rezan.

The Reformer of Russia carried a law which puts to shame many a civilized state; by this law no member of the civil service, no "bourgeois" with an established position, and no minor, might enter a monastery. Peter quite grasped the importance of not allowing useful subjects to take up idleness as a profession, nor those who had not yet command of the least part of their fortune to renounce liberty for ever.

The Czar not only, after the example of the Turkish Sultans, subjected the Church to the State, but, by a greater stroke of policy, he destroyed a band of troops like the Janissaries; and that which the Ottoman Emperors failed to do, he succeeded in very rapidly; he disbanded the Russian Janissaries, called Strelitz, who had dominated the Czars. This band, feared rather by its masters than its neighbours, consisted of about 30,000 infantry, half stationed at Moscow, and the other half at various points on the frontier; a member of the Strelitz only drew pay at the rate of four roubles a year, but privileges and abuses amply made up for this.

Peter at first formed a band of mercenaries, in which he had himself enrolled, and was not too proud to begin as drummer-boy, so much were the people in need of good example. He became officer by degrees, made new regiments from time to time, and at last, finding himself at the head of disciplined troops, broke up the Strelitz, who were afraid to disobey him.

The cavalry resembled that of Poland, and that of France in the days when France was only a collection of fiefs. Russian noblemen took the field at their own expense, and engaged without discipline, and sometimes unarmed but for a sabre and a quiver; they were quite unused to discipline, and so were always beaten.

Peter the Great taught them to obey, both by example and by punishment. For he himself served as a soldier and subordinate officer, and as Czar severely punished the "boyards," as the noblemen were called, who argued that the privilege of the nobility was to serve the State in their own way. He instituted a regular corps of artillery, and seized 500 church bells to cast cannon. By the year 1714 he had 13,000 brass cannon. He also formed a corps of dragoons, a form of arm both suited to Russian capacity and for which their horses, which are small, are particularly fit.

Russia has, at the present day (1738), thirty well-equipped regiments of dragoons of 1,000 men each.

He it was, too, who established the hussars in Russia; he even got a school of engineers in a country where he was the first to understand the elements of geometry.

He was a good engineer himself; but he excelled especially in seamanship. As he was born with an extreme fear of the sea, it is all the greater credit to him that he was a good captain, a skilful pilot, a good seaman, and a clever carpenter. Yet in his young days he could not cross a bridge without a shudder; and he had the wooden shutters of his carriage closed on these occasions. It was his courage and will which led him to overcome this constitutional weakness.

He had built on the Gulf of Tanais, near Azov, a fine port; his idea was to keep a fleet of galleys there, and as he considered that these long, flat, light craft would be successful in the Baltic, he had 300 of them built in his favourite town of Petersburg. He taught his subjects how to construct them from ordinary fir, and then how to manage them.

The revenue of the Czar was inconsiderable, compared with the immense size of his empire. It never exceeded twenty-four millions, reckoning the mark as £50, as we do at the present moment; but, after all, only he is rich who can do great deeds. Russia is not densely populated, though the women are prolific and the men are strong. Peter himself, by the very civilization of his empire, contributed to its population. The causes of the fact that there are still vast deserts in this great stretch of the continent are to be sought in frequent recruiting for unsuccessful wars, the transporting of nations from the Caspian to the Baltic, the destruction of life in the public works, the ravages wrought by disease (three-quarters of the children dying of small-pox), and the sad result of a means of government long savage, and barbarous even in its civilization. The present population of Russia consists of 500,000 noble families, 200,000 lawyers, rather more than 5,000,000 "bourgeois" and peasants paying a kind of poll-tax, and 600,000 men in the provinces conquered from the Swedes; so that this immense realm does not contain more than 14,000,000 men; that is to say, two-thirds of the population of France.

The Czar Peter, having transformed the manners, laws, militia, and the very face of his country, wished also to take a prominent part in commerce, which brings both riches to a State and advantages to the whole world. He intended to make Russia the centre of Asian and European trade. The Volga, Tanais, and Duna were to be united by canals, of which he drew the plans, and new ways were to be opened from the Baltic to the Euxine and the Caspian, and from these to the Northern Ocean.

In the year 1700 he decided to build on the Baltic a port which should be the mart of the North, and a town which should be the capital of his empire, because the port of Archangel, ice-bound for nine months in the year, and the access to which necessitated a long and dangerous circuit, did not seem to him convenient. Already he was seeking a passage to China through the seas of the north-east, and the manufactures of Paris and of Pekin were to enrich his new town.

A road of 754 versts, made across marshes which had to be first filled, led from Moscow to his new town. Most of his projects were carried out by his own hand, and two Empresses who succeeded him successively carried out his policy whenever practicable, and only abandoned the impossible.

He made tours throughout his empire whenever he was not engaged in active warfare. But he travelled as lawgiver and natural philosopher. He carefully investigated natural conditions everywhere, and tried to correct and to perfect. He himself plumbed rivers and seas, had locks made, visited the timber-yards, examined mines, assayed metals, planned accurate maps, and worked at them with his own hand.

He built, in a desolate district, the imperial town of Petersburg, which, at the present day, contains 60,000 houses, and where there has arisen in our day a brilliant Court, and where the greatest luxury is to be had. He built the port of Cronstadt on the Neva, Sainte-Croix on the frontiers of Persia, and forts in the Ukraine and in Siberia, docks at Archangel, Petersburg, Astrakan, and at Azov; besides arsenals and hospitals. His own residences he built small and in bad style, but his public buildings were magnificent and imposing. The sciences, which in other parts have been the slow product of centuries, were, by his care, introduced into his empire in full perfection. He made an academy, modelled on the famous institutions of Paris and London; at great expense men like Delisle, Bilfinger, Hermann, Bernoulli, were summoned to Petersburg. This academy is still in existence, and is now training Russian scholars.

He compelled the younger members of the nobility to travel to gain culture, and to return to Russia polished by foreign good breeding. I have met young Russians who were quite men of the world, and well-informed to boot.

It is shocking to realize that this reformer lacked the cardinal virtue of humanity. With so many virtues he was yet brutal in his pleasures, savage in his manner, and barbarous in seeking revenge. He civilized his people, but remained savage himself. He carried out his sentences with his own hands, and at a debauch at table he displayed his skill in cutting off heads. There are in Africa kings who shed the blood of their subjects with their own hands, but these monarchs pass for barbarians. The death of one of his sons, who ought to have been punished or disinherited, would make his memory odious, if the good he did his subjects did not almost atone for his cruelty to his own family.

Such a man was Peter the Czar, and his great plans were only sketched in outline when he united with the kings of Poland and Denmark against a child whom they all despised.

The founder of Russia resolved to be a conqueror; he believed the task an easy one, and felt that a war so well launched would help him in all his projects. The art of war was a new art in which his people needed lessons.

Besides, he wanted a port on the east side of the Baltic for the execution of his great plans. He needed Ingria, which lies to the north-east of Livonia. The Swedes possessed it, and it must be seized from them. His ancestors, again, had had rights over Ingria, Estonia, and Livonia; it seemed the right time to revive these claims, which not only dated from a hundred years back, but had also been annulled by treaties. He therefore concluded a treaty with the King of Poland to take from Sweden the districts which lie between the Gulf of Finland, the Baltic, Poland and Russia.

BOOK II

Sudden and extraordinary transformation in the character of Charles XII—At the age of eighteen he carries on war with Denmark, Poland and Russia—He concludes the war with Denmark in six weeks—Beats an army of 80,000 Russians with 8,000 Swedes, and proceeds to Poland—Description of Poland and its Government—Charles wins several victories, and conquers Poland, where he makes preparations to nominate a king.

THUS three powerful kings were threatening the throne of the boy-king, Charles XII. Rumours of these preparations dismayed the people, and alarmed the King's Council. The great generals were dead; everything was to be feared under a young king who had so far made a bad impression on people. He was hardly ever present at the Council without crossing his legs on the table; he seemed too absent-minded and callous to take part in any business.

The dangerous position of affairs was deliberated by the Council in his presence, and, as some Councillors were proposing to divert the storm by means of negotiation, Charles suddenly rose from his seat with the determined air of a man of resolution who has decided on a course of action. "Gentlemen," he said, "I have resolved never to engage in an unjust war, but, on the other hand, never to conclude a just war but by the ruin of my foes. I have made up my mind. I intend to attack the first who declares war against me, and when I have conquered him I hope to strike terror into the rest." This speech amazed the old Councillors; they exchanged glances without venturing a reply, and finally, astonished at this revelation of their king's courage, and ashamed to show less courage than he, they received his orders for the war cordially.

They were still more surprised when they observed that he suddenly renounced all the most innocent, youthful pleasures. From the moment that he began to prepare for war he entered on a new mode of life, from which he never afterwards departed in one particular. With Alexander and Cæsar as his ideals, he set himself the task of imitating those conquerors in everything but their vices.

He renounced all magnificence, pastimes and recreations, and reduced his menu to the utmost frugality. He had affected display in dress, but in future wore the uniform of a common soldier. There had been a rumour that he had entertained a passion for a lady of the Court. But whether this was true or not, it is certain that he abstained from the society of women for ever after, not only to avoid coming too much under their influence, but that he might prove to his soldiers his determination to live under the severest discipline; possibly, too, he wished to pose as the only Prince who had conquered so difficult a temptation. He also resolved to abstain from wine for the rest of his life. Some people say that he made this resolve in order to curb nature in every particular, and to add a new virtue to his heroism; but the majority say that he took this means of punishing himself for an excess which he had once committed, leading to an insult offered to a lady at table in the presence of his mother. If that was so, his self-condemnation and the life-long deprivation which he imposed on himself are none the less to be admired.

He began operations by a promise of relief to his brother-in-law, the Duke of Holstein. Eight thousand men were immediately sent to Pomerania, a province bordering on Holstein, to protect the Duke against the attacks of the Danes. The Duke certainly needed them; his dominions were already ravaged, his castle at Gottorp taken and the town of Tonning closely besieged, the King of Denmark being there in person, to enjoy a conquest of which he felt certain. This spark enflamed the empire. On one side the Saxon troops of the King of Poland and those of Brandenburg, Volfenbuttel and Hesse-Cassel marched to join the Danes. On the other the King of Sweden's 8,000 men, the troops of Hanover and Zell, and three Dutch regiments came to the help of the Duke.

While the little country of Holstein was thus made the theatre of war two squadrons, one from England and the other from Holland, appeared in the Baltic.

These two States were guarantors of the treaty of Altena, which the Danes had broken, and they were all the more eager to relieve the oppressed Duke, as it was to the interest of their trade to prevent the growth of the power of the King of Denmark. For they knew that the Danes, when they once had control of the Sound, would lay heavy dues on the trading nations, as soon as they were strong enough to do so.

The English and the Dutch had, for this reason, kept, as far as possible, the balance of power equal between the princes of the North; they joined the King of Sweden, who seemed on the point of being overwhelmed by many enemies acting in concert, and helped him for the same reason that the others attacked him, viz. because they thought him incapable of self-defence.

He was bear-hunting when he got news of the invasion of Livonia by the Saxons. He was conducting the hunt in a way as dangerous as novel; the only arms used were forked cudgels, behind a net stretched between trees; a bear of enormous size rushed straight at the King, who, after a long struggle, brought it to the ground, with the help of his net and cudgel.

He started for his first campaign on the 8th of May, new style, in the year 1700. He left Stockholm never to return.

An immense crowd of people went with him as far as Carlscroon, praying for him and weeping and praising him. Before he left Stockholm he established a Council of Defence, composed of Senators. This commission was to have charge of all that concerned the fleet, the troops and fortifications. The Senate was to provisionally regulate all other internal affairs. Having thus arranged all securely within his dominions he concentrated entirely on the war. His fleet consisted of forty-three vessels, that in which he embarked, called the King Charles, was the largest they had ever seen, and carried 120 guns; Count Piper, his Prime Minister, and General Renschild embarked with him. He joined the squadron of the allies; the Danish fleet refused an engagement, and gave the united fleets the opportunity of coming so near Copenhagen that they could throw some bombs into the town.

There is no doubt that it was the King himself who then proposed to General Renschild that they should disembark and besiege Copenhagen by land while it was invested by sea. Renschild was astonished at a proposal which displayed in a young and inexperienced Prince as much skill as courage. Soon all was ready for the disembarkment; orders were given for the embarkation of 3,000 men who were stationed on the coast of Sweden, and who were added to the men they had on board. The King left his large ship and embarked on a lighter frigate; then they sent 300 grenadiers in small vessels along the coast. Among these vessels were small, flat-bottomed boats, which carried the fagots, *chevaux de frise* and the weapons of the pioneers.

Five hundred picked men followed in other shallops. Then came the King's men-of-war with two English and two Dutch frigates, whose cannon were to cover the landing of the troops. Copenhagen, the capital of Denmark, is situated in the island of Zeeland, in the midst of a beautiful plain, which has the Sound on the north-west and the Baltic on the east, where the King of Sweden then had his position. At the unexpected movement of the vessels which threatened invasion, the inhabitants, dismayed by the inactivity of their own fleet and by the motion of the Swedish ships, looked round in terror to see on what point the storm would burst. Charles's fleet stopped before Humblebek, seven miles from Copenhagen. The Danes immediately drew up their cavalry on this spot. The infantry were placed behind deep entrenchments, and all the artillery forthcoming was directed against the Swedes.

The King then left his frigate to embark on the first boat at the head of his guards. The ambassador of France was constantly at his elbow. "Sir," said the King to him in Latin, for he never would speak French, "you have no quarrel with the Danes, and must now oblige me by retiring." "Sir," answered the Count de Guiscard, in French, "the King my master has commanded me to attend your Majesty; and I flatter myself that you will not banish me from your Court, which has never been so brilliant as to-day." With these words he gave his hand to the King, who leapt into the boat, followed by Count Piper and the ambassador.

They advanced supported by the broadsides of the vessels which were covering the descent. The small boats were within a hundred yards of the shore when Charles, impatient of the delay in landing, threw himself from the boat into the sea, sword in hand, and with the water up to his waist, and in spite of a shower of musket-shot, discharged by the Danes, his ministers, the ambassador of France, and officers and soldiers followed his example. The King, who had never before heard a discharge of loaded muskets, asked Major Stuart, who stood next to him, what that whistling was in his ears. "It is the sound of the muskets they are firing at you," said the Major. "Ah!" remarked the King, "that shall henceforth be my band." At that very moment the Major, who had explained the noise to him, was shot in the shoulder, and a lieutenant fell dead at the other side of the King.

Troops attacked in entrenchments are generally beaten, because the attacking party has an impetus which defenders cannot have; besides, waiting for the enemy in one's lines is often a confession of inferiority.

After a faint resistance the Danish horse and foot fled. As soon as the King had seized their entrenchments he fell on his knees to thank God for the first success of his arms. He immediately had redoubts formed in the direction of the town, and himself marked out the line of the encampment. At the same time he sent his fleet back to Scania, a part of Sweden not far from Copenhagen, to get reinforcements of 9,000 men. Everything conspired to second Charles's energetic efforts; the 9,000 men were on the shore ready to embark, and the very next day a favourable wind brought them to him.

All this happened within sight of the Danish fleet, which had not dared to advance. Copenhagen, in consternation, sent deputies to the King to ask him not to bombard the town. He received them on horseback at the head of his regiment of guards, and the deputies fell on their knees before him. He demanded of the town four hundred thousand dollars, with all sorts of provisions for the camp, for which he gave his word of honour to pay. They brought him the provisions, because they dare not refuse, but did not expect that the conquerors would condescend to pay for them; and those who brought them were astonished to find that they were paid generously by the humblest soldier in the army. The Swedish troops had long been accustomed to the strict discipline which contributed not a little to their victories, but the young King increased its severity. A soldier would not have dared to refuse payment for what he bought, much less maraud, or even go out of the camp. He even easily brought his troops to keep his rule that the dead should not be stripped after a victory without his permission. Prayers were said in camp twice a day, at seven in the morning and five in the afternoon, and he never failed to be present at them himself and to give his soldiers an example of piety as well as of valour.

His camp, which was far better governed than Copenhagen, had everything in abundance; and the country folk preferred to sell their goods to their enemies the Swedes than to their own countrymen, who did not pay so good a price for them. So it happened that the townsmen were often obliged to fetch goods, which were unobtainable in their own markets, from the King of Sweden's camp.

The King of Denmark was then in Holstein, whither he seems to have marched only to raise the siege of Tonning. He saw the Baltic covered with his enemies' ships, and a young conqueror already master of Zeeland and ready to take possession of the capital. He published a declaration that whoever took up arms against the Swedes should gain their liberty. This declaration had great influence in a country which had once enjoyed freedom, but where all the peasants and many even of the townsmen were then serfs. Charles sent word to the King of Denmark that he must make up his mind either to do justice to the Duke of Holstein, or have his kingdom laid waste with fire and sword.

The Danes were, indeed, fortunate in dealing with a conqueror who prided himself on his justice. A congress was summoned to meet in the town of Tevendal on the frontiers of Holstein. The Swedish King would not allow diplomacy on the part of the ministers to lengthen the proceedings; he wanted the treaty settled with the same rapidity with which he had invaded Zeeland. As a matter of fact it was concluded on the 5th of August to the advantage of the Duke of Holstein, who was indemnified for all the expenses of the war and freed from oppression. The King of Sweden would make no claims on his own behalf, being satisfied with having helped his ally and humbled his enemy. Thus Charles XII, at eighteen years old, began and ended this war in less than six weeks.

Just at the same time the King of Poland laid siege in person to the town of Riga, the capital of Livonia, and the Czar was marching from the East at the head of 100,000 men. Riga was defended by the old Count D'Alberg, a Swedish general who, at the age of eighty, combined the enthusiasm of youth with the experience of sixty campaigns. Count Fleming, afterwards minister for Poland, a man great both in the field and at the council board, together with M. Patkul, carried on the siege under the directions of the King; in spite of several advantages gained by the besiegers the experience of the old Count D'Alberg counteracted all their efforts, and the King of Poland despaired of gaining the town. At last he got an honourable pretext for raising the siege; Riga was full of merchandise belonging to the Dutch; the States-General ordered their ambassador at the Court of Augustus to make representations to him on the subject. The King of Poland did not require much pressing, but consented to raise the siege rather than occasion the least inconvenience to his allies, who were not much surprised at his ready compliance, as they knew the cause of it.

The only thing left to Charles to complete his first campaign was to march against his rival for glory, Peter Alexiowitz. He was the more angry with him because there were at Stockholm three ambassadors who had just sworn to an inviolable peace: he who prided himself on his probity could not understand how a legislator like the Czar could make light of what should be held sacred. The young and honourable Prince never dreamed that there might be one code of morality for princes and another for private individuals. The Russian Emperor published a manifesto which he had much better have suppressed: he gave as reason for war that he had not been sufficiently honoured when he passed incognito to Riga, and also that provisions were sold too dear to his ambassadors. These were the grievances for which he ravaged Ingria with 80,000 men.

It was on the 1st of October, a month in which the weather is more severe in that climate than is January in Paris, that he appeared before Narva. The Czar, who in such weather would often ride 400 leagues to see a mine or a canal, spared his men no more than himself. Besides, he knew that the Swedes, ever since the time of Gustavus Adolphus, fought in the depth of winter as well as in summer, and he wanted to accustom his Russians not to care about the seasons, so that some day they might at least equal the Swedes. So at a time when frost and snow force nations in temperate climates to suspend hostilities Peter was besieging Narva, thirty degrees from the Pole, and Charles was advancing to its relief. The Czar had no sooner arrived before the place than he hastened to put into practice all that he had lately learned on his travels: he drew out his camp, fortified it on all sides, built walls at intervals, and opened the trench with his own hands. He had given the command of the army to the Duke of Croy, a German, and a clever general, who got little support from the Russian officers.

The Czar himself had only the ordinary rank of lieutenant in his own army. He thought it necessary to give an example of military obedience to his nobility, who up till then had been undisciplined and accustomed to lead bands of ill-armed slaves without experience or order. There is nothing surprising in the fact that he who at Amsterdam turned carpenter to procure fleets for himself should at Narva turn lieutenant in order to teach his people the art of war.

The Russians are strong and indefatigable, and perhaps as brave as the Swedes, but it requires time to make veterans, and discipline to make them invincible. The only fairly reliable regiments were commanded by German officers, but there were very few of them; the rest were savages torn from their forests, clothed in the skins of wild beasts, some armed with arrows and others with clubs. Few had muskets, none had seen a regular siege, there was not one good gunner in the whole army.

A hundred and fifty cannon, which ought to have reduced the little town of Narva to ashes, hardly made a breach, while every moment the artillery of the town were destroying whole lines at work in the trenches. Narva was practically unfortified, and Count Horn, who was in command, had not a thousand regular troops, and yet this immense army was not able to reduce it in ten weeks.

On the 15th of November the Czar heard that the King of Sweden had crossed the sea with 200 transports and was on his way to the relief of Narva. There were not more than 20,000 Swedes, but superiority of numbers was the Czar's only advantage. He was far, therefore, from despising his enemy, and used all his skill to crush him; and not content with 100,000 men he levied another army to oppose him and harass him in his advance. He had already sent for 30,000 men who were advancing from Plescow by forced marches. He then took a step which would render him contemptible if so great a legislator could be so. He left his camp, where his presence was necessary, to go to meet these reinforcements, which could quite well reach the camp without his aid; this step made it appear that he was afraid of fighting, in an entrenched camp, a young and inexperienced prince, who might attack him.

However that may be, his plan was to hem in the King between two armies. Nor was this all: a detachment of 30,000 men from the camp before Narva was posted at a league's distance from the town, on the King of Sweden's route, 20,000 Strelitz were further off on the same route, and 5,000 others formed an advanced guard. Charles would have to force his way through all these troops before he could reach the camp, which was fortified by a rampart and a double ditch. The King of Sweden had landed at Pernaw, on the Gulf of Riga, with about 15,000 foot and more than 4,000 horse. From Pernaw he made a forced march to Revel, followed by all his horse and only 4,000 of his foot. He continually advanced without waiting for the rest of his troops.

Soon he found himself, with only 8,000 men, in presence of the enemy's outposts. He did not hesitate to attack them one after the other, without giving them time to find out with how small a number they had to contend. The Russians, when they saw the Swedes advancing against them, took it for granted that they had a whole army to encounter, and the advanced guard of 5,000 men, who were holding a pass between the hills where 100 men of courage might have barred the passage of a whole army, fled at the first approach of the Swedes. The 20,000 men behind them, terrified at the flight of their countrymen, were overcome by fear and caused panic in the camp to which they fled. All the posts were carried in three days and a half, and what would have been on other occasions reckoned three distinct victories did not delay the King an hour. At last he appeared with his 8,000 men, wearied with the fatigues of so long a march, before a camp of 80,000 Russians, protected by 150 cannon. He hardly allowed them time for rest before he gave orders for an instant attack.

The signal was two musket-shots, and the word in German, "With God's help." A general officer pointed out to him the greatness of the danger. "Surely you have no doubt," he replied, "but that I with my 8,000 brave Swedes shall trample down 80,000 Russians!" Then a moment after, fearing that his speech was boastful, he ran after the officer. "Do you not agree with me," he said, "that I have a double advantage over the enemy? First because their horse will be useless to them, and secondly because, as the position is cramped, their numbers will only incommode them, so that I shall really possess the advantage." The officer thought it best not to differ from him, and so they attacked the Russians about noon, on the 30th November.

As soon as the cannon of the Swedes had made a breach in the entrenchments they advanced with fixed bayonets, having the snow, which drove full in the face of the enemy, behind them. The Russians stood the fire for half-an-hour without quitting their posts. The King attacked the Czar's quarters, on the other side of the camp, and hoped to meet him in person, for he was ignorant of the fact that he had gone to meet his 40,000 reinforcements who were expected shortly. At the first discharge the King received a ball in the shoulder; but it was a spent ball which rested in the folds of his black cravat and did him no harm.

His horse was killed under him, and it is said that the King leapt nimbly on another, exclaiming, "These fellows make me take exercise." Then he continued to advance and give orders with the same presence of mind as before. Within three hours the entrenchments were carried on all sides: the King chased the enemy's right as far as the river Narva with his left, if one may speak of "chasing" when 4,000 men are in pursuit of nearly 50,000. The bridge broke under them as they fled; in a moment the river was full of dead bodies; the rest in despair returned to their camp without knowing the direction in which they were going. They found some huts behind which they stationed themselves; there they defended themselves for a time because they had no mean of escape; but finally their generals, Dolgorouky, Gollofkin and Federowitz surrendered to the King and laid down their arms at his feet. Just then the Duke of Croy arrived to surrender with thirty officers.

Charles received all these prisoners with as charming and engaging a manner as if he were feting them in his own Court. He only put the general officers under a guard; all the under officers and soldiers were disarmed and taken to the river Narva, where they were provided with boats to convey them to their own country. In the meantime night came on, and the right wing of the Russian force was still fighting. The Swedes had not lost 1,500 men; 18,000 Russians had been killed in their entrenchments, many had been drowned, many had crossed the river; but still there remained enough to entirely exterminate the Swedes. But it is not the number lost, but the panic of survivors which spells defeat in war. The King made haste to seize the enemy's artillery before nightfall. He took up an advantageous position between their camp and the town, and there got some hours' sleep on the ground, wrapped in his cloak, waiting till at daybreak he could fall on the enemy's left wing, which was not yet completely routed.

At two o'clock in the morning General Wade, who was in command of that wing, having heard of the King's gracious reception of the other generals and his sending home of the subalterns and soldiers, asked the same favour of him. The conqueror sent him word that he need only approach at the head of his troops and surrender his arms and standards. Soon the general appeared with his Russians, to the number of about 30,000. Soldiers and officers marched bare-headed in front of less than 7,000 Swedes. As the soldiers passed before him they threw down their muskets and swords; the officers surrendered their ensigns and colours.

He let the whole band cross the river without keeping one single prisoner. Had he put them under guard the number of prisoners would have been at least five times that of the conquerors.

He then victoriously entered Narva, attended by the Duke of Croy and the other Russian officers; he ordered their swords to be restored to them, and when he heard that they wanted money, because the tradesmen of Narva refused to trust them, he sent the Duke of Croy 1,000 ducats, and 500 to every Russian officer, who were full of admiration for this treatment, which they had never conceived possible. An account of the victory was at once drawn up to send to Stockholm, and to the allies, but the King erased with his own hands whatever redounded too much to his own credit or to the discredit of the Czar. His modesty could not hinder them from striking several medals to commemorate the event at Stockholm. One of these represented him, on one face, standing on a pedestal, to which a Russian,

Dane and Pole were chained; and on the reverse a Hercules, armed with a club, trampling a Cerberus, and the inscription, "Tres uno contudit ictu."

Among the prisoners made on the day of the battle of Narva was one who was typical of the revolutions of fortune. He was the eldest son and heir of the King of Georgia. He was called the "Czarafis," a name which means son of the Czar among all the Tartars as well as in Russia; for the word Czar meant King among the ancient Scythians, from whom all these peoples are descended, and is not derived from the name of the Cæsars, so long unknown to these barbarians. His father, Mitelleski, who was master of the most beautiful part of the country between the mountains of Ararat and the eastern extremity of the Black Sea, had been driven from his kingdom by his own subjects in 1688, and preferred throwing himself on the mercy of the Emperor of Russia, to applying to the Turks. This king's son, at the age of nineteen, helped Peter the Great in his expedition against the Swedes, and was taken in battle by some Finnish soldiers, who had already stripped him, and were on the point of killing him, when Count Renschild rescued him from their hands, supplied him with clothes, and presented him to his master. Charles sent him to Stockholm, where the wretched prince died shortly after. When he took leave, the King made aloud a natural reflection on the strangeness of the fate of an Asiatic prince, born at the foot of the Caucasus, and going to live a prisoner among the snows of Sweden:

"It is just," he said, "as if I were to be one day prisoner among the Tartars of the Crimea." At that time these words made no impression, but afterwards, when the prediction had been justified in the event, there was but too much reason to remember them.

The Czar was advancing by long marches with a force of 40,000 Russians, expecting to surround his enemy on all sides. When he had got half-way he heard of the battle of Narva, and the dispersal of his whole camp. He thought it best not to attack a victor who had shortly before destroyed 100,000 entrenched troops, with a force of 40,000 raw and undisciplined men. He retraced his steps, hoping to discipline his troops at the same time as civilize his subjects. "I know," he remarked, "that the Swedes will long beat us, but in time they will teach us to beat them." Moscow, his capital, was terror-stricken to hear of this defeat. So great was the pride and ignorance of the people that they were convinced they had been conquered by superhuman agency, and that the Swedes had secured their victory by magic. This opinion was so widespread that a public prayer to Saint Nicholas, patron saint of Russia, was ordered. This prayer is too singular to be omitted. It runs thus—

"O thou, our perpetual consolation in all our adversities, great Saint Nicholas, of infinite power, how have we offended thee in our sacrifices, our genuflections, our bowings, our thanksgivings, that thou hast thus forsaken us? We have implored thine assistance against these terrible, insolent, savage, dreadful, invincible destroyers, when, like lions and bears who have lost their young, they have fallen upon us, terrified us, wounded us, slain us by thousands, who are thy people. As it is impossible that this should have happened without sorcery and witchcraft, we beseech thee, O great Nicholas, to be our champion and standard-bearer, to deliver us from this band of sorcerers, and to drive them from our coasts with the reward they deserve."

While the Russians were thus complaining of their defeat to St. Nicholas, Charles XII returned thanks to God, and prepared himself for fresh victories.

The King of Poland fully expected that his enemy, who had conquered the Danes and Russians, would next turn his arms against him. He made a firmer alliance with the Czar, and the two princes arranged an interview at which they could agree on some policy. They met at Brizen, a small town in Lithuania, without any of the formalities which only delay business, and for which they were in no humour under the circumstances. The princes of the North met with a familiarity which is not yet the fashion in the south of Europe. Peter and Augustus passed fifteen days together in pleasures which passed all bounds; for the Czar, who had set himself to reform his kingdom, could not restrain his own dangerous inclination to riotous living.

The King of Poland promised to furnish the Czar with 50,000 German troops, which were to be hired from several princes, and which the Czar was to pay. He, on the other hand, was to send 50,000 Russians to Poland to be trained in the art of war, and was also to pay the King of Poland 3,000,000 rixdollars within two years. Had this treaty been carried out it might have been fatal to the King of Sweden. It was a ready and sure way of making good soldiers of the Russians, and might perhaps have forged irons for half Europe.

Charles XII set himself to prevent the King of Poland from getting the benefit of this treaty. After passing the winter in Narva, he marched into Livonia, to the very town of Riga which King Augustus had failed to take. The Saxon troops were posted along the river Dwina, which is very broad at this spot, and their task was to dispute the passage with Charles, who lay on the other bank. The Saxons were not then commanded by their Prince, who was at that time ill; but their leader was Marshal Stenau, who was general; under him commanded Prince Ferdinand, Duke of Courland, and the same Patkul, who, after having maintained his rights on paper, defended his country against Charles sword in hand at the peril of his life.

The King of Sweden had great boats made, after a new model, so that the sides were far higher than ordinary, and could be let down and drawn up like a drawbridge. When raised they protected the troops they carried, and when let down they formed a bridge to land by.

He also employed another artifice. Having noticed that the wind blew straight from the north, where his troops lay, to the south, where his enemies were encamped, he fired a large heap of wet straw, which spread a thick smoke over the river and prevented the Saxons from seeing his troops, or guessing at his actions. Under cover of this cloud he sent out boats filled with smoking straw, so that the cloud increased, and being right in the enemy's face, prevented them from knowing whether the King had started on the passage or not. Meanwhile, he himself led the execution of his scheme; and when he was in the middle of the river, "Well," he said, "the Dwina is going to be as kind to us as the sea of Copenhagen; take my word for it, General, we shall beat them." He got to the other side in a quarter of an hour, and was vexed to see three people leap to shore before him. He had his cannon landed at once, and drew up his line without any opposition from the enemy, who were blinded by the smoke. When the wind dispersed the smoke the Saxons saw the King of Sweden already on his march against them. Marshal Stenau lost not a moment, but at the first appearance of the Swedes fell furiously upon them with the best part of his horse. The violent shock coming upon the Swedes just as they were forming, threw them into disorder. They gave way, were broken, and pursued up to the river. The King of Sweden rallied them instantly in the midst of the stream, with as much ease as if he were holding a review. Then his troops, marching in closer formation than before, beat back Marshal Stenau, and advanced into the plain. Stenau felt that his men were beginning to waver, and, like a skilful commander, drew them off into a dry place flanked by a marsh, and a wood where his artillery were posted. The advantage of their position, and the time they had to recover their spirits, restored the Swedes' courage. Charles attacked at once with 15,000 men, while the Duke had about 12,000. The battle was hard fought and bloody; the Duke had two horses killed under him; he three times penetrated into the centre of the King's guards, but at last, having been unhorsed by a musket blow, his army fell into confusion, and he disputed the field no longer. His cuirassiers carried him off from the thick of the battle with difficulty, all bruised, and half dead, from the horses' feet, as they were trampling him.

After the victory the King of Sweden hastened to Mittau, the capital of Courland, and took it. All the towns of the Duchy surrendered at discretion; it was rather a triumphal passage than a conquest. He passed rapidly on to Lithuania, and conquered wherever he passed. And he acknowledged that it was a great satisfaction to him to enter in triumph the town of Birzen, where the King of Poland and the Czar had plotted his ruin. It was here that he planned to dethrone the King of Poland by the agency of the Poles themselves. When one day he was at table, quite absorbed in the thought of his enterprise, and observing his usual rule of abstinence in the midst of a profound silence, appearing engrossed in his great plans, a German colonel, who was present, said loud enough for the King to hear, that the meals which the Czar and the King of Poland had made in the same place were very different from these.

"Yes," said the King, rising, "and I shall the more easily disturb their digestions." In fact, using a little diplomacy to assist his arms, he did not delay to prepare for the event about which he had been busy thinking.

The Government of Poland is an almost exact image of the old Celtic and Gothic Government, which has been altered almost everywhere else. It is the only state which has retained the name "republic," with the royal dignity.

Every nobleman has the right to vote at the election of the king, and to stand for election himself. These fine privileges have corresponding abuses; the throne is almost always put up for sale, and as a Pole is seldom rich enough to buy it, it is often sold to foreigners. The nobility defend their liberty against the king, and tyrannize over the rest of the nation. The body of the people are slaves; such is the fate of mankind, that the great majority are, in some way or another, kept under by the minority. There the peasant does not sow his crops for himself but for his lord, to whom he and his land and his very work belong, and who can sell him, or cut his throat as if he were a beast of the field. A lord is answerable to none but himself. Judgment can only be given against him for a criminal action by an assembly of the whole nation.

Nor can he be arrested until after his condemnation, so that he is hardly ever punished. Many among them are poor, in which case they let themselves out to the richer, and do the basest duties for a salary. They would rather serve their equals than engage in trade, and while taking care of their masters' horses they call themselves electors of kings and destroyers of tyrants.

Whoever saw a King of Poland in the pomp of his majesty, would think him the most absolute prince in Europe; yet he is certainly the least so. The Poles really make with him the same contract which is supposed to exist between a sovereign and his subjects. The King of Poland at the moment of his consecration, and when he swears to keep the "pacta conventa," releases his subjects from their oath of allegiance if he should break the laws of the republic. He nominates to all public offices, and confers all honours. Nothing is hereditary in Poland, except estates and noble rank. The sons of a count or of a king have no claim to the dignities of their father. But there is this great difference between the king and a republic, that he cannot deprive of any office after having conferred it, and that the republic may depose him if he breaks the constitution.

The nobility, jealous of their liberty, often sell their votes and seldom their affections. They have scarcely elected a king before they fear his ambition and make plots against him. The great men whose fortunes he has made, and whom he cannot degrade, often become his enemies instead of remaining his favourites; and those who are attached to the Court, become objects of hatred to the rest of the nobility. This makes the existence of two parties the rule among them; a condition which is inevitable, and even a necessity, in countries where they will have kings and at the same time preserve their liberty. What concerns the nation is regulated by the States-General, which they call Diets. These Diets are by the law of the kingdom to be held alternately in Poland and Lithuania. The deputies do business there with sword in hand, like the old Sarmatæ, from whom they are descended; and sometimes too in a state of intoxication, a vice to which the Sarmatæ were strangers. Every nobleman deputed to these States-General has the right the Roman tribunes had of vetoing the laws of the Senate. One nobleman, by saying "I protest," can put a stop to the unanimous resolutions of all the rest; and if he leaves the place where the Diet is held they are obliged to separate.

To the disorders arising from this law they apply a remedy still more dangerous. There are almost always two factions in Poland; as unanimity in the Diet is almost impossible, each party forms confederacies, in which decisions are made by the majority's votes, without regard to the minority.

These assemblies, which are unconstitutional but authorized by precedent, are held in the king's name, though often without his consent and against his interests, much in the same way as the League in France made use of Henry III's name to undermine his power, or as the Parliament in England, which executed Charles I, began by putting the King's name at the head of all the Acts they passed to destroy him. When the troubles are ended, then it is the function of the General Diets to annul the acts of these cabals; any Diet can also repeal the acts of its predecessors, because one king can abolish the laws of his predecessors, or his own laws.

The nobility which makes the laws for the State is also its defence. They muster on horseback on great occasions, and can make a corps of more than 100,000 men. This great body, called "Pospolite," moves with difficulty, and is ill-governed. Difficulties of provisions and forage make it impossible for them to keep together long; they lack discipline, experience and obedience, but their strong love of liberty makes them always formidable. They may be conquered, dispersed, or even kept for a time in bonds, but they soon shake off the yoke; they compare themselves to reeds, which a storm will bend to the ground, and which will rise when the wind drops. It is for this reason that they have no fortified towns—they themselves are to be the only bulwarks of the State; they never let their king build fortresses, lest he should use them rather for their oppression than for their defence; their country is quite open, except for two or three frontier towns, and if in any of their wars, civil or foreign, they resolve to sustain a siege, they are obliged to hastily raise earth fortifications, repair old half-ruined walls, and enlarge the half-choked ditches; then the town is taken before the entrenchments are finished.

The Pospolite is not always on horses to guard the country; they only form by order of the Diet, or, in times of great danger, by that of the king.

The ordinary protection of Poland is in the hands of a force which the State is obliged to support. It is composed of two bodies independent of each other under two different generals. The two generals are independent of each other, and though they are nominated by the king, are responsible to the State alone and have supreme authority over their troops. The colonels are absolute masters of their regiments, and it is their affair to get them what sustenance they can, and to pay them; but as they are seldom paid themselves, they ravage the country, and ruin the farmers to satisfy their own rapacity, and that of their soldiers. The Polish lords appear in these armies with more magnificence than in civil life, and their tents are finer than their houses. The cavalry, which makes up two-thirds of the army, is almost entirely composed of noblemen, and is remarkable for the gracefulness of the horses and the richness of the accoutrements.

Their men-at-arms especially, who are called either hussars or pancernes, are always attended by several valets, who lead their horses, which have ornamented bridles with plates of silver and silver nails, embroidered saddles, saddle-bows and gilt stirrups, sometimes made of massive silver, with saddle-cloth trailing in the fashion of the Turks, whose magnificence the Poles imitate as nearly as possible.

But though the cavalry is so gorgeous the foot are wretched, ill-clad, ill-armed, without uniform clothes or anything regular; at least that is how they were up to 1710. These foot-soldiers, who are like wandering Tartars, bear hunger, cold, fatigue, and all the hardship of war with incredible endurance. The characteristics of the ancient Sarmatæ, their ancestors, can still be seen in the Poles; the same lack of discipline, the same fury in assault, the same readiness to run away and to return to the field, the same mad fury of slaughter when they are victorious.

The King of Poland at first consoled himself with the idea that these two armies would fight for him, that the Polish Pospolite would arm at his orders, and that all these forces, united with his Saxon subjects and his Russian allies, would make up a multitude before whom the small Swedish force would not dare to appear. But he saw himself suddenly deprived of this means of succour through the very pains which he had taken to have them all at once.

Accustomed in his hereditary dominions to absolute power, he was perhaps too confident that he could govern Poland like Saxony.

The beginning of his reign raised malcontents, his very first acts irritated the party which was opposed to his election, and alienated almost all the rest. The Poles resented the fact that their towns were filled with Saxon garrisons and their frontiers with troops. The nation, far more anxious to maintain their own liberties than to attack their neighbours, did not consider the king's attack on Sweden and his invasion of Livonia as advantageous to the State. It is difficult to deceive a free nation concerning its interests. The Poles saw that if this war, undertaken against their wishes, was unsuccessful, their country, unprotected on every side, would fall a prey to the King of Sweden, and that if it succeeded they would be subdued by their own king, who as soon as he was master of Livonia as well as Saxony would be able to hem in Poland between these two countries.

In the face of this alternative, of either being enslaved by the king whom they had elected, or of having their land ravaged by Charles who was justly enraged, they raised a great outcry against a war which they believed was rather declared against themselves than against Sweden. They regarded the Saxons and the Russians as the instruments of their bondage. And when the King of Sweden had overcome all that opposed him, and was advancing with a victorious army into the heart of Lithuania, they opposed the King violently, and with the more freedom because they were in misery.

Lithuania was then divided into two parties, that of the Princess Sapieha, and that of Oginski. These two factions had begun by private quarrels, and degenerated into civil war.

The King of Sweden was on the side of the Princess Sapieha; and Oginski, ill supported by the Saxons, found his party almost destroyed. The Lithuanian army, which these troubles and lack of money was reducing to a small number, was partly dispersed by the conqueror. The few who sided with the King of Poland were small bodies of wandering troops, who lived by spoil. So that Augustus found nothing in Lithuania but the weakness of his own party, the hate of his subjects, and a foreign army led by an offended, victorious and implacable king.

There was certainly an army in Poland, but instead of 38,000 men, the number prescribed by law, there were not 18,000. Then it was not only ill-armed and ill-paid, but the generals were undecided on any course of action. The King's best course was to command the nobility to follow him; but he dare not run the risk of a refusal, which would increase his weakness by disclosing it.

In this state of trouble and uncertainty, all the counts and dukes demanded a Parliament of the King, just as in England, in times of crisis, the different bodies of the State present addresses to the King beseeching him to call a Parliament. Augustus was more in need of an army than of a Parliament where the actions of kings are criticized. But he was forced to call one, that he might not provoke the nation irretrievably. A Diet was therefore summoned to meet at Warsaw, on the 2nd of December, 1701. He soon saw that Charles XII had as much influence in the Assembly as he had himself. The party of the Sapieha, the Lubomirski, and their friends, Count Leczinski, treasurer of the crown, who owed his fortune to King Augustus, and above all the partisans of the Sobieski, were all secretly for the King of Sweden.

The most influential of them, and the most dangerous enemy that the King of Poland had, was Cardinal Radjouski, archbishop of Gnesna, primate of the kingdom and president of the Diet; his conduct was full of duplicity and artifice, and he was entirely dominated by an ambitious woman whom the Swedes called Madame la Cardinale, and who never ceased to urge him to intrigue and faction. King John Sobieski, Augustus's predecessor, had first made him archbishop of Varmia and vice-chancellor of the kingdom. By favour of the same Prince, the Bishop got a Cardinal's hat; this dignity soon opened his way to the primacy, and thus uniting in his person all that impresses people, he was able to undertake great enterprises with impunity.

On the death of John he exerted his interest to place Jacques Sobieski on the throne; but the great hate they bore the father, great as he was, led to the rejection of the son. Then the Cardinal-Primate united with the Abbé Polignac, ambassador from France, to give the crown to the Prince of Conti, who actually was elected.

But the money and the troops of the Saxons got the better of him. At last he allowed himself to be drawn into the party which crowned the Elector of Saxony, and waited impatiently for a chance of sowing dissension between the nation and the new king.

The victories of Charles XII, protector of Prince James Sobiesky, the civil war in Lithuania, the general dissatisfaction of all his people with King Augustus, made the Cardinal-Primate hope that the time had come when he might send Augustus back into Saxony, and open the way to the throne for Prince John. This Prince, who had formerly been the innocent object of the Poles' hatred, was beginning to be their idol, in proportion as King Augustus lost their favour; but he dare not even conceive such a revolution, of which the Cardinal had insensibly laid the foundations.

At first he seemed to wish to reconcile the King with the republic. He sent circular letters apparently dictated by the spirit of concord and charity, a common and well-known snare, but one by which men are always caught; he wrote a touching letter to the King of Sweden, imploring him, in the name of Him whom all Christians adore, to give peace to Poland and her King. Charles XII answered the Cardinal's intentions rather than his words, for he remained with his victorious army in the Grand Duchy of Lithuania, declaring that he had no desire to disturb the Diet, that he was making war on Augustus and the Saxons, and not on Poland, and that far from attacking the State he had come to save it from oppression. These letters and answers were for public perusal. The springs which made the Diet act were the emissaries, who continually came and went between the Cardinal and Count Piper, and the private meetings held at this prelate's house. They proposed to send an embassy to Charles XII, and were unanimous in their demands that their King should not call in the aid of any more Russians, and that he should send his Saxon troops away.

Augustus's bad luck had already brought about what the Diet asked him. The treaty made secretly with the Russians at Birzen had turned out to be as useless as it had seemed formidable. He was far from being able to send the Czar the 15,000 men he had promised to raise in the Empire.

The Czar himself, a dangerous enemy of Poland, was not at all anxious at that time to help a divided kingdom, hoping to have some share in the spoils. He contented himself with sending 20,000 Russians into Lithuania, and they did more mischief than the Swedes, fleeing continually before the conqueror, and ravaging Polish territory, till at last, being chased by the Swedish generals and finding nothing else to ravage, they returned in bands to their own country. As to the scattered remains of the Saxon army which had been beaten at Riga, King Augustus sent them to winter and recruit in Saxony, that this sacrifice might regain him the affections of the Polish nation in his present difficult position.

Then the war was abandoned for a series of intrigues, and the Diet divided into almost as many factions as there were dukedoms. One day the interests of King Augustus were paramount, the next they were rejected. Everybody clamoured for liberty and justice, yet they had no conception of either; the time was spent in secret cabals and public debate. The Diet knew nothing about what they might or should do; great assemblies seldom agree on good measures in time of civil uproar, because bold men in such assemblies are generally factious, while more reliable men are usually timid.

The Diet broke up in disorder on the 17th of February, 1702, after three months' plotting and irresolution. The senators, that is, the dukes and the bishops, remained at Warsaw. The Polish Senate has the right of making laws provisionally, which the Diets seldom disannul; this body, much less cumbrous and more used to business, was far less disturbed, and quickly came to a resolution.

They agreed to send the embassy proposed in the Diet to the King of Sweden, and also that the Pospolite should mount and hold themselves ready for any emergency. They also made several regulations to appease the troubles in Lithuania, and still more to diminish the King's authority, though it was less to be feared than Charles's.

Augustus preferred to receive hard conditions from his conqueror than from his subjects; he therefore determined to sue for peace with the King of Sweden, and was on the point of negotiating with him. He was obliged to keep this step secret from the Senate, whom he regarded as a still more implacable foe. As the affair was difficult he intrusted it to the Countess of Königsmarck, a Swedish lady of high rank to whom he was then attached. This lady, who was celebrated throughout the world for her wit and beauty, was more capable than any minister of bringing a negotiation to a successful issue. Besides, as she had some property in Charles's dominions, and had been long a member of his Court, she had a plausible reason for waiting on the Prince. She came then to the Swedish camp in Lithuania, and first applied to Count Piper, who too lightly promised her an audience of his master.

The Countess, among the talents which made her one of the most delightful persons in Europe, had a gift for speaking several languages like a native, and would sometimes amuse herself by making French verses which might have been written at Versailles. She made some for Charles XII. She introduced the gods of antiquity, praising his different virtues, and ended as follows—

"Enfin chacun des Dieux discourant à sa gloire,

Le plaçait par avance au temple de mémoire:

Mais Venus ni Bacchus n'en dirent pas un mot."

All her wit and charm were lost on such a man as the King of Sweden; he obstinately refused to see her. She planned to intercept him when he was taking his usual horse-exercise. Thus meeting him one day in a very narrow lane she alighted as soon as she saw him. The King bowed without a word, turned his horse and rode straight back. So that the only satisfaction the Countess got from her journey was the conviction that she was the only person of whom the King was afraid.

The King of Poland was then obliged to throw himself into the arms of the Senate. He made them two proposals by means of the Count of Mariemburg; either that they should leave him the control of the army, which he would pay two quarters in advance out of his own pocket, or else that they should allow him to bring 12,000 Saxons into Poland. The Cardinal replied as severely as the King of Sweden had done. He told the Count of Mariemburg, in the name of the Assembly, "That they had decided to send an embassy to Charles XII, and that it was not his affair to introduce Saxons."

In this extremity the King was anxious to preserve at least a semblance of royal authority. He sent one of his chamberlains to Charles to inquire when and how his Swedish Majesty would receive the embassy of the King, his master, and of the State. Unfortunately they had neglected to provide this messenger with a passport; so Charles threw him into prison, with the remark that he was waiting for an embassy from the State, and none from King Augustus.

Then Charles, leaving garrisons behind him in some of the Lithuanian towns, advanced to Grodno, a town famous in Europe for the Diets held there, but ill-built and worse fortified. Some miles away from Grodno he met the embassy sent by the Polish State. Charles XII received them in his tent with some display of military pomp; their proposals were full of evasion and obscurity, they seemed afraid of Charles, and disliked Augustus, but they were ashamed of deposing a king whom they had elected at the order of a foreigner. Nothing was settled, and Charles gave them to understand that he would give them a decision at Warsaw.

His march was preceded by a manifesto which the Cardinal and his party spread over Poland in eight days. By this document Charles invited all the Poles to join him in vengeance, pretending that their interests were the same. They were, as a matter of fact, very different, but the manifesto, seconded by a great party, by disorder in the Senate and by the approach of the conqueror, made a great impression. They were obliged to own Charles for a protector, since it was his will, and it was well for them that he was content with this title. The Senators who were opposed to Augustus advertised the manifesto in his very face, and those who were on his side kept silence. At last when they heard that Charles was advancing by forced marches, they all took panic, and prepared to flee. The Cardinal was one of the first to leave Warsaw, the majority hastened to flee, some to await the issue of affairs on their own estates, some to arm their adherents. With the King there remained only the Imperial and Russian ambassadors, the Pope's Legate, and some few bishops and counts, who were attached to him. He was forced to flee, and nothing had yet been decided in his favour. Before his departure, he hastened to take counsel with the small number of Senators who remained. But though they were anxious to serve him they were still Poles, and had all got so great an aversion for Saxon troops, that they dare not allow him to bring 6,000 men for his defence, and they further voted that these 6,000 men should be commanded by the Grand Duke of Poland, and immediately sent back after peace had been made. As to the armies of the republic, they put them at his disposal.

After this settlement the King left Warsaw, being too weak to oppose the enemy, and little satisfied with his own party. He at once published his orders for assembling the Pospolite and the armies, which were little more than a name.

There was nothing to be hoped from Lithuania, where the Swedes were posted; while the Polish army, reduced in number, lacked arms, provisions and the will to fight. The majority of the nobles, intimidated, undecided, or disaffected, stayed on their own lands. It was in vain that the King, authorized by law, ordered every noble to appear on horseback under pain of death, and to follow him; they began to argue that they need not obey him. His chief trust was in the troops of the Electorate, where, as the form of government was absolute, he did not fear disobedience. He had already given orders to 2,000 Saxons, who were marching rapidly. He also recalled 8,000, which he had promised to the Emperor for the French war, but which in his difficult position he was forced to withdraw. The introduction of so many Saxons into Poland meant the provocation of general disaffection, and the violation of the law made by his own party, allowing him a force of only 6,000. But he realized that if he were victor they would not dare to complain, while if he were beaten they would never forgive the introduction of 6,000 men. While his soldiers were arriving in groups, and he was passing from county to county collecting the nobles who adhered to him, the King of Sweden at last arrived before Warsaw on the 5th of May, 1702. The gates were opened to him at the first summons; he sent away the Polish garrison, disbanded the militia, set up military posts of his own everywhere, and ordered the inhabitants to disarm; then content with that, and not wishing to exasperate them, he only demanded a tribute of 100,000 livres. King Augustus was at that time assembling his forces at Cracow, and was very surprised to see the Cardinal-Primate among them. This man wished, perhaps, to maintain an external reputation to the last, and to dethrone his King with every mark of outward respect. He gave him to understand that the King of Sweden would grant reasonable terms, and humbly asked permission to go to see the King. King Augustus granted what he was powerless to refuse, and so left him free to do him an injury. The Cardinal hastened immediately to see the King of Sweden, to whom he had not yet ventured to present himself. He met the Prince at Prague, not far from Warsaw, but without the ceremony which had been shown towards the ambassadors of the State.

He found the conqueror clad in a dress of coarse blue cloth with brass buttons, jack-boots, and buffalo-skin gloves reaching to the elbow, in a room without hangings, together with the Duke of Holstein, his brother-in-law, Count Piper, his prime minister, and several officers. The King came forward to meet the Cardinal, and they stood talking for a quarter of an hour, when Charles concluded by saying aloud, "I will never grant the Poles peace till they have elected another king." The Cardinal, who had expected this, immediately reported it to all the counts, saying that he was most sorry about it, but pointing out the necessity for complying with the conqueror's wishes.

At this news the King of Poland saw that he must either lose his crown or defend it in battle, and he put forth his best resources for this last contest. All his Saxon forces had arrived from the frontiers of Saxony. The nobility of the Palatinate of Cracow, where he still was, came in a body to offer him their services. He personally exhorted every one of these to remember the oaths they had taken, and they promised him that they would fight to the last drop of their blood in his defence. Fortified by this help, and by the troops called the crown corps, he went for the first time to attack the King of Sweden, and soon found him advancing towards Cracow.

The two Kings met on the 19th of July, 1702, in a large plain near Clissau, between Warsaw and Cracow. Augustus had nearly 20,000 men, and Charles not more than 12,000; the battle began by a discharge of artillery. At the first volley, discharged by the Saxons, the Duke of Holstein, who commanded the Swedish cavalry, a young prince of great courage and valour, received a cannon-shot in his loins. The King asked if he were dead, and when they answered in the affirmative he said nothing, the tears fell from his eyes, and then covering his face with his hands for a moment, he spurred his horse furiously, and rushed into the thick of the fight at the head of his guards.

The King of Poland did all that could be expected of a prince fighting for his crown; he thrice personally led his men in a charge, but the good fortune of Charles carried the day, and he gained a complete victory. The enemy's camp, artillery and flags, and Augustus's war-chest were left in his hands.

He did not delay on the field of battle, but marched straight to Cracow, pursuing the King of Poland, who fled before him. The citizens of Cracow were brave enough to shut the gates upon the conqueror. He had them broken open, the garrison did not dare to fire a single shot; they were chased with whips and sticks to the castle, where the King entered with them. One gunner ventured to prepare to fire a cannon; Charles rushed up to him and snatched the match away; he then threw himself at the King's feet. Three Swedish regiments were lodged at free quarters in the town, and the citizens were taxed by a tribute of 100,000 rixdollars. Count Steinbock, having heard that some treasure had been hidden in the tomb of the Polish kings, in the Church of Saint Nicholas at Cracow, had them opened; they only found gold and silver ornaments belonging to the church; they took some of them and Charles sent a golden chalice to a Swedish church; this would have raised the Polish Catholics against him, if anything could have withstood the terror inspired by his arms. He left Cracow fully resolved to pursue Augustus without intermission, but within a few miles of the city his horse fell and broke his thigh-bone, so that he had to be carried back to Cracow, where he lay in bed in the hands of the surgeons six weeks. This accident gave Augustus breathing space. He had the report immediately spread throughout Poland and Germany that Charles had been killed by his fall. This false report, which was believed for some time, filled all men's minds with astonishment and uncertainty.

During this slight interval he assembled all the orders of the kingdom to Mariemburg. The meeting was a large one, and few of the Counts refused to send their deputies.

He regained popularity by presents, promises, and the affability which is so necessary to absolute kings to make them popular, and to elective kings as an added support to their power. The Diet was soon undeceived concerning the false report, but the impulse had already been given to that great body, and they allowed themselves to be carried along by the impulse, and all the members swore fidelity to the King.

The Cardinal himself, pretending to be still attached to King Augustus, came to the Diet. He kissed the King's hand, and did not scruple to take the oath with the rest. The oath implied that they had never attempted, and never would attempt anything against Augustus. The King excused the Cardinal from the first part of the oath, and he blushed as he swore to the rest.

This Diet resolved that the republic of Poland should maintain an army of 50,000 men at their own expense for the service of the State, that they should give the Swedes six weeks to declare for peace or war, and the same time to the Princess Sapieha, the authors of the troubles in Lithuania, to come and beg pardon of the King of Poland.

In the meantime the King of Sweden was cured of his wound, and carried everything before him. Still pursuing his plan of making the Poles dethrone their King themselves, he had, by means of the intrigues of the Cardinal, a new assembly called at Warsaw, to oppose that of Lubin. His generals pointed out to him that the affair might still be protracted and might at last prove abortive, that during this time the Russians were daily attacking the troops he had left behind in Livonia and Ingria, that the Swedes were not invariably successful, and that his presence there would in all probability shortly be necessary. Charles, who was as dogged in the carrying out of his plans as he was brisk in his action, answered, "Should I stay here fifty years, I would not leave the place till I have dethroned the King of Poland."

He left the Assembly of Warsaw to dispute with that of Lubin in debates and writings, and to seek precedents to justify their proceedings in the laws of kingdoms, laws which are always equivocable, and interpreted by each party at will.

For himself, having increased his victorious troops by 6,000 cavalry and 8,000 infantry, he marched against the rest of the Saxon army he had beaten at Clissau, and which had time to rally and recruit while he had been kept in bed by his fall.

This army avoided him and withdrew towards Brussels on the north-west of Warsaw. The river Bug lay between him and the enemy. Charles swam across at the head of his horse, while the infantry sought a ford higher up.

On May 1, 1703, he came upon the Saxons at a place called Pultask. They were commanded by General Stenau and were about 10,000 in number. The King of Sweden in his precipitate march had not brought more with him, being sure that fewer would have sufficed. The fear of his arms was so great that one half of the army ran away at his approach.

General Stenau held his ground for a few minutes with two regiments; but the moment after he was drawn into the general retreat of his army, which was dispersed before it was beaten. The Swedes did not make 1,000 prisoners, nor were there 600 killed; they had more difficulty in pursuing than in defeating them.

Augustus, who had nothing left but the scattered remnants of the Saxons who had been beaten on all sides, hastily withdrew to Thorn, a town in the kingdom of Prussia, on the Vistula, and under Polish protection. Charles at once prepared to besiege it. The King of Poland, realizing his danger, withdrew to Saxony, but Charles, in spite of brisk marches, swimming across rivers, hurrying along with his infantry, and riding behind his cavalry, was not able to bring his cannon up to Thorn; he was obliged to wait till it was sent him from Sweden by sea.

In the meantime, he took up a position within some miles of the town, and would often advance too near the ramparts to reconnoitre; the plain coat that he always wore was of greater service to him than he had ever expected on these dangerous walks; it protected him from being marked out by the enemy for a shot. One day, when he had gone very near with one of his generals, called Lieven, who was dressed in blue trimmed with gold, he feared that he would be seen. With the magnanimity which was natural to him, which prevented him from remembering that he was exposing his own life for a subject, he told Lieven to walk behind him. Lieven, realizing too late the mistake he had made in putting on a noticeable uniform which brought those near him also into risk, and being equally afraid for the King's safety in whatever place he was, hesitated as to whether he ought to obey him. While he was debating with himself for a second, the King took him by the arm, and screened him: at that very instant a discharge of cannon took them in the flank, and struck the general dead on the very spot which the King had just left. The death of this man, killed directly in his stead, and because he was trying to save him, confirmed him in the opinion he had always had about predestination, and made him believe that his fate which had saved him under such extraordinary circumstances was reserving him for the execution of great designs.

All his schemes succeeded, and he was equally fortunate in negotiations and in war; his influence was felt throughout the whole of Poland, for his Grand Marshal Renschild was in the heart of those dominions with a large section of the army. Nearly 30,000 generals, scattered through the north and east on the Russian frontier, withstood the efforts of the whole Russian Empire; and Charles was in the west, at the other end of Poland, at the head of picked troops.

The King of Denmark, tied down by the treaty of Travendal, which he was too weak to break, remained quiet. He was prudently afraid of showing his vexation at seeing the King of Sweden so near his estates. Further, towards the south-west, between the Elbe and Weser, lay the Duchy of Bremen, the last territory formerly acquired by the Swedes, filled with strong garrisons, and opening the way for the conqueror to Saxony and the Empire. Thus from the German Ocean almost to the Gulf of Borysthenes, that is, across the whole breadth of Europe, and up to the gates of Moscow, all was in consternation, and a general revolution was imminent. His vessels were masters of the Baltic, and employed in transporting prisoners from Poland into his own country. Sweden alone, at peace during these great doings, was rejoicing in deep peace, and in the glory of her King, for which she did not have to pay the price, for his victorious troops were maintained at the expense of the conquered.

During this general peace of the North before the arms of Charles XII, the town of Dantzig ventured to offend him. Fourteen frigates and forty transports were bringing the King reinforcements of 6,000 men, with cannon and ammunition to finish the siege of Thorn. These had to pass up the Vistula; at the mouth of that river lies the rich town of Dantzig, a free town, enjoying the same privileges in Poland as the Imperial towns have in Germany. Its liberty had been alternately attacked by the Danes, Swedes, and some German princes, and was only saved by the mutual jealousy of these Powers. Count Steinbock, one of the Swedish generals, assembled the magistrates in the name of the King, and demanded a passage and ammunition for his troops. The magistrates, showing an unusual rashness in those treating with their superior, dare neither absolutely refuse nor yet exactly grant what he demanded. The general compelled them to give him more than he had asked; and even exacted from the town a contribution of 100,000 crowns to make up for their rash denial.

At last the recruits, the cannon and the ammunition having arrived before Thorn, the siege was begun on the 22nd of September. Robel, governor of the place, defended it for a month with a garrison of 5,000 men, and then it was forced to surrender at discretion. Robel was presented unarmed to the King. His Majesty never missed a chance of honouring merit in a foe, and gave him a sword with his own hand, together with a considerable present of money, and sent him away on parole. But the town, which was small and poor, was condemned to pay 40,000 crowns, an excessive sum for it.

Elbing, standing on an arm of the Vistula, was founded by the Teutonic Knights, and had been annexed to Poland. It did not take advantage of the mistake of the Dantzig townsfolk, hesitated too long about giving passage to the Swedes, and was more severely punished than Dantzig.

Charles entered it in person on the 13th of December, at the head of 4,000 men armed with bayonets. The inhabitants, in terror, threw themselves upon their knees in the streets, and begged for mercy. He disarmed them, quartered his troops in their houses, and then summoning the chief magistrate he demanded a sum of 260,000 crowns, to be handed over that very day. He seized the 200 pieces of cannon, and the 400,000 charges of powder, which were in the town; a victory gained would not have brought him so many advantages. All these successes were the precursors to the dethroning of King Augustus.

The Cardinal had scarcely taken the oath of fealty to his King when he repaired to the assembly at Warsaw, still under pretence of making peace. He talked of nothing but peace and obedience, but was attended by 3,000 soldiers raised on his own estate. At last he threw off the mask, and declared in the name of the Assembly that "Augustus, Elector of Saxony, was incapable of wearing the crown of Poland." They then unanimously pronounced the throne vacant.

The intention of the King of Sweden, and so necessarily of this Diet, was to give the throne to the Prince Jacques Sobieski, whose father Jean had possessed it.

Jacques Sobieski was then at Breslau, in Silesia, impatiently waiting for the crown which his father had worn.

One day he was hunting some miles from Breslau, with Prince Constantine, one of his brothers, when thirty Saxon cavaliers, sent secretly by King Augustus, suddenly rushed from a neighbouring wood, surrounded the two princes, and carried them off without resistance. Relays of horses were ready a little distance off, on which they were at once taken to Leipzig, and closely guarded.

This step upset the plans of Charles, the Cardinal and the Assembly of Warsaw.

Fortune, which sports with crowned heads, almost brought the King of Poland to the point of being taken himself. He was at table, three miles from Cracow, relying on an advanced guard, posted at a distance, when General Renschild appeared suddenly, after having surprised this guard. The King of Poland had only time to mount with eleven others. The general pursued him for eight days, expecting to seize him at any moment. The King had almost reached Sendomir; the Swedish general was still in pursuit, and it was only through extraordinary good luck that the Prince escaped.

In the meantime the King's party and that of the Cardinal were calling each other traitors to their country.

The army of the Crown was divided into two factions. Augustus, forced at last to accept help from the Russians, regretted that he had not applied to them sooner; he hurried alternately into Saxony, where his resources were at an end, and into Poland where they dare not help him. On the other hand, the King of Sweden was ruling calmly and successfully in Poland. Count Piper, who was as great a politician as his master was a hero, seized the opportunity to advise Charles to take the crown of Poland for himself; he pointed out to him how easily he could carry out the scheme with a victorious army and a powerful party in the heart of a kingdom which he had already subdued; he tempted him by the title of Defender of the Reformed Faith, a name which flattered Charles's ambition. He could, he said, easily play (in Poland) the part which Gustavus Vasa had played in Sweden, and introduce Lutheranism, and break the tyranny of the nobility and the clergy over the people. Charles was tempted for a moment; but glory was his idol; he sacrificed to it both his interests and the pleasure he would have had in taking Poland from the Pope. He told Count Piper that he would rather give away kingdoms than gain them, and added smiling, "You were born to be the minister of an Italian prince."

Charles was still near Thorn, in that part of the kingdom of Prussia which belongs to Poland; from there he had an eye on what was going on at Warsaw, and kept his powerful neighbours in awe. Prince Alexander, brother of the two Sobieskis, who had been carried off to Silesia, came to ask vengeance of him. The King was all the more ready to grant it, because he thought it easy, and that he would gain his own vengeance too. But as he was eager to give Poland a king, he proposed that Prince Alexander should take the crown, which fortune seemed bent on denying to his brother. He did not in the least expect a refusal, but Prince Alexander told him that nothing would ever persuade him to take advantage of his elder brother's misfortune. The King of Sweden, Count Piper, all his friends, and especially the young

Palatine of Posnania, Stanislas Leczinski, pressed him to accept. But he was decided. The neighbouring princes were astonished at the news, and did not know which to admire most—a king who at the age of twenty-two gave away the crown of Poland, or Prince Alexander who refused it.

BOOK III

Stanislas Leczinski chosen King of Poland—Death of the Cardinal-Primate—Great retreat of General Schullemburg—Exploits of the Czar—Foundation of Petersburg—Charles's entry into Saxony—The peace of Altranstadt—Augustus abdicates in favour of Stanislas—General Patkul, the Czar's plenipotentiary, is broken on the wheel, and quartered—Charles receives the ambassadors of foreign princes in Saxony—He also goes to Dresden to see Augustus before his departure.

YOUNG Stanislas Leczinski was therefore deputed by the Assembly at Warsaw to give the King of Sweden an account of several differences that had arisen among them since Jacques had been carried off. Stanislas' personal appearance was pleasing, full of courage and sweetness, with that frank open air which is the greatest of outward advantages, and a better seconder of a man's words than eloquence itself. Charles was impressed by his discreet allusions to King Augustus, the Assembly, the Cardinal and the different interests which rent Poland. King Stanislas did the writer the honour of relating his conversation with the King, which took place in Latin. "How can we hold an election if the two Princes and Constantine are absent?" he inquired. "How can you get the State out of the difficulty without an election?" answered the King.

This conversation was the only intrigue which placed Stanislas on his throne. Charles prolonged the conversation purposely, that he might the better sound the young deputy's genius. After the conference he said aloud that he had never met a man so fit to reconcile all parties. He immediately made inquiries about the character of Leczinski, and found that he was brave and inured to fatigue, that he always slept on a kind of straw mattress, and that he required no personal service from his attendants; that he was more temperate than is usual in that climate, economical, adored by his servants, and perhaps the only popular prince in Poland, at a time when all ties were broken but those of interest and faction. This character, which corresponded in many respects with his own, made him make up his mind finally. He remarked aloud after the meeting, "There is a man who will always be my friend," and people knew that that meant, "There is a man who shall be king."

When the Primate of Poland heard that the King had nominated the Palatine Leczinski, he hastened to Charles to try to make him change his mind, for he wished to put the crown on the head of a certain Lubomirski. "But what objection have you to Stanislas?" asked the conqueror. "Sire," said the Primate, "he is too young." "He is much about my own age," answered the

King dryly, turning his back on the Prelate. Then he sent Count Horn to Warsaw at once to notify the Assembly that they must elect a king in three days, and that they must choose Stanislas Leczinski. Count Horn arrived on the 7th July, and fixed the election for the 12th, just as if he were arranging the decampment of a battalion. The Cardinal-Primate, disappointed of the fruit of so many intrigues, returned to the Assembly, where he left no stone unturned to ruin the election in which he had had no share; but the King of Sweden arrived incognito at Warsaw, so that he had to be silent. All that the Primate could do was to absent himself from the election: he took up the position of a neutral, being unable to oppose the conqueror and unwilling to assist him.

On Saturday, 12th July, the day appointed for the election, the Assembly met at Colo, at about three in the afternoon. They met there by arrangement, and the Bishop of Posnania presided instead of the Cardinal. Count Horn and two other officers were present at the ceremony, as ambassadors extraordinary from Charles to the Republic. The session lasted till nine in the evening, and the Bishop brought it to an end by declaring in the name of the Diet that Stanislas was elected King of Poland. They all threw their caps into the air, and the acclamations stifled the cries of the opposers.

It was no use for the Cardinal and his party to stay away from the elections; they were all obliged the next day to come and pay homage to the new King, who received them as if he were quite satisfied with their conduct; their greatest mortification was that they had to attend him to the King of Sweden's quarters. His Majesty gave all honours to the King he had just made, and, to add weight to his new dignity, assigned money and troops for his use.

Charles XII left Warsaw at once to proceed to the completion of the conquest of Poland. He had ordered his army to meet before Leopold, the capital of the great Palatinate of Russia, a place important in itself, but still more so for the riches it held. It was thought that by means of the fortifications, which King Augustus had made there, it would hold out fifteen days. The conqueror invested it on the 5th, and took it the following day by assault. All who resisted were put to the sword. The victors, who were now masters of the town, did not disperse for pillage, in spite of the reports concerning treasure in Leopold: they ranged themselves in battle array in the great square. The King then proclaimed, by sounding a trumpet, that all who had anything belonging to King Augustus or his adherents should bring them themselves before sunset on pain of death. The arrangements were so well made that few dare disobey him, and they brought him 400 chests, filled with gold and silver coin, plate and other things of value.

The beginning of Stanislas' reign was contemporaneous with a very different event. Some business for which he must be present had forced him to remain in Warsaw: he had with him his mother, his wife and two daughters; the Cardinal, the Bishop of Posnania and some prominent Poles made up his new court. His guards were 6,000 Poles of the royal army, who had lately entered his service, but whose fidelity had not yet been tried. General Horn, governor of the town, had only about 1,500 Swedes with him. They were at Warsaw in peace, and Stanislas was reckoning on starting in a few days for the conquest of Leopold, when suddenly they heard that an immense army was approaching the town. It was King Augustus, who was making a fresh effort; by one of the finest marches ever made he was coming up with 20,000 men to fall on Warsaw, after having eluded the King of Sweden; his purpose was to kidnap his rival.

Warsaw was not fortified, and the Polish troops who were defending it were not reliable. There were those in the town from whom Augustus got information, and if Stanislas delayed he would be ruined. He sent his family to Posnania, under the guard of Polish troops upon which he could absolutely rely. It was in this disorder that he feared he had lost his second daughter, aged one; she was lost by a nurse, and they discovered her in a manger, in a neighbouring village, where she had been left. That is the story that I have often heard him tell. It was this child who, after many vicissitudes, became Queen of France. Several gentlemen took different roads. The new King went to join Charles XII, learning early to suffer disgrace, and forced to leave his capital six weeks after he had been made King.

Augustus entered the capital as a victorious and enraged sovereign. The inhabitants, already fleeced by the King of Sweden, were more heavily taxed still by Augustus. The Cardinal's palace and all the houses of the confederate lords were given over to plunder. The most extraordinary thing about this transient revolution was that the Papal Legate, who had come with King Augustus, demanded in the name of his master that the Bishop of Posnania should be handed over to him as responsible to the Court of Rome for having abetted a Prince who had been put on the throne by the arms of a Lutheran.

The Court of Rome, which had always endeavoured to increase its temporal power by means of the spiritual, had long established a kind of jurisdiction in Poland, with the Papal Legate at the head of it. These ministers never missed a chance of extending their power, which was revered by the majority, but always resisted by those of greater discernment. They had claimed the right of judging all ecclesiastical cases, and had, especially during periods of disturbance, usurped many other privileges which they maintained until about 1728, when they were deprived of them: for such abuses are seldom reformed till they have become intolerable.

King Augustus, very glad to be able to punish the Bishop with decency, and at the same time to do something acceptable to the Roman Court, though he would have opposed it on any other occasion, delivered up the Polish Prelate into the hands of the Legate. The Bishop, having seen his palace plundered, was taken by the soldiers into Saxony, where he died.

Count Horn endured the continual fire of the enemy in the castle where he was enclosed for some time, but at last the place could hold out no longer, and he sounded a parley and gave himself up with his 15,000 Swedes. This was the first advantage which King Augustus gained in the torrent of his misfortune against the victorious Swedes.

Charles, accompanied by King Stanislas, went to meet his enemy at the head of the best part of his troops. The Saxon army fled before him; the towns for thirty miles round sent him their keys, and every day brought word of some advantage gained. Success became too familiar to Charles: he said it was hunting rather than fighting, and complained of never having to contest a victory.

For some time Augustus entrusted the command of his army to Count Schullemburg, a very able general: he certainly needed all his experience at the head of a discouraged army. He seemed more anxious to safeguard his master's troops than to conquer: he made war by means of stratagem, while the two kings acted with vigour. He stole marches on them, seized advantageous posts, and sacrificed some of his cavalry to give time to his foot to withdraw in safety. He saved his troops by splendid retreats before an enemy with whom one could only gain this sort of glory.

Scarcely had he arrived in the Palatinate of Posnania than he heard that the two Kings, whom he had believed to be fifty leagues off, had covered the fifty leagues in nine days. He had not more than 8,000 foot and 1,000 horse; he had to hold his own against a superior force, the King of Sweden's reputation and the fear which so many defeats had naturally inspired in the Saxons. He was always of opinion, in spite of the German generals, that the foot might hold their own against the horse in an open field, even without the benefit of *chevaux de frise*: and he ventured to try the experiment on that day against a victorious horse commanded by the two Kings and the most experienced of the Swedish generals. He took up such an advantageous position that he could not be surrounded; his first line knelt on the ground, and were armed with pikes and muskets; the soldiers were in close formation, and presented to the enemy's horse a kind of rampart bristling with pikes and muskets; the second line bending a little over the shoulders of the first, shot over their heads, and the third, standing upright, fired simultaneously from behind the other two. The Swedes fell upon the Saxons with their usual impetuosity, but they awaited them without flinching. By this means the

Swedes advanced in disorder, and the Saxons warded off the attack by keeping their ranks.

Schullemburg drew up his men in an oblong battalion, and, though wounded in five places, he retired in good order at midnight to the little town of Gurau, three leagues from the battle-field. He had scarcely time to breathe here before the two Kings appeared close behind him.

Beyond Gurau, towards the river Oder, lay a thick wood through which the Saxon general led his exhausted troops; the Swedes, without being nonplussed, pursued him through the thickets of the woods, finding their way without difficulty through places scarcely passable by foot-passengers. Yet the Saxons had not crossed the wood more than five hours before the Swedish cavalry appeared.

On the other side of the wood runs the river Parts, at the foot of a village named Rutsen. Schullemburg had sent forward in haste to get the boats ready, and had got his troops across the river: they were already lessened by half. Charles arrived just as Schullemburg had reached the other side; never had a conqueror pursued his enemy so rapidly.

The reputation of Schullemburg depended on his escaping from the King of Sweden, while the King thought his glory concerned in taking him and the rest of his army. He lost no time in making his cavalry swim the river. Thus the Saxons found themselves enclosed between the river Parts and the great river Oder, which rises in Silesia, and is very deep and rapid at this spot.

The ruin of Schullemburg seemed inevitable: but after having lost few soldiers he crossed the Oder during the night. Thus he saved his army, and Charles could not help saying, "To-day Schullemburg has conquered us."

It was this same Schullemburg who was afterwards general of the Venetians, and he in whose honour the Republic erected a statue in Corfu, because he defended this rampart of Italy against the Turks. None but republics confer such honours; kings do not give rewards.

But what thus brought glory to Schullemburg was of little use to King Augustus. He once more abandoned Poland to his enemies, withdrew into Saxony and hastily prepared the fortifications of Dresden, for he already feared, not without reason, the loss of the capital of his hereditary dominions.

Charles XII found Poland submissive; his generals, following his example, had engaged in Courland with several small bodies of Russians, who, since the great battle of Narva, had only shown themselves in small companies, and who in this part only made war like the Tartar vagabonds, who plunder and flee and reappear only to flee again. Wherever the Swedes were they thought they were certain to win, though they numbered only twenty against a hundred.

Under these fortunate circumstances Stanislas prepared for his coronation; fortune, which had had him elected king at Warsaw and then had driven him thence, recalled him thither to the acclamation of a crowd of nobles which the fortune of war attached to him; a Diet was convoked there; all other obstacles were removed, only the Court of Rome was disposed to thwart it.

It was naturally expected that this Court would declare in favour of King Augustus, who from a Protestant had become a Catholic to gain the crown in opposition to Stanislas, who was placed upon the throne by the great enemy of the Catholic faith. The then Pope, Clement XI, sent dispatches to all the prelates of Poland, and especially to the Cardinal-Primate, threatening them with excommunication if they presumed to assist at the consecration of Stanislas or take part in any plot against King Augustus.

If these dispatches were delivered to the bishops who were at Warsaw, it was to be feared that, while some would obey them through weakness, the majority would seize the opportunity to become more exacting in proportion as they were necessary. All possible precautions were therefore taken to prevent the letters of the Pope from being received at Warsaw. A Franciscan got possession of them secretly, undertaking to deliver them into the bishops' own hands: he first gave one to the suffragan of Chelm. This prelate, who was a great partisan of King Stanislas, gave it to his Majesty unopened. The King sent for the monk, and asked how he dare take charge of such a document. The Franciscan answered that he did it by order of his general. Stanislas told him to in future take his orders from his King rather than from his Superior, and banished him immediately from the town.

The same day a placard was published by the King of Sweden, by which all ecclesiastics, secular and regular, were forbidden to take part in politics under the severest penalties.

For greater security he had guards posted at the doors of all the prelates' houses, and forbad the entry of any stranger into the town. He exercised these small severities so that Stanislas should not fall out with the clergy on his accession; he said that he refreshed himself from the fatigue of campaigns by checking the intrigues of the Roman Curia, and that he must fight it on paper, just as he attacked other sovereigns with actual weapons.

The Cardinal was asked by Charles and Stanislas to perform the ceremony of coronation. But it did not seem to him seemly that he should quit Dantzig to consecrate a king who had been elected against his wish; but, as it was always his policy to act a part in all that he did, he wanted to get a legitimate excuse for his refusal: he therefore caused the Pope's dispatch to be fixed, in the night, to the gate of his own house. The magistrate of Dantzig in great indignation had search made for the culprits, which were not found; the Primate feigned irritation and was really very pleased: he had an excuse for not consecrating the new King, and at the same time remained on good terms with Charles, Augustus, Stanislas and the Pope.

He died a few days after, leaving his country in turmoil. The only result of all his intrigues was that he had offended simultaneously three Kings, Charles, Augustus, Stanislas, the Polish State and the Pope, who had commanded him to come to Rome to account for his conduct. But, as even politicians sometimes experience remorse in their last moments, he wrote to King Augustus on his death-bed asking his pardon.

The coronation was solemnized quietly and magnificently in Warsaw in spite of the Polish custom of crowning kings in Cracow. Stanislas Leczinski and his wife Charlotte were consecrated King and Queen of Poland at the hands of the Archbishop of Leopold assisted by several other bishops. The only reward Charles reaped from his conquest was to be present at the ceremony incognito.

While he was thus providing Poland with a king, and the King of Denmark dare not harrass him, while the King of Prussia was courting his friendship and Augustus was withdrawing to his hereditary dominions, the Czar became daily more formidable. His assistance of Augustus in Poland had been feeble, but he had made powerful diversions in Ingria.

As for him, he not only began to be a great soldier himself, but also to teach his soldiers the art of war: discipline was established among his forces; he had good engineers, experienced artillery and many good officers; he had also learned the great art of supporting his armies. Some of his generals had learned both to fight well and, if necessary, to abstain from fighting; more than all, he had built up a fleet capable of making head against the Swedes in the Baltic.

Confident in all these advantages, due both to his genius and to the absence of the King of Sweden, he took Narva by assault after a regular siege and a blockade by land and sea. When the soldiers had taken the town they plundered it, and gave themselves to horrible barbarities: the Czar hastened from one place to another to stop the disorder and massacre. He rescued by force from the hands of the soldiers women whose throats they were going to cut after having outraged them; he was obliged to kill with his own hands some Russians who would not listen to his commands. In the town hall at Narva they still show the table where he laid his sword, as he said to the citizens who flocked after him, "This sword is not wet with the blood of the citizens I have slain, but with that of the Russians whom I have killed to save your lives."

Had the Czar always shown such humanity he would have been the greatest of heroes. His ambition went beyond the destruction of towns. In the midst of his new conquests he was laying the foundations of a city not far from Narva. This was the city of Petersburg, which was henceforth his seat and the centre of his trade. It is between Finland and Ingria, in a marshy island, around which the Neva flows in several branches before it falls into the Gulf of Finland. He himself made the plan of the town, of the fortress, the port, the quays, which adorn it, and the fortifications defending its entry. This desert, uncultivated island, which is nothing but a mud heap during the short summer of that climate, and a pool of ice in winter, unapproachable by land except across wild forests and deep morasses, and till then the habitation of bears and wolves, was, in 1703, filled with more than 300,000 men whom the Czar had called together from the farthest limits of his dominions. The peasants of the kingdom of Astrakan and those who live on the frontiers of China were transported to Petersburg. Before he could lay the foundations of a town he was obliged to pierce forests, make roads, drain marshes and raise banks. Nature was subjugated in every direction. But the Czar was bent on peopling a country which did not seem meant for man's habitation; he was not to be diverted from his resolve either by the floods, which ruined his works, or by the barrenness of the soil, or by the ignorance of the workmen, or by the mortality which swept away 200,000 men at the very beginning. The town was founded in spite of the obstacles which existed in nature herself, in the genius of the people, and an unfortunate war. Already in 1705 Petersburg was a considerable town, and its port was full of vessels. The Emperor attracted strangers in large numbers by the rewards which he gave them, giving some lands, others houses, and encouraging all the arts which might civilize life in that cruel climate. Above all, he made it inaccessible to the enemy. The Swedish generals, who frequently beat his troops in every other district, were not able to do the least harm to this increasing colony. It was at peace in the midst of the war which surrounded it.

The Czar, by thus creating new dominions for himself, still held out a helping hand to King Augustus, who was losing his. He persuaded him by the instrumentality of General Patkul, who had lately joined the Russian side, and was then the Czar's ambassador in Saxony, to come to Grodno to confer with him once more on the unhappy state of affairs.

King Augustus came thither with some troops, attended by General Schullemburg, whose passage across the Oder had got him a reputation in the north, and in whom he placed his great hope. The Czar arrived followed by 100,000 men. The two monarchs formed new plans of war. As King Augustus was dethroned he was no longer afraid of exasperating the Poles by delivering their country to the Russian troops. It was decided that the Czar's army should be divided into several bodies to oppose every action of the King of Sweden. During this interview King Augustus instituted the order of the White Eagle, a feeble resource to bring over to his side certain Polish lords who wanted real advantages rather than an empty honour, which becomes ridiculous when derived from a prince who is king only in name. The conference of the two Kings ended in a strange manner. The Czar departed suddenly, leaving his troops to his ally, in order to extinguish a rebellion with which he was threatened in Astrakan. He had scarcely started when King Augustus ordered the arrest of Patkul at Dresden.

All Europe was amazed that, in opposition to the law of nations, and apparently to his own interest, he should venture to imprison the ambassador of the only prince who afforded him protection. The secret history of the affair was this: Patkul, proscribed in Sweden for having maintained the privileges of his country, Livonia, had become general to Augustus: but his high spirit not according with the proud disposition of General Fleming, the King's favourite, and more imperious than himself, he had passed into the Czar's service, and was then his general and ambassador to Augustus. He was a man of great discernment, and had found out that the proposal of Fleming and the Chancellor of Saxony was to offer Charles peace on his own terms. He at once formed a plan to prevent this and to bring about some arrangement between the Czar and Sweden. The Chancellor got wind of his project, and obtained leave to seize him. King Augustus told the Czar that Patkul was a wretch and would betray them both. His only fault was that he served his master too well: but an ill-timed piece of service is often punished as a treason.

In the meantime, the 100,000 Russians, on one side, divided into several small bodies, burnt and ravaged the estates of Stanislas' adherents: while Schullemburg, on the other, was advancing with fresh troops. But the fortune of the Swedes dispersed these two armies in less than two months. Charles XII and Stanislas attacked the separate corps of the Russians one after another, but so swiftly that one Russian general was beaten before he had heard of the defeat of his colleague. No obstacle could check the conqueror's advance. If he found a river in the way he and his Swedes swam across it.

One party of the Swedes took the baggage of Augustus in which were 400,000 crowns of silver coin; Stanislas seized 800,000 ducats belonging to Prince Menzikoff, the Russian general, Charles, leading his cavalry, would often march thirty leagues in twenty-four hours, every soldier leading another mount to use when his own should be spent. The Russians, panic-stricken and reduced to a small band, fled in confusion beyond the Borysthenes.

While Charles was thus driving the Russians into the heart of Lithuania, Schullemburg at last repassed the Oder and came at the head of 20,000 men to offer battle to the great Marshal Renschild, who was considered Charles's best general, and was called the Parmenio of the North. These two famous generals, who seemed to share the fate of their respective masters, met near Punits, at a place called Frauenstadt, a territory which had already proved fatal to the troops of Augustus. Renschild had only thirteen battalions and twenty-two squadrons, which made a total of about 10,000 men, and Schullemburg had twice that number.

It must be remembered, too, that he had in his army between 6,000 and 7,000 Russians, who had been under discipline a long time, and were as reliable as veterans. This battle of Fraustadt was fought on 12th February, 1706: but the same General Schullemburg, who with 4,000 men had to a certain extent harassed the King of Sweden, was completely defeated by General Renschild. The battle did not last a quarter of an hour, in a moment the Saxons wavered, and the Russians threw down their arms on the first appearance of the Swedes. The panic was so sudden and the confusion so great that the conquerors found on the field 7,000 muskets ready loaded, which they had thrown away without firing. There never was a rout more sudden, more complete or more disgraceful: and yet all the Saxon and Swedish officers acknowledged that no general had ever arranged his men better; it was that day that they realized how little human foresight can pre-arrange events.

Among the prisoners there was a whole regiment of French. These poor wretches had been taken by the Saxon troops in 1704 at the famous battle of Hochstet, which was so fatal to the greatness of Louis XIV. They had since enlisted under King Augustus, who had formed them into a regiment of dragoons, and put them under the command of a Frenchman called Joyeuse. The colonel was killed at the first and only charge of the Swedes, and the whole regiment became prisoners of war. From that day these Frenchmen petitioned to be taken into the service of the King of Sweden; they were received into that service by a singular fate, which preserved them for a further change of their conqueror to their master.

As to the Russians they begged for their life on their knees, but they were inhumanly massacred in cold blood, six hours after the battle, to punish them for the outrages of the compatriots, and to get rid of prisoners which the conquerors did not know what to do with.

Augustus was now absolutely without resources. He had nothing left but Cracow, where he was shut up with two regiments of Russians, two of Saxons and some troops of the regal army, by whom he was afraid of being handed over to the conqueror; but his misfortune was at its height when he heard that Charles had at last entered Saxony, on the 1st September, 1706.

He had crossed Silesia without deigning to even warn the Court of Vienna. Germany was in consternation: the Diet of Ratisbon, which represents the Empire, and the resolutions of which are often as ineffectual as they are solemn, declared the King of Sweden an enemy to the Empire if he crossed the Oder with his army; this very resolution was a further inducement to him to march into Germany.

Upon his approach the villages were deserted and the inhabitants fled in all directions. Charles acted as he had at Copenhagen: he had proclamations made everywhere that he only wanted to procure peace, and that all those who returned to their houses and paid the contributions that he would demand should be treated as his own subjects, while the rest should be pursued with no quarter. This declaration from a prince who had never been known to break his word brought back in large numbers all those of the inhabitants who had been dispersed by fear. He encamped at Altranstadt, near the plains of Lutzen, the field of battle famous for the victory and death of Gustavus Adolphus. He went to see the place where this great man fell, and when he reached the spot he said, "I have endeavoured to live like him; perhaps God may one day grant me a death as glorious."

From this camp he commanded the estates of Saxony to meet, and to send him without delay the register of Finance of the Electorate. As soon as he had them in his power, and had information of exactly what Saxony could supply, he levied a tax on it of 625,000 rixdollars a month.

Besides this contribution the Saxons were obliged to supply every Swedish soldier with two pounds of meat, two pounds of bread, two pots of beer and fourpence a day, together with forage for his horse. When the contributions had been thus fixed the King arranged a new method of protecting the Saxons from the insults of his soldiers. He ordered that in all the towns where his soldiers were quartered every housekeeper with whom the soldiers were lodged should give certificates of their behaviour each month, without which the soldier could not draw his pay; further, inspectors went round once a fortnight to inquire if the Swedes had done any damage, and housekeepers were carefully indemnified and culprits punished.

The severe discipline under which Charles's troops lived is well known; they did not pillage towns taken by assault without permission; they pillaged in an orderly way, and desisted at the first signal. The Swedes boast to this day of the discipline they kept in Saxony: yet the Saxons complain that the most terrible outrages were committed among them. These contradictory statements would be irreconcilable if we did not remember that men look at the same thing from different points of view.

It would have been very strange had not the conquerors sometimes abused their privileges, and had not the conquered regarded the smallest damage as the most terrible injury. One day as the King was riding near Leipzig a Saxon peasant threw himself at his feet to ask justice against a grenadier, who had just gone off with what he had intended for his family dinner. The King had the soldier called. "Is it true," he asked sternly, "that you have robbed this man?" "Sire," answered the soldier, "I have not done him so much harm as your Majesty has done his master, for you have stolen a kingdom from him, while I have only taken a turkey from this rustic." The King gave the peasant ten ducats, and pardoned the soldier for the boldness of the repartee, but he added, "Remember, friend, that I have taken a kingdom from King Augustus, but I have taken nothing for myself."

The great Leipzig fair was held as usual, tradesmen attended it in perfect security; not one Swedish soldier was to be seen in the fair; it might have been said that the only object of the Swedish army in Saxony was to keep the peace: the King ruled throughout the Electorate with as absolute a power and as deep a tranquillity as in Stockholm.

King Augustus, a wanderer in Poland, and deprived both of his kingdom and his electorate, at last wrote a letter with his own hand to Charles XII to ask for a peace.

He commissioned Baron Imhof, accompanied by M. Finsten of the Privy Council, secretly to deliver this letter; he gave them full powers and *carte blanche*, directing them to try to obtain for him reasonable and Christian conditions. He was obliged to conceal his overtures for peace and to refrain from having recourse to the mediation of any prince, for being then in Poland, at the mercy of the Russians, he had reason to fear that the dangerous ally whom he had abandoned would take vengeance on him for his submission to the conqueror. His two plenipotentiaries came by night to Charles's camp and had a private audience. The King read the letter, and said, "Gentlemen, you shall have your answer in a moment." Then he went into his office and wrote as follows—

"I consent to grant peace on the following conditions, in which it must not be expected that I will make the least alteration:—

"1. That King Augustus renounce for ever the crown of Poland, that he acknowledge Stanislas as lawful king; and that he promise never to recover the throne, even after the death of Stanislas.

"2. That he renounce all other treaties, and especially those he has made with Russia.

"3. That he send back with honour into my camp the Princess Sobieski, and any other prisoners he may have taken.

"4. That he deliver into my hands all the deserters who have taken service with him, particularly Jean Patkul; and that proceedings be stopped against all such as have passed from his service to mine."

He gave this paper to Count Piper, bidding him negotiate the rest with King Augustus's plenipotentiaries. They were overwhelmed by the severity of the terms, and tried with the small skill which is possible to the powerless, to lessen the rigour of the King of Sweden. They had several conferences with Count Piper, the only answer he would give to all their suggestions was, "Such is the will of the King my master, and he never changes his mind."

While this peace was being negotiated secretly in Saxony, chance seemed to give King Augustus the opportunity of gaining more honourable terms, and of treating with his conqueror on a more equal footing.

Prince Menzikoff, commander-in-chief of the Russian army, went to join him in Poland with 30.000 men, at a time when he not only did not expect their assistance but even feared it. He was accompanied by Polish and Saxon troops, 6,000 in all. Surrounded by Prince Menzikoffs army, and with only this small body-guard, he was in terror lest they should discover his negotiation; he pictured himself simultaneously dethroned by his enemy, and in danger of being taken prisoner by his ally. In this critical state of affairs the army found itself in the near neighbourhood of one of the Swedish generals, called Meyerfield, who was at the head of 6,000 troops at Calish, near the Palatinate of Posnania. Prince Menzikoff pressed the King to give battle. The King, in this most difficult position, delayed under various pretexts, for though the enemy had only one third of his numbers, there were 4,000 Swedes in the army of Meyerfield, and that was enough to make the result doubtful. On the other hand, to fall upon the Swedes during the negotiations and to lose the day, would mean irretrievable ruin. He therefore resolved to send a reliable messenger to the enemy's general to let him know the secret of the peace and to warn him to retreat. But this advice had a very different effect from what had been expected. General Meyerfield believed that it was a snare to intimidate him, and on that supposition alone he dared to risk a battle.

That day the Russians for the first time conquered the Swedes in a pitched battle. This victory, which King Augustus had gained in spite of himself, was complete; in the midst of his ill-fortune he entered in triumph into Warsaw, formerly his capital, but now a dismantled and ruined town, ready to receive any conqueror whatever, and to acknowledge the strongest as king. He was tempted to seize this moment of prosperity, and to attack the King of Sweden in Saxony with the Russian army. But when he remembered that Charles was at the head of a Swedish army, which had till then been invincible; that the Russians would forsake him directly they had information that the treaty had been begun; that Saxony, his hereditary dominions, already drained of men and money, would be ravaged by the Russians as well as by the Swedes; that the Empire, occupied with the French war, could not help him; and that he would be left without dominions, friends, or money, he considered it better to accept the King of Sweden's terms.

These terms were made even more severe when Charles heard that King Augustus had attacked his troops during the negotiations. His rage and the pleasure of still further humbling an enemy who had just conquered his troops, made him more inflexible about all the articles of the treaty. Thus the victory of King Augustus was wholly to his own disadvantage, a circumstance in which his experience was unique.

He had just had the Te Deum sung in Warsaw, when Finsten, one of his plenipotentiaries, arrived from Saxony, with the treaty of peace which deprived him of his crown. Augustus signed it after some hesitation, and then started for Saxony, in the vain hope that his presence might soften the King of Sweden, and that his enemy might recall the former bonds between their houses, and their common blood.

The two Princes first met at Gutersdorf, in Count Piper's quarters. The meeting was unceremonious; Charles was in jack-boots, with a piece of black taffeta tied carelessly round his neck instead of a cravat; his coat was as usual made of coarse blue cloth with brass buttons. He was wearing the long sword which he had used in the battle of Narva, and often leaned upon it.

The conversation turned entirely upon those great boots. Charles told Augustus that he had not had them off for six years, except at bed-time. These details were the only subject discussed by two kings, whereof one had taken the crown from the other.

Augustus adopted during the whole interview that air of delight and satisfaction which princes and great men accustomed to business know how to assume in the midst of the cruelest mortifications. The two kings dined together several times afterwards. Charles always pretended to give the place of honour to Augustus, but far from relaxing his terms, he made them even more severe. It was bad enough for a sovereign to be forced to hand over a general and a public minister, it was a great humiliation to be forced to send to his successor, Stanislas, the crown jewels and archives, but it was the finishing touch to this humiliation to be forced to congratulate on his accession him who had taken his place on the throne. Charles insisted on a letter from Augustus to Stanislas: the King showed no haste to comply with this demand; but Charles had made up his mind, and it had to be written.

Here is a faithful copy of the original, which King Stanislas still keeps, and which I have lately seen.

"SIR AND BROTHER,

"We do not consider it was necessary to enter upon a detailed correspondence with your Majesty; but to please the King of Sweden, and that it may not be said that we have been unwilling to satisfy him, we hereby congratulate you on your accession, and hope that your subjects will prove more faithful to you than ours have been to us. Every one will do us the justice to believe that we have only been paid with ingratitude for all our benefits, and that the majority of our subjects have only aimed at our ruin. We hope that you will not be exposed to like misfortunes, and commit you to God's keeping.

"Your brother and neighbour,

"AUGUSTUS, King.

"*Dresden: April* 8, 1707."

Augustus was further obliged to command all the magistrates to no longer style him King of Poland, and to efface the title he renounced from the liturgy. He was less concerned about liberating the Sobieskis; on coming out of prison these princes refused to see him. But the sacrifice of Patkul was a great hardship to him; on the one hand, the Czar was clamouring for him to be sent back as his ambassador; on the other, the King of Sweden threatened terrible penalties if he were not handed over. Patkul was then imprisoned in the castle of Konigstein in Saxony. Augustus thought he could satisfy Charles and his own honour at the same time. He sent his guards to deliver up the wretched prisoner to the Swedish troops; but sent, in advance, a secret message to the Governor of Konigstein to let him escape. Patkul's bad luck frustrated the care they took to save him. The governor, knowing him to be very rich, wished him to buy his liberty. The prisoner, still relying on the law of nations, and informed of the intentions of King Augustus, refused to pay for what he thought he could obtain for nothing. During the interval, the guards appointed to deliver him to the Swedes arrived, and handed him over at once to the four Swedish officers, who took him straight to head-quarters at Altranstadt, where he stayed three months, tied to a stake by a heavy iron chain. Then he was taken to Casimir.

Charles XII, forgetting that he was the Czar's ambassador, and only remembering that he had been his own subject, commanded the court-martial to pass sentence upon him with the greatest rigour. He was condemned to be broken on the wheel and quartered. A chaplain came to tell him he must die, without informing him of the form of his execution. Then the man who had braved death in so many battles, finding himself alone with a priest, and his courage no longer supported by the incitements of glory or passion, wept bitterly.

He was engaged to a Saxon lady, named Madame D'Einstedel, who had birth, merit, and beauty, and whom he had hoped to marry at the time that he was given up to execution. He asked the chaplain to visit her and comfort her, and assure her that he died full of the tenderest affection for her. When he was led to the place of execution, and saw the wheels and stakes in readiness for his death, he fell into convulsions of fear, and threw himself into the arms of the minister, who embraced him, and covering him with his cloak wept over him. A Swedish officer then read aloud a paper as follows—

"This is to declare that the express order of his Majesty, our merciful lord, is, that this man, who is a traitor to his country, be broken and quartered for the reparation of his crimes, and as an example to others. Let every man beware of treason, and faithfully serve his King."

At the words "most merciful lord," Patkul cried out, "What mercy!" and at "traitor to his country," "Alas, I have served it too well." He received sixteen blows, and endured the longest and most dreadful tortures imaginable. So perished the unfortunate Jean Patkul, ambassador and general to the King of Russia.

Those who regarded him only as a revolted subject who had rebelled against his King, thought that he deserved his death, but those who regarded him as a Livonian, born in a province with privileges to defend, and who remembered that he was driven from Livonia just for supporting these rights, called him the martyr to the liberties of his country. All agreed that the title of ambassador to the Czar should have rendered his person sacred. The King of Sweden alone, trained in despotic principles, believed that he had only done an act of justice, while all Europe condemned his cruelty.

His quartered members were exposed on gibbets till 1713, when Augustus, having regained his throne, ordered these testimonials of the straits he was reduced to at Altranstadt to be collected. They were brought to him in a box at Warsaw, in the presence of the French ambassador. The King of Poland showed the box to him, simply remarking, "These are the members of Patkul," without one word of blame or regret for his memory, so that none present dare refer to so sad and terrible a subject.

About this time Paikel, a Livonian officer of Saxon troops, taken prisoner in the field, was condemned at Stockholm by a decree of the Senate; but his sentence was only to lose his head. This difference of punishment in the same cases made it only too plain that Charles, in putting Patkul to so cruel a death, had thought rather of vengeance than of punishment.

However that may be, Paikel, after his condemnation, proposed to the Senate to disclose to the King in exchange for a pardon the secret of the manufacture of gold; he made the experiment in prison, in the presence of

Colonel Hamilton and the magistrates of the town; and whether he had really discovered some useful art, or whether he had learned the art of cunning deception, as seems most probable, certain it is that they carried the gold which was found at the bottom of the crucible to the mint at Stockholm, and made such a circumstantial report to the Senate that the Queen, Charles's grandmother, ordered that the execution should be suspended till the King had been informed of this curious fact, and should send his orders from Stockholm. The King answered that he had refused to pardon a criminal for the entreaties of his friends, and that he would never do for the sake of profit what he could not do for friendship. There was something heroic in this inflexibility on the part of a prince who, it must be remembered, thought the secret possible. When King Augustus heard of the incident he remarked that he was not surprised that the King of Sweden was so indifferent about the philosopher's stone, as he had found it in Saxony.

When the Czar heard of the strange peace that Augustus, in spite of their treaties, had concluded at Altranstadt, and that Patkul, his ambassador and plenipotentiary, had been handed over to the King of Sweden, in defiance of international law, he advertised his complaints in all the Courts of Europe. He wrote to the Emperor of Germany, to the Queen of England, and to the States-General of the United Provinces. He said that the unfortunate necessity to which Augustus had yielded were merely cowardice and treachery. He called upon all these Powers to mediate that his ambassador might be sent back, and to resist the affront which, through him, was offered to all crowned heads; he appealed to their honour not to stoop so low as to guarantee the Peace of Altranstadt, which Charles was urging upon them by threats. The only effect of these letters was to make the power of the King of Sweden more obvious. The Emperor, England and Holland, were then carrying on a destructive war against France; they thought it inexpedient to exasperate Charles by refusing him the vain form of guaranteeing a treaty. As for the wretched Patkul, not one Power mediated for him, which proves both the danger of a subject's reliance on a prince, and also the great prestige of Charles.

A proposal was made in the Czar's Council to retaliate on the Swedish officers who were prisoners at Moscow. The Czar would not consent to a barbarity which would have had such fatal results; there were more Russians prisoners in Sweden than Swedes in Russia.

He sought for a more useful vengeance. The great army of his enemy lay idle in Saxony. Levenhaupt, general to the King of Sweden, who was left in Poland at the head of about 20,000 men, could not guard the passes in a country which was both unfortified and full of factions. Stanislas was at the camp of Charles. The Russian Emperor seized the chance, and entered Poland with more than 60,000 men; he split them into several corps, and marched with a flying camp as far as Leopold, which was not garrisoned by the Swedes. All Polish towns are at the mercy of whoever may present himself at their gates at the head of an army. He had an assembly called together at Leopold, like the one which had dethroned Augustus at Warsaw.

Poland then had two primates, as well as two kings, the one nominated by Augustus, the other by Stanislas. The primate nominated by Augustus summoned the assembly at Leopold, and got together there all those men whom the Prince had abandoned by the Peace of Altranstadt, and also those who had been bribed to the Czar's side. It was proposed to elect a new king. So that Poland was very near having three kings at one time, and no one could say which was the right one.

During the conferences of Leopold, the Czar, whose interests were closely connected with those of the Emperor of Germany, through their mutual fear of the King of Sweden, secretly obtained from him a number of German officers. These gradually considerably strengthened his force, by the discipline and experience they brought with them.

He attached them to his service by great rewards; and for the greater encouragement of his own troops he gave his portrait set in diamonds to all the generals who had fought in the battle of Calish; the subaltern officers had gold medals, and every private soldier had a silver medal.

These monuments of the victory at Calish were all struck in the new town of Petersburg, where arts and sciences flourished in proportion as he taught his troops of emulation and glory. The confusion, multiplicity of factions, and frequent ravages in Poland hindered the Diet of Leopold from coming to any conclusion. The Czar transferred it to Lubin. But the change of place made no alteration in the disorder and uncertainty which every one felt. The assembly contented themselves with owning neither Augustus, who had abdicated, nor Stanislas, who had been elected contrary to their wishes.

But they lacked both the unanimity and the resolution to name another king. During these futile deliberations the party of the Princess Sapieha, Oginski's party, those who secretly supported King Augustus, and the new subjects of Stanislas, were all at war with one another, ravaging each other's estates, and completing the ruin of their country.

The Swedish troops, commanded by Levenhaupt, of which one part was in Livonia, another in Lithuania, and a third in Poland, were seeking the Russian troops, and burning the property of Stanislas' enemies. The Russians ruined friends as well as enemies, and nothing was to be seen but towns in ashes, and vagrant troops of Poles, deprived of all their possessions, who hated their two kings Charles and the Czar, equally.

King Stanislas set out from Altranstadt on the 15th of July, 1707, with General Renschild, sixteen Swedish regiments and much money. His object was to appease the troubles in Poland, and to make his authority owned by peaceable means. He was acknowledged wherever he went; the discipline of his troops, which threw into stronger contrast the cruelty of the Russians, gained all hearts; his extreme affability brought round to him, in proportion as it was realized, almost all factions, and his money gained him the majority of the royal forces. The Czar, fearing that he would lack supplies in a country ravaged by his own troops, withdrew into Lithuania, where he had told the various parts of the army to meet, and established magazines. This retreat left King Stanislas in peaceable possession of all Poland.

The only one who then troubled him in his dominions was Count Siniawski, Grand General by nomination of Augustus. He was extremely able and very ambitious, and, heading a third party, he recognized neither Augustus nor Stanislas. He had used all his influence to get himself elected, but was now content to lead a party, as he could not be king.

The crown troops, who continued under his command, had hardly any other pay but licence to ravage their own country with impunity. All who suffered from their ravages or were afraid of them, immediately submitted to Stanislas, whose power was daily increased.

The King of Sweden was then receiving in his camp at Altranstadt ambassadors from almost all the princes of Christendom. Some begged him to retire from the Imperial dominions, others to turn his arms against the Emperor. It was reported on all sides that he meant to join France in crushing the House of Austria.

Amongst these ambassadors was the famous John, Duke of Marlborough, who was sent by Anne, Queen of Great Britain. This man, who took every town that he besieged, and gained every battle that he fought, was a prominent courtier at St. James, the leader of a Parliamentary party, and the most able foreign minister of his time. He did France as much damage by his diplomatic talent as by his arms; and M. Fagel, Secretary of the States-General, has been heard to say that, on more than one occasion, the States having resolved to oppose what the Duke intended to lay before them, the Duke, when he appeared, though he spoke very poor French, brought them all round to his way of thinking.

Together with Prince Eugene, his fellow-victor, and the Grand Pensioner of Holland, Heinsius, he bore the whole weight of the enterprises of the allies against France. He knew that Charles was angry with the Emperor and the

Empire, that he was being secretly approached by the French, and that if the conqueror joined Louis XIV the allies would be overwhelmed.

It is true that Charles had given his word to take no part whatever in the war between Louis XIV and the allies; but the Duke did not believe that any prince would be so great a slave to his word as not to sacrifice it to his greatness and interest. He therefore started for the Hague in order to sound the King of Sweden.

As soon as he arrived at Leipzig, he went secretly, not to Count Piper, first minister, but to Baron Gortz, who was beginning to share the King's confidence with Piper. When he was presented to the King with the English minister Robinson, he spoke French, saying that he would be happy to have the opportunity of acquiring under his direction what he had yet to learn of the art of war. The King made no polite remark in answer to this compliment, and seemed to forget that he was being addressed by Marlborough. The conversation was tedious and trivial, Charles using Swedish, and Robinson acting as interpreter. Marlborough, who was never in a hurry to propose things, and who had learned by long experience the art of reading men, and discovering the connection between their inmost thoughts and their actions, gestures and speech, studied the King carefully. When he spoke on war in general he thought he remarked in his Majesty a natural dislike of France, and he saw, too, that he was talking with pleasure of the conquests of the allies. He noticed that his eyes kindled when he mentioned the Czar, in spite of the restraint shown in the conversation; and he noticed a map of Russia before him on the table. This quite convinced him that the real intention of the King of Sweden, and his only ambition, was to dethrone the Czar, just as he had dethroned the King of Poland. He understood that his object in remaining in Saxony was to impose on the Emperor of Germany certain severe conditions. But he knew that the Emperor would accept them, and that thus matters would be satisfactorily settled. He left Charles to follow his own bent, and, satisfied with having fathomed his intentions, he did not make any proposal to him.

As few negotiations are concluded without money, and as ministers have been known to sell the hatred or friendship of their masters, all Europe believed that the Duke of Marlborough had succeeded with the King of Sweden by means of the gift of a large sum of money to Count Piper, and the Count's reputation has suffered for it to this very day. For my part I have traced this report to its source, and I have it on authority that Piper received a small present from the Emperor, with the consent of the King his master, and nothing from the Duke of Marlborough. It is certain that Charles was bent on dethroning the Czar of Russia, that he took counsel of no one, and that he had no need of advice from Count Piper to wreak his long-meditated vengeance on Peter Alexiowitz. Lastly, the minister's reputation is absolutely vindicated by the fact that Charles paid honour to his memory long after, when, hearing of his death in Russia, he had his body taken to Stockholm, and buried with great pomp and magnificence at his own expense.

The King, who had as yet experienced no ill-fortune, nor even any hindrance to success, thought that one year would dethrone the Czar, and that then he could retrace his steps as the arbiter of Europe; but his aim was first to humiliate the Emperor of Germany.

Baron Stralheim, Swedish ambassador at Vienna, had quarrelled at table with Count Zobor, the Emperor's chamberlain; the latter, having refused to drink to the health of Charles, and having accused him of treating his master too badly, Stralheim had given him the lie with a box on the ears, and had dared, after this insult, to demand reparation at the Imperial Court.

Fear of the displeasure of the King of Sweden had forced the Emperor to banish the subject whom it was his duty to avenge. Charles was not satisfied, but insisted that the Count of Zobor should be handed over to him. The Court of Vienna had to swallow its pride and hand over the Count to the King, who sent him back, after having kept him prisoner some time at Stettin. Contrary to international law he further demanded that 1,500 wretched Russians, who had escaped his arms and fled to the Empire, should be given up to him. The Court of Vienna would have had to consent to this strange demand, and they would have been handed over to the enemy, had not the Russian ambassador at Vienna arranged for their escape by different routes.

The third and last of his demands was the most exorbitant. He declared himself protector of the Emperor's Protestant subjects in Silesia, a province of the House of Austria, and not of the Empire; he wanted the Emperor to grant them the liberties and privileges which had been gained by the Treaty of Westphalia, but nullified, or at least eluded, by the Treaty of Ryswick. The Emperor, whose great aim was to get rid of so dangerous a neighbour, still assented, and granted him all that he wanted. The Lutherans obtained more than 100 churches, which the Catholics were obliged to cede by this treaty, but many of these concessions, secured for them by the King of Sweden's fortune, were taken from them as soon as he could no longer impose laws.

The Emperor, who was forced to make these concessions, and who submitted to Charles's wishes in everything, was Joseph, the eldest son of Leopold, and brother of Charles VI, who succeeded him. The Pope's nuncio, who then resided in the court of Joseph, reproached him severely for ceding, as a Catholic, the interests of his own religion to the heretics. "It is very lucky for you," answered the Emperor, smiling, "that the King of Sweden did not propose that I should turn Protestant, for had he done so I do not know what I might have done."

Count Wratislau, his ambassador to Charles XII, brought the treaty in favour of the Silesians, and signed by his master, to Leipzig. Charles then said he was satisfied, and the firm friend of the Emperor. But he was disgusted that Rome had opposed him to the utmost of her ability. He felt the greatest contempt for the weakness of the Court, which being at present the irreconcilable enemy of half Europe, always distrusts the other half, and only maintains its credit by its skilful diplomacy. He seemed determined on vengeance. He told Count Wratislau that the Swedes had once subjugated Rome, and that they had not degenerated as she had done.

He let the Pope know that he would one day demand the effects which Queen Christina had left at Rome. It is impossible to say how far this young conqueror would have carried his resentment and his arms, had fortune seconded his designs. Nothing then seemed an impossibility to him; he even sent several officers secretly to Asia, and as far as Egypt, to take plans of the towns and inform him of the strength of those countries. Certainly, if any one were capable of overturning the empire of the Persians and Turks, and then going on into Italy, it was Charles XII. He was as young as Alexander, as great a soldier, and as daring; but he was more indefatigable, stronger, and more temperate; then the Swedes, too, were perhaps better men than the Macedonians. But such plans, which are called divine when they succeed, are regarded as chimeras when they fail.

At last, all difficulties having been overcome, and all his plans carried out, after having humiliated the Emperor, dictated to the Empire, protected the Lutherans in the midst of Roman Catholics, dethroned one king and crowned another, and made himself the terror of all princes, he prepared to start. The luxuries of Saxony, where he remained idle a whole year, had made no alteration in his mode of life. He rode out thrice a day, got up at four o'clock in the morning, dressed unaided, never drank wine, only spent a quarter of an hour at table, exercised his men every day, and indulged in no other pleasure than that of making Europe tremble.

The Swedes did not yet know what was to be their destination, but it was rumoured in the army that Charles might go to Moscow. Some days before he started he commanded the Grand Marshal of the Household to write out for him the route from Leipzig, then he paused, and, that the Grand Marshal should have no idea of his project, he added, with a smile, "and to all the capitals of Europe." The marshal brought him a list of them all, at the head of which he had purposely placed "Route from Leipzig to Stockholm." The majority of the Swedes longed to return thither, but it was far from the King's intention to take them back home. "Monsieur le Maréchal," he said, "I see whither you would lead me; but we shall not return to Stockholm so soon."

The army was already on the march, and passed near Dresden. Charles was at their head, riding, as was his habit, two or three hundred paces in advance of his guards. Suddenly they lost sight of him; some officers advanced at full gallop to see what had become of him, but they could not find him. In a minute the whole army took the alarm. They halted; the generals assembled; they were in a state of great consternation when they learned from a Saxon peasant what had become of him.

As he was passing so near Dresden, he had taken it into his head to pay a visit to King Augustus; he rode into the town, followed by three or four generals. Count Fleming, seeing them pass, had only time to run and let his master know. He suggested to Augustus a suitable reception on this occasion, but Charles came into the room in his boots, before Augustus had time to recover from his surprise. He was then ill, and in a nightshirt, but he hastily dressed. Charles breakfasted with him as a traveller taking leave of a friend, then he expressed a wish to see the fortifications. During the short time that they were going round them, a Livonian, exiled from Sweden, who was serving in the Saxon army, thought that he could not have a better chance of pardon. He felt sure that his Majesty would not refuse so small a favour to a prince from whom he had taken a crown, and in whose power he had placed himself. Augustus readily undertook the office—he was a short distance from Charles, talking to General Hord. "I believe," he said, smiling, "that your master would not refuse me." "You don't know him," answered the General; "he would rather refuse you here than anywhere else." This did not prevent Augustus from asking a pardon for the Livonian in the most pressing way. Charles refused, in such a way that it was impossible to ask again. After having spent some hours on this strange visit, he embraced Augustus and departed.

On rejoining his army, he found all his generals panic-stricken. He inquired the reason; they told him that they had determined to besiege Dresden, in case he had been detained prisoner there. "Pshaw!" said the King; "they dare not." The next day they got news that Augustus was holding a Council extraordinary at Dresden. "You see," remarked Renschild, "they are deliberating as to what they ought to have done yesterday." Some days later, Renschild, in an interview with the King, spoke with astonishment of the journey to Dresden. "I had confidence in my good fortune," said Charles; "but at one moment it looked critical. Fleming was not at all anxious that I should leave Dresden so soon."

BOOK IV

Charles leaves Saxony—Pursues the Czar—Advances into Ukrania—His losses and wounds, and the battle of Pultowa—The consequences of the battle—Charles forced to escape into Turkey—His reception in Bessarabia.

AT last Charles left Saxony in September 1707, with an army of 43,000 men, formerly steel-clad, but now shining resplendent in gold and silver, and enriched with the spoils of Poland and Saxony. Every soldier had with him fifty crowns ready money; not only, too, were all the regiments complete, but there were several supernumeraries to each company. Besides this army Count Levenhaupt, one of his best generals, was waiting for him in Poland with 20,000 men; he had, too, another army of 15,000 in Finland, and recruits were on their way from Sweden. With all these forces it was not doubted that he would dethrone the Czar.

The Emperor was then in Russia, trying to keep up the spirits of a party which King Augustus seemed to have deserted. His troops, divided into several corps, fled in all directions on the first report of the approach of the King of Sweden. He had advised his generals never to wait for the arrival of the conqueror with a superior force, and he was well obeyed.

The King of Sweden, in the midst of his march, received an embassy from the Turks. The ambassador was received in Piper's quarters; he kept up his master's dignity by a certain display of magnificence, and the King, who was worse lodged, worse served, and more plainly clad than the humblest officer in his army, would often say that Count Piper's quarters were his palace. The Turkish ambassador presented Charles with 100 Swedish soldiers, who had been taken by the Calmouks and sold in Turkey, redeemed by the Grand Master, and sent by him to the King as the most agreeable present he could make him. Not that the proud Ottoman meant to pay homage to the glory of Charles, but because the Sultan, the natural enemy of the Emperors of Russia and Germany, wished to strengthen himself against them by the friendship of the King of Sweden and alliance with Poland.

The ambassador complimented Stanislas on his accession; so that he had been owned as King, in a short time, by Germany, France, England, Spain and Turkey. But the Pope deferred acknowledging him till time had confirmed him in a kingship of which a sudden fall might deprive him.

Scarcely had Charles interviewed the ambassador of the Ottoman Porte than he went in search of the Russians. The Czar's troops had left and returned to Poland more than twenty times during the war; as the country lay open on all sides, without strongholds to cut the retreat of an enemy, the Russians were often able to return to the very spot where they had suffered defeat, and could even penetrate as far into the country as the conqueror. During Charles's stay in Saxony, the Czar had advanced to Leopold, on the southern frontier of Poland. He was at that time in the north, at Grodno, in Lithuania, about 100 leagues from Leopold.

Charles left Stanislas in Poland with about 1,000 Swedes and his new subjects to help him preserve his kingdom against his enemies at home and abroad; he himself, at the head of his horse, marched through ice and snow to Grodno, in January 1708. He had already passed the Niemen, within two leagues of the town, before the Czar knew anything of his march. Directly the news came that the Swedes were upon them, the Czar left the town by the north gate, while Charles entered by the south. The King had only six hundred of his guards with him, the rest being unable to follow him. The Czar, imagining that a whole army was entering Crodno, fled with 2,000 men; but he heard that very day from a Polish deserter that he had abandoned the place to not more than six hundred men, the body of the enemy's army being still more than five leagues away. He did not lose time, but sent a detachment of 15,000 cavalry in the evening to surprise the King of Sweden in the town. The 15,000 Russians, helped by the darkness of the night, advanced as far as the first Swedish guard without recognition. This guard consisted of thirty men, and they alone supported the charge of the 15,000 for seven minutes. The King, who was at the other end of the town, came up presently with his six hundred guards, and the Russians fled in haste. In a short time his army joined him, and he pursued the enemy. All the Russians dispersed throughout Lithuania, retiring hastily into the Palatinate of Minski, where they had a rendezvous. The Swedes, whom the King also divided into several corps, continued to pursue them for about thirty leagues of their way. The fleers and the pursuers made forced marches almost every day, though it was midwinter.

The soldiers of Charles and the Czar had long become indifferent to the seasons: it was only the terror inspired by the name of Charles which made the difference between the Russians and the Swedes.

From Grodno eastward to the Borysthenes there is nothing but marshes, deserts, mountains and immense forests. Even where the ground is cultivated no provision was to be found; the country folk hid all their grain and other dry goods underground. In order to find these subterranean magazines, they had to sound the earth with long poles tipped with iron. The Russians and the Swedes used these provisions by turns, but they were not always discovered, nor were they always sufficient when they were.

The King of Sweden, who had foreseen these difficulties, had provided biscuit for his army, so that nothing hindered his march. After he had crossed the forest of Minski, where his men were obliged every moment to cut down trees to make way for the troops and baggage, he found himself, on the 25th of June, 1708, near Borislou, in front of the river Berezine.

The Czar had assembled the best part of his troops in this spot and had entrenched himself to advantage; his aim was to hinder the Swedes from crossing the river. Charles placed some of his regiment on the banks of the Berezine, close to Borislou, as though he intended to attempt the crossing in face of the enemy. At the same time he led his army about three leagues up the river, threw a bridge across it, cut his way through a body of 3,000 men who defended that post, and marched straight against the enemy without a halt. The Russians did not wait for his arrival, but immediately decamped and withdrew towards Borysthenes, spoiling all the roads, and destroying all on their line of march, so that they might at least delay the Swedes' advance.

Charles surmounted all difficulties, continually advancing towards Borysthenes. On his way he met 20,000 Russians, entrenched at a spot called Hollosin, behind a marsh, which could not be reached without crossing a river. Charles did not wait till the rest of his infantry had arrived to make the attack, but threw himself into the water at the head of his foot-guards, and crossed the river and the morass, though the water was sometimes above his shoulders. While he thus attacked the enemy, he ordered his cavalry to pass round the morass and take them in the flank.

The Russians, amazed that no barrier could defend them, were simultaneously routed by the King on foot, and by the Swedish horse. The horse, having made their way through the enemy, joined the King in the midst of the fray. He then mounted, but some time after, finding a young Swedish noble named Gyllenstein, for whom he had great affection, wounded in the fray and unable to walk, he insisted on his taking his horse, and continued to command on foot at the head of his infantry. Of all the battles he had ever fought, this was in all probability the most glorious—that in which he was exposed to the greatest risks, and in which he showed the greatest ability. The memory of it is kept by a medal with the inscription, "Silvæ, paludes, aggeres, hostes, victi" on one side and "Victrices copias alium laturus in orbem" on the other.

The Russians, driven out everywhere, recrossed the Borysthenes, which separates Poland from their own country. Charles lost no time in following them; he crossed the great river after them at Mohilou, the last town in Poland, which is sometimes in the hands of the Poles, sometimes in those of the Czar, after the usual fate of frontier places.

The Czar, seeing his empire, into which he was introducing arts and commerce, becoming a prey to a war which might in a short time ruin his plans, and perhaps lose him his throne, was thinking of peace, and even made proposals by a Polish nobleman whom he sent to the Swedish army. Charles, who had been unaccustomed to granting peace to his enemy except in their capitals, only replied, "I will treat with the Czar at Moscow."

When the Czar heard this haughty answer, "My brother Charles," he said, "would still pose as Alexander, but I flatter myself he will find me no Darius."

From Mohilou, where the King crossed the Borysthenes, turning north along the river, upon the frontiers of Poland and Russia, is situated the country of Smolensko, through which lies the main road from Poland to Moscow. The Czar fled by this road, and the King followed by forced marches. Part of the Russian rearguard was more than once engaged with the dragoons of the Swedish vanguard. Generally the latter got the advantage, but they weakened themselves by these skirmishes, which were never decisive, and always meant the loss of some of their men.

On the 22nd of September this year, 1708, the King attacked a body of ten thousand horse and six thousand Calmouks near Smolensko.

These Calmouks are Tartars, living between Astrakan, which is part of the Czar's dominions, and Samarcande, the country of the Usbeck Tartars. The Calmouks' country stretches from the east to the mountains which separate the Mogul from the western part of Asia. Those who dwell near Astrakan are tributary to the Czar. He pretends to absolute dominion over them, but their wandering life hinders him from subduing them, and forces him to treat them as the Grand-Seignior treats the Arabs, sometimes bearing with their robberies, and at others punishing them.

There are always some of the Calmouks in the Russian army, and the Czar had even succeeded in reducing them to discipline like the rest of his soldiers.

The King fell on this army with only six regiments of horse and four thousand infantry; he broke the Russian ranks at the head of his Ostrogothic regiment and forced the enemy to retreat. The King advanced upon them by rough and hollow ways where the Calmouks lay hid; they then appeared and threw themselves between the regiment where the King was fighting and the rest of the Swedish army. In an instant both Russians and Calmouks had surrounded this regiment and made their way close up to his Majesty. They killed two aides-de-camp who were fighting near him. The King's horse was killed under him, and as one of the equerries was offering him another, both equerry and horse were struck dead on the spot. Charles fought on foot, surrounded by some of his officers who immediately hastened to rally round him.

Several were taken, wounded or slain, or swept off to a distance from the King by the crowd which attacked them; so that there were only five men left near him. By that extraordinary good luck which till then had never deserted him, and on which he always relied, he had killed more than a dozen of the enemy with his own hand without one wound. At last Colonel Dardoff forced his way, with only one company of his regiment, through the Calmouks, and came up just in time to save the King. The rest of the Swedes put the Tartars to the sword. The army reformed, Charles mounted, and, fatigued as he was, pursued the Russians two leagues.

The conqueror was still on the main road to the capital of Russia. The distance from Smolensko, where this battle was fought, to Moscow, is about 100 French leagues; the army had scarcely any provisions. The King was pressed to wait till General Levenhaupt, who was to bring up reinforcements of 15,000 men, came to join him. Charles, who rarely listened to advice, not only refused to listen to this wise counsel, but, to the great amazement of the whole army, left the Moscow road, and marched south towards Ukrania into the country of the Cossacks, between lesser Tartary, Poland and Russia.

This country is about 100 French leagues from north to south, and about the same from east to west. It is divided into two nearly equal parts by the Borysthenes, which crosses from north-west to south-west; the chief town is Baturin, on the little river Sem. The northernmost part of Ukrania is under cultivation, and rich; the southernmost part, in the forty-eighth degree, is one of the most fertile and at the same time the most deserted districts in the world; bad management quite counteracts its natural advantages.

The inhabitants of those parts, which border on lesser Tartary, neither plant nor sow lest the Tartars of Budziac, Precop and Moldavia, who are all brigands, should carry off their harvests.

Ukrania has always aspired to freedom; but being hedged in by Russia, the dominions of the Grand-Seignior, and Poland, it has been obliged to seek for a protector (who is, of course, a master) in one of those States. First it put itself under the protection of Poland, who treated it too much as a subject-state; then they appealed to the Russians, who did their best to reduce them to serfdom. At first the Ukranians had the privilege of choosing a prince, called general, but soon they were deprived of this privilege, and their general was nominated by the Russian Court.

The office was then filled by a Pole called Mazeppa; he had been brought up as page to King John Casimir, and had got a little learning at his Court. On the discovery of an intrigue with the wife of a Polish nobleman, the latter had him tied, stark naked, to a wild horse, and set him free in that state. The horse, which had been brought from Ukrania, returned to its own country, carrying Mazeppa with him half dead from hunger and fatigue. Some of the peasants gave him relief, and he stayed a long time among them, and distinguished himself in several attempts against the Tartars. The superiority of his intelligence made him a person of consideration in the eyes of the

Cossacks, and as his reputation daily increased the Czar was forced to make him Prince of Ukrania.

One day, as he was sitting at table with the Czar at Moscow, the Emperor proposed to him to drill the Cossacks and make them more independent. Mazeppa pointed out the situation of Ukrania and the nature of the people as insurmountable obstacles. The Czar, who was over-heated with wine, and had not always sufficient self-control, called him a traitor, and threatened to have him impaled. On his return into Ukrania Mazeppa planned a revolt. The Swedish army appearing shortly after on the frontier facilitated matters for him, and he resolved to gain independence, and to form for himself a powerful kingdom from Ukrania and the ruins of the Russian Empire. He was a man of great courage, of considerable enterprise, and most painstaking, though he was advanced in years.

He made a secret league with the King of Sweden, to hasten the Czar's downfall and gain something himself out of it. He gave him a rendezvous near the river Desna; Mazeppa promised to meet him there with 30,000 men, ammunition and provisions, and all his treasure, which was immense. The Swedish army was therefore ordered to march towards that part of the country, to the great regret of the officers, who knew nothing of the King's treaty with the Cossacks.

Charles sent orders to Levenhaupt to bring his troops and provisions with all haste to Ukrania, where he intended passing the winter, that, having subdued that country, he might conquer Russia the following spring; meanwhile he advanced towards the river Desna, which flows into the Borysthenes at Kiouw.

The obstacles they had hitherto encountered on their march were trifles to those they met on this new route; they had to cross a forest fifty leagues broad, which was full of marshes. General Lagercron, who led the van with 5,000 men and pioneers, led the army thirty leagues too far to the east. They had marched four days before the King discovered their mistake. They regained the right road with some difficulty, but almost all the artillery and wagons were stuck fast or sunk in the mud.

They then marched for twelve days in this painful and laborious fashion till they had eaten the little biscuit they had left, and so they arrived, spent with hunger and fatigue, on the banks of the Desna, where Mazeppa was to meet them. Instead of the Prince, however, they found a body of Russians advancing towards them on the other side of the river. The King was much astonished, and decided to cross the Desna and attack the enemy. The banks of this river were so steep that they were obliged to let the soldiers down by cords; then they crossed in their usual manner, some by swimming, some on hastily constructed rafts.

The band of Russians, which arrived at the same time, were only 8,000, so that their resistance was feeble, and this obstacle was also overcome.

Charles advanced further into this desolate country, uncertain of his route and of Mazeppa's fidelity; at last the latter appeared, but rather as a fugitive than as a strong ally. The Russians had discovered and prevented his plan: they had fallen upon the Cossacks and cut them in pieces; his chief friends were taken red-handed, and thirty of them had been broken on the wheel. His towns were reduced to ashes, his treasures plundered, and the provisions he was preparing for the King of Sweden seized. He himself escaped with difficulty, accompanied by 6,000 men, and some horses laden with gold and silver. But he held out to the King the hope that he would be of some service from his knowledge of this unknown country, and by the affection of the natives, who, enraged with the Russians, came in troops to the camp, and brought provisions.

Charles hoped that at least General Levenhaupt would come to repair this ill fortune; he was to bring about 15,000 Swedes (of more use than 100,000 Cossacks), with stores and ammunition. He arrived at last, but almost in the same condition as Mazeppa. He had already passed the Borysthenes above Mohilou, and advanced about twenty leagues further on the road to Ukrania. He brought the King a convoy of 8,000 wagons, with the money he had raised in Lithuania and on march. On reaching Lesno, near the spot where the rivers Pronia and Sossa unite to flow into the Borysthenes far below, the Czar appeared at the head of 50,000 men.

The Swedish general, who had not quite 16,000, decided not to entrench. Their many victories had given the Swedes so much confidence that they never inquired as to the enemy's numbers, but only their position. Levenhaupt marched against them on the 7th of October, 1708, in the afternoon. At the first attack they killed 15,000 Russians; the Czar's army took panic and fled in all directions, and the Emperor of Russia thought he would be entirely defeated. He saw that the safety of his dominions depended upon the action of the day, and that he could be ruined if Levenhaupt joined the King of Sweden with a victorious army.

As soon as he saw his troops fall back he ran to the rear, where the Cossacks and Calmouks were posted, and said, "I order you to fire on every man who runs away, and even to shoot me, should I be so cowardly as to turn my back." Then he returned to the van and rallied the troops in person, assisted by the Prince Menzikoff and Prince Gallitsin. Levenhaupt, who had pressing orders to join his master, chose to continue his march rather than to renew the battle, thinking that he had done enough to discourage the enemy from pursuit.

No later than eleven the next morning the Czar attacked him on the entrance to a morass, and spread his lines to surround him. The Swedes faced about, and the fight lasted two hours with equal resolution on both sides. The Russians lost three times as many men, but still held their position, and the victory was undecided. At four General Bayer brought the Czar reinforcements. The battle was then renewed for the third time with greater fury than before, and lasted till nightfall. Then the force of numbers carried the day; the Swedes were broken, routed, and driven back on their baggage. Levenhaupt rallied his men behind his chariots, and though they were conquered they did not flee.

Not one from an army of about 9,000 men took to flight. The general formed them up as easily as if they had not been beaten. The Czar, on the other hand, passed the night under arms, and ordered his soldiers on pain of death, and his officers on pain of dismissal, to abstain from plunder.

Next morning at daybreak he ordered a fresh attack. Levenhaupt had retired to a strong position some miles distant, after having spiked some of his cannon and fired some of his wagons. The Russians came up just in time to hinder the whole convoy from being burned, and seized six thousand wagons which they saved. The Czar, who wished to utterly crush the Swedes, sent one of his generals, called Phulg, to attack them for the fifth time, and he offered them honourable terms if they would capitulate. Levenhaupt refused, and the fifth battle was as bloody as any of the former ones. Of the 9,000 soldiers he had left he lost half, the other half not breaking line. At last night came on, and Levenhaupt, after having fought five battles against 50,000 men, crossed the Sossa by swimming, followed by the 5,000 men remaining to him. The wounded were carried over on rafts. The Czar lost about 20,000 Russians in these engagements, in which he had the glory of conquering the Swedes, and Levenhaupt the credit of disputing the victory for three days, and of retreating without being forced from his last position. So that he came to his master's camp with the honour of having made so good a defence, but without ammunition or forces. The King of Sweden, therefore, without provisions, and cut off from communication with Poland, was surrounded by enemies in the midst of a country where he had scarcely any resource but his own courage.

In this extremity the memorable winter of 1709, which was still more severe in those frontiers of Europe than it was in France, destroyed a part of his army. Charles resolved to defy the season as he had his enemies; he ventured on long marches with his troops during the bitter cold. It was on one of these marches that 2,000 of his men died of cold before his very eyes. The cavalry had no boots, and the foot no shoes, and hardly any clothes. They were forced to make footgear of the skins of beasts as best they could, and they often went hungry. They had even been obliged to throw the best part of their cannon into quagmires and rivers for want of horses to draw them; so that this once flourishing army was reduced to 24,000 men at the point of starvation. They neither got news from Sweden, nor were they able to send there. In this state of affairs one officer only complained. "What," said the King to him, "are you miserable at being so far from your wife? If you are really a soldier I will lead you to such a distance that you will not hear from Sweden once in three years."

The Marquis of Brancas, now Swedish ambassador, told me that a soldier ventured to present the King, before the whole army, with a piece of bread that was black and mouldy. It was made from barley and oats, and was the only food they then had, and that in scanty quantities. The King received the piece of bread unmoved, ate it all, and then said coolly to the soldier, "It is not good, but one can eat it." This characteristic touch, insignificant as it is (if, indeed, that should be called insignificant which increases respect and confidence), did more than all the rest to help the Swedish army to bear hardships which would have been insupportable under any other general.

In these circumstances he at last received news from Stockholm, but only that his sister the Duchess of Holstein, aged 27, had been carried off by small-pox. She was as gentle and pitiful as her brother was imperious and implacable in revenge. He had always been very fond of her; he felt her loss the more as, now that the tide of his fortune had turned, he was more susceptible. He learned also that they had carried out his orders and raised troops and money, but could not send them to his camp; for there lay between him and Stockholm nearly five hundred leagues and an enemy with a superior force to encounter.

The Czar, who was as energetic as the King, after having sent fresh forces into Poland to assist the confederates, united under General Siniawski against Stanislas, and soon advanced into Ukrania, in the middle of this severe winter, to oppose the King of Sweden. He stayed there with the object of weakening the enemy by small engagements, for by this means he thought the Swedish army must be quite wrecked at last, as he was able to draw fresh forces every moment from his dominions, while they could not get recruits. The cold there must have been excessive, since it forced the two enemies to suspend hostilities. But on the first of February, amid ice and snow, they began to fight again.

After several small skirmishes and some reverses, the King's army was reduced in April to 18,000 men. Mazeppa alone, the Prince of the Cossacks, supplied them with the necessaries of life; without his assistance the army must have perished from hunger and destitution.

At this moment, the Czar, to attract Mazeppa to his service again, offered him terms; but the Cossack stood by his new ally, either from fear of the terrible punishment of the wheel, by which his friends had perished, or because he sought revenge.

Charles, with his 18,000 Swedes and as many Cossacks, had not abandoned his plan of reaching Russia. Towards the end of May he went to siege Pultawa, on the river Vorskla, on the extreme eastern frontier of Ukrania, about thirteen full leagues from the Borysthenes, where the Czar had a magazine. This country is that of the Zaporavians, the strangest people in the world. They are a collection of former Russians, Poles, Tartars, and all make profession of a kind of Christianity, and of a kind of freebooting brigandage. They elect a chief, whom they depose or assassinate; they allow no women to live among them, but they kidnap all the children for twenty or thirty leagues round, and train them in their ways. During summer they are always in the field, during winter they sleep in vast barns, containing 400 or 500 men. They fear nothing, and live at liberty; they risk death for the smallest booty, with the same boldness with which Charles XII faced it to bestow crowns. The Czar sent them 60,000 florins in the hope that they would side with him; they took the money and then, through the exertions of Mazeppa, declared for Charles: but they proved of very little use, for they think it ridiculous to fight for anything but booty. It was a great point gained that they did no harm: there were about 2,000 of them at most who did regular duty. Ten of their chiefs were one day presented to Charles, but they had great difficulty in finding those who were not intoxicated, for they always began the day in that condition. They were taken into the trenches, and showed their skill in shooting with long rifles, for they could pick off the enemies they singled out at 600 paces away. Charles added to these bandits some 1,000 Valaques; then he laid siege to Pultawa, with an army of about 30,000 men, in a wretched condition and wanting all necessaries. The Czar had made Pultawa a magazine: if the King took it it would open the road to Moscow for him, and he could await, well supplied, the recruits he expected from Sweden, Livonia, Pomerania and Poland. As, then, his sole resource lay in the taking of Pultawa, he carried on the siege with vigour. Mazeppa, who had informants in the town, assured him that he would soon master it, and hope began to reanimate the army. His soldiers regarded the taking of Pultawa as the end of all their miseries.

From the beginning of the siege the King realized that he had given his enemies some useful lessons in the art of war. Prince Menzikoff, in spite of all his precautions, threw reinforcements into the town, and the garrison then amounted to almost 10,000 men. They made sorties, sometimes successfully; but what made the town impregnable was the approach of the Czar, who was advancing with 10,000 combatants. Charles XII went to meet him on the 27th of May, his birthday, and beat one of their corps; but as he was returning from his camp he got a musket-shot, which pierced his boot and shattered his heel-bone. There was not the least sign on his face that he had been shot; he continued calmly to give his orders, and remained mounted nearly six hours after the accident. One of his servants at last noticing that the sole of his boot was covered with blood, ran for the doctor; then the King's pain was so acute that they had to take him off his horse and carry him to his tent. The surgeons examined the wound and saw that it had already begun to mortify, and thought that the leg must be cut off. The consternation in the army was great. But one of the surgeons, called Newman, better skilled and braver than the rest, was certain that he could save the leg by means of a deep incision.

"Begin at once, then," said the King; "cut boldly, fear nothing." He held his leg with his own hands, looking at the incisions made as if they were in the leg of another.

As they were putting on the dressing he gave orders for an assault next morning, but scarcely had he given the order than they brought him word that the whole army of the enemy was upon him. He was therefore obliged to alter his plan. Wounded and incapable of action, he found himself shut in between the river Borysthenes and the river which runs to Pultawa, in a desert district, with no forts or ammunition, and opposed to an army which cut him off from retreat or provisions. In this terrible position he did not, as might have been expected, assemble a council of war, but on the night of 7th July he sent for Marshal Renschild, and ordered him, without deliberation, but without uneasiness, to prepare to attack the Czar next morning. Renschild did not argue, but went to carry out his orders.

At the door of the King's tent he met Count Piper, with whom, as often happens between the minister and the general, he had long been on bad terms. Piper asked him if there were anything new. "No," said the General coldly, and passed on to give his orders. As soon as Piper entered the royal tent the King asked if Renschild had told him anything. "Nothing," answered Piper. "Well, then," answered the King, "I tell you that to-morrow we shall give battle." Count Piper was astonished at so desperate a resolve, but he knew that his master could never be made to change his opinion; he only expressed his astonishment by his silence, and left the King to sleep till dawn.

The battle of Pultawa was fought on the 8th of July, 1709, between the two most famous monarchs in the world: Charles XII, distinguished by a course of nine years' victories, and Peter Alexiowitz by nine years of painstaking training of his troops to an equality with the Swedes; the one famed for having given away the dominions of others, the other for having civilized his own; Charles loving danger and fighting only for the sake of glory, Alexiowitz not running away from difficulties, and making war from interested motives only; the Swedish King liberal from a generous temperament, the Russian never generous but with some object in view; the former sober and temperate in an extraordinary degree, naturally brave and only once showing cruelty, the latter not having thrown off the roughness of his education or his race, as terrible to his subjects as he was wonderful to strangers, and addicted to excess which, as a matter of fact, shortened his days. Charles bore the title "Invincible," which he might lose at any moment; the nations had already given Peter the title "Great," which he could not lose by any defeat, as he did not owe it to his victories.

To get a clear idea of this battle and the place where it was fought, one must imagine Pultawa to the north, the King of Sweden's camp to the south, slightly to the east; his baggage about a mile behind him, and the river Pultawa on the north side of the town, running from east to west. The Czar had passed the river about a league from Pultawa, towards the west, and was beginning to form his camp. At daybreak the Swedes appeared above their trenches with four cannon for their artillery; the rest were left in the camp with about 3,000 men, and 4,000 remained with the baggage. So that the Swedish army marching against the enemy consisted of about 25,000 men, of whom not more than 12,000 were regulars. Generals Renschild, Roos, Levenhaupt, Slipenbak, Hoorn, Sparre, Hamilton, the Prince of Wirtemburg, a relation of the King, and some others, most of whom had been at the battle of Narva, reminded the subalterns of that day, when 8,000 Swedes had destroyed an army of 100,000 Russians in entrenchments. The officers remarked it to the soldiers, and all encouraged one another on the march.

The King conducted the march, carried in a litter at the head of his infantry. By his order a party of horse advanced to attack that of the enemy; the battle began with this engagement. At half-past four in the morning the enemy's cavalry lay to the west, on the right of the Russian camp: Prince Menzikoff and Count Golowin had placed them at intervals between redoubts fortified with cannon. General Slipenbak, at the head of the Swedes, fell upon them. All who have served with the Swedes know that it is almost impossible to resist their first onset. The Russian squadrons were broken and put to flight. The Czar himself ran to rally them, and his hat was pierced by a musket shot. Menzikoff had three horses killed under him, and the Swedes shouted victory.

Charles was sure that the battle was gained; he had sent General Creuts about midnight with five thousand horse to attack the enemy's rear while he attacked their front, but, as ill-luck would have it, Creuts lost his way and did not appear.

The Czar, who had thought that all was lost, had time to rally his cavalry, and fell on the King's horse in his turn; unsupported by Creuts' detachment it was broken, and Slipenbak taken prisoner. At the same time seventy-two cannon from the camp played on the Swedish horse, and the Russian foot, issuing from their lines, advanced to attack Charles.

The Czar then detached Menzikoff and sent him to take up a position between Pultawa and the Swedes. He carried out his master's orders dexterously and promptly: not only did he cut the communication between the Swedish army and the troops remaining in the camp at Pultawa, but meeting a body of 3,000 reserves he cut them to pieces. Meanwhile, the Russian foot issued from their lines and advanced in order into the plain on the other side; the Swedish horse rallied within a quarter of a league of the enemy's army, and the King, assisted by General Renschild, gave orders for a general engagement.

He ranged his remaining troops in two lines, his foot in the centre, his horse on the two wings. The Czar arranged his forces in the same way; he had the advantage in numbers and also seventy-two cannon, while the Swedes had only four, and were running out of powder.

The Czar was in the centre of his army, and at that time bore the title of Major-General, and was apparently in the service of General Czeremetoff; but as Emperor he went from rank to rank, mounted on a Turkish horse, a present from the Grand-Seignior, exhorting his officers and soldiers and promising them all rewards. At nine in the morning the battle began again. One of the first discharges of the Russian cannon carried off the two horses of the King's litter; he had two others harnessed in, and a second volley shattered the litter and threw the King out. The troops who were fighting near him believed he was killed; in the consternation the Swedes lost ground, and, their powder failing and the enemy's cannon keeping up fire, the first line fell back on the second, and the second fled. In this last action of the Swedish army they were routed by a single line of 10,000 Russian infantry; so much had matters changed. Prince Wirtemburg, General Renschild and several leading officers were already prisoners; the camp before Pultawa was forced, and all in utterly hopeless confusion. Count Piper and other officers had left the camp and did not know what to do, nor what had become of their King. They ran from one side of the field to the other; Major Bere offered to lead them to the baggage, but the clouds of dust and smoke which covered the field, and their own confusion, carried them to the other side of the town, where they were taken prisoners by the garrison.

The King was unwilling to flee, and would not defend himself. General Poniatowski chanced to be with him at that moment. He was a colonel of King Stanislas' Swedish guards, and a person of remarkable merit, who was so attached to Charles XII that he had accompanied him as a volunteer to Ukrania. He was a man who in all the chances of life, and in danger, where others would at most have only shown courage, always made his plans at once and met with success; he signed to two soldiers, who took the King under the arms and put him on horseback in spite of the great pain of his wound.

Poniatowski, though he had no command in the army, being made general by necessity on this occasion, rallied 500 horse round the King's person: some were dragoons, some ordinary troopers, some officers. This band, inspired by the misfortune of their Prince, made their way through more than ten regiments of Russians and took Charles through the midst of the enemy, the distance of a league, to the baggage of the Swedish army.

This amazing retreat was an achievement in such a disastrous situation, but it was necessary for the King to flee further.

Though the King had never had a coach since he left Stockholm, they found Count Piper's among the baggage. They put him into it and started for the Borysthenes with all haste. The King, who had not spoken a single word from the time he was put on horseback till he came to the baggage, then asked what had become of Count Piper. "He has been taken prisoner with all his chancery officers," they told him. "And General Renschild and the Duke of Wirtemburg?" he asked. "They too are prisoners," said Poniatowski. "Prisoners of the Russians!" exclaimed Charles, with a shrug; "let us rather escape to Turkey." His expression did not change, however, and whoever had seen him and been ignorant of his position would never have suspected that he had been either conquered or wounded.

While he was escaping the Russians seized his artillery in the camp before Pultawa, his baggage and his military chest, containing 6,000,000 in specie, the spoil of Poland and Saxony. Nearly 9,000 Swedes were killed in the battle, about 6,000 were taken prisoners. There still remained some 18,000, including Swedes and Poles, as well as Cossacks, who escaped to the Borysthenes under the direction of General Levenhaupt. He went one way with these fugitives while the King, with some of his cavalry, took another direction. The coach in which he was riding broke down by the way, and they put him on horseback again. To complete his misfortunes he got lost in a wood during the night; there his courage could no longer make up for his spent strength, the pain of his wound was intensified by fatigue, and his horse fell under him from exhaustion. He lay for some hours at the foot of a tree, each moment in danger of a surprise from the conquerors who were looking for him everywhere.

At last, on the night of July 9th, he found himself on the banks of the Borysthenes, and Levenhaupt had just come up with the remnants of the army. The Swedes saw with joy mingled with grief, their King whom they had thought to be dead. The enemy drew near; they had no bridge to pass the river, nor time to make one, nor powder to defend themselves with, nor provisions to save the army from perishing with hunger, for they had eaten nothing for two days.

At all events, the rest of the army were Swedes, and the conquered King was Charles XII. Almost all the officers advised that a stand should be made to meet the Russians, and that they should die or conquer on the banks of the Borysthenes. Doubtless Charles would have decided on this course had he not been overcome with weakness; his wound mortified and he had fever; and it has been remarked that most men, when attacked with the fever of suppuration, lose the instinct of valour which, like other virtues, needs a calm head. Charles was no longer master of himself. They carried him like a sick man who has lost consciousness.

Happily they had still a miserable calash, which they had brought to that spot at great risk; they embarked it in a little boat, and the King and General Mazeppa in another. The latter had saved several coffers full of money, but as the current was very rapid and the wind began to blow the Cossack threw more than three parts of his treasure into the river to lighten the boat. Mullen, the King's chancellor, and Count Poniatowski, who was now more than ever indispensable to the King, for his remarkable presence of mind in difficulties, crossed over in other boats with some of the officers. Three hundred horsemen and a large number of Poles and Cossacks, relying on the strength of their horses, ventured to cross by swimming. Their troop, keeping close together, resisted the current and broke the waves, but all who tried to cross separately a little lower down were carried away and sank. Of the foot that tried to cross not one got to the other side.

While the routed army was in this difficult position Prince Menzikoff came up with 10,000 horse, each with a foot soldier behind him. The bodies of the Swedes who had died on the way of wounds, fatigue and hunger were an index to the Prince of the route that the army had taken. The Prince sent a herald to the Swedish General to offer capitulation. Immediately four generals were sent by Levenhaupt to receive the conqueror's order. Before that day 16,000 of King Charles's soldiers would have attacked the whole force of the Russian empire and have perished to a man, rather than have surrendered; but after a battle lost and a flight of two days, and after having lost their Prince who had been forced to flee himself, the strength of every soldier being spent and their courage no longer supported by hope, the love of life overcame courage. The whole army was made prisoners of war. Some of the soldiers, in despair at falling into Russian hands, threw themselves into the Borysthenes, and the rest were made slaves. They defiled in Prince Menzikoff's presence and laid their arms at his feet, as 30,000 Russians had done nine years before at the King of Sweden's at Narva.

But while the King then sent back all the Russian prisoners he was not afraid of, the Czar kept all the Swedes that were taken at Pultawa. These poor wretches were dispersed throughout the Czar's dominions, and particularly in Siberia, a vast province of greater Tartary which stretches eastward to the frontiers of the Chinese empire. In this barbarous country, where the use of bread was unknown, the Swedes, ingenious through necessity, exercised the trades and arts they had formerly been brought up to. All the distinctions which fortune makes between men were then banished, the officer who had no handicraft was forced to cut and carry wood for the soldier, who had now turned tailor, draper, joiner, mason, or smith, and got a livelihood by his labour. Some officers became painters and some architects, some taught languages and mathematics; they even went so far as to erect public schools, which gradually became so useful and famous that they sent children there from Moscow. Count Piper, the King's first minister, was long imprisoned at Petersburg. The Czar, like the rest of Europe, believed that this minister had sold his master to the Duke of Marlborough, and so brought the arms of Sweden, which might have pacified Europe, on Russia, and he made his captivity more severe on this supposition. Piper died some years after at Moscow, having received little assistance from his family, which lived in great opulence at Stockholm, and uselessly lamented by his King, who would never humble himself by offering a ransom, which he feared the Czar would not accept, for there was never any challenge of exchange between Charles and the Czar. The Emperor of Russia, elated by a joy which he took no pains to conceal, received on the battle-field the prisoners whom they brought to him in troops, and asked every moment, "Where, then, is Charles my brother?"

He paid the Swedish Generals the compliment of inviting them to his table; among other questions he asked Renschild: What were the numbers of the army of the King his master before the battle? Renschild answered that only the King had the list of them and never gave information to any one, but that he thought the whole number might be 35,000 men, of whom 18,000 were Swedes and the rest Cossacks. The Czar seemed surprised, and asked how they dare invade so distant a country and lay siege to Pultawa with so small a force. "We were not always consulted," answered the Swedish General, "but like faithful servants we obeyed our master's orders without ever contradicting him." On this answer the Czar turned to certain courtiers, who had been suspected of conspiring against him, "Ah!" he said, "see how a sovereign should be obeyed."

Then, taking a glass of wine, "To the health of my masters in the art of war," he said. Renschild asked who they were whom he honoured with so high a title? "You, gentlemen, the Swedish Generals," answered the Czar. "Your Majesty is very ungrateful to handle your masters so severely," replied Renschild. When dinner was over the Czar ordered their swords to be restored to all the officers, and treated them as a Prince who had a mind to give his subjects lessons in generosity and good breeding. But this same Prince, who treated the Swedish Generals so well, had all the Cossacks he caught broken on the wheel.

Thus the Swedish army, which left Saxony in such triumph, was now no more: one half having perished from want, and the other half being enslaved or massacred. Charles XII had lost in one day the fruit of nine years' labours and almost a hundred battles.

He fled in a wretched calash, with General Hoorn, dangerously wounded; the rest of his troops followed, some on horseback, some in wagons, across a desert where there were neither huts, tents, men, animals nor roads; everything, even water, was lacking.

That was at the beginning of July. The country is in the forty-seventh degree of latitude; the sun's heat was made less endurable by the dry sand of the desert; horses fell by the way, and men were near dying of thirst. Towards night they found a spring of muddy water; they filled bottles with the water, which saved the lives of the King's little troop. After five days' march he found himself on the banks of the river Hippais, now called the Bogh by the barbarians, who have disfigured even the names of the countries to which Greek colonies had brought prosperity. This river joins the Borysthenes some miles lower, and with it falls into the Black Sea. Beyond the Bogh, towards the south, is the little town of Oczakou, frontier-town of the Turkish empire. The inhabitants, seeing approach a troop of men-at-arms whose dress and language were strange to them, refused to carry them over to Oczakou without an order from the Governor of the town, Mahomet-Bacha. The King sent this Governor an express message, asking for a passage. But the Turk, not knowing how to act in a country where a false step often costs a man his life, dare not act on his own responsibility without the permission of the Pasha of the province, who lived at Bender, in Bessarabia, thirty leagues from Oczakou. While they were awaiting this permission the Russians had crossed the Borysthenes, and approached to seize the King himself.

At last the Pasha sent word to the King saying that he would send a small boat for him and for two or three of his suite. Then the Swedes seized by force what they could not obtain by gentle means: some went to the other bank in a little skiff, and seizing some boats brought them to their bank. This was the means of their rescue, for the owners of the Turkish boats, fearing to lose the chance of some gain, came in crowds to offer their services; just at this moment the favourable reply of the Governor of Bender arrived. But the Russians came up, and the King had the misfortune of seeing 500 of his followers who had not been able to get over in time seized by the enemy, whose insulting boasts he heard. The Pasha of Oczakou asked his pardon, by an interpreter, for these delays, which had caused the capture of the 500 men, and besought him not to mention it to the Grand-Seignior. Charles promised, after scolding him as if he were one of his own subjects.

The Commander of Bender sent in haste an aga to wait on the King, and offer him a magnificent tent, provisions, wagons, all conveniences, officers and attendants, necessary to bring him with splendour to Bender. For it is customary with the Turks not only to defray the expenses of ambassadors to their place of residence but plentifully to supply, during the time of their sojourn, the needs of the Princes who take refuge among them.

BOOK V

The state of the Ottoman Porte—Charles retires to Bender—His occupations—His intrigues at the Porte—His plans—Augustus restored—The King of Denmark attacks Sweden—All the King's other territories are invaded—The Czar keeps festival at Moscow—The affair of Pruth—History of the Czarina.

ACHMET the third was then Emperor of the Turks. He had been placed on the throne in 1703, replacing his brother Mustapha, by a revolution like that which in England transferred the crown from James II to his son-in-law William. Mustapha was under the control of his Mufti, whom the people hated, and made his whole empire revolt against him. His army, with which he had reckoned to punish the malcontents, joined them, and he was seized, unceremoniously deposed, and his brother taken from the seraglio to be made Sultan, almost without bloodshed. Achmet confined the deposed Sultan in Constantinople, where he survived for several years, to the great surprise of the Turks, who had been accustomed to see the dethronement of their kings followed by their death. The only return the new Sultan made to the ministers, the generals, the officers of janissaries, and to those who had part in the revolution, was to execute them one after the other, for fear they should subsequently attempt another revolution. By the sacrifice of so many brave men he weakened the empire but strengthened his throne. Henceforth his mind was bent on amassing treasure. He was the first of the sultans who ventured to make a small alteration in the money, and to impose a new tax; but he was obliged to give up both these plans for fear of a rebellion, for the rapacity and tyranny of the Grand Seignior is felt only by the officers of the empire, who, whoever they may be, are slaves of the sultan; but the rest of the Mussulmans live in absolute security, with no fears for their lives, fortunes and liberty.

Such was the Emperor of the Turks, to whom the King of Sweden fled for refuge. He wrote to him as soon as he arrived in his territory. His letter is dated 13th of July, 1709. Several different copies of it are extant, which are all condemned as mere fabrications, but of all those which I have seen there is not one which does not display pride, and which was not rather in accordance with his courage than with his situation.

The Sultan did not reply till towards the end of September. The pride of the Ottoman Porte made Charles feel the gulf that it considered existed between the Turkish Emperor and a Christian fugitive and conquered King of part of Scandinavia.

Charles was, as a matter of fact, treated as an honourable prisoner. But he formed the design of turning the Ottoman arms against his enemies; he believed he could subdue Poland again, and reduce Russia to submission; he sent an envoy to Constantinople, but his best helper in his great project was Poniatowski, who went to Constantinople unofficially, and soon made himself indispensable to the King, agreeable to the Porte, and dangerous to the grand vizirs themselves.

One of those who seconded his designs most cleverly was a Portuguese doctor, Fonseca, living at Constantinople, a learned and able man, who had knowledge of men as well as of his own art, and whose profession gave him access to the Court, and often intimacy with the vizirs. I knew him well at Paris, and he confirmed all the details which I am going to relate. Count Poniatowski told me himself that he was clever enough to get letters through to the Sultana Valida, mother of the reigning Emperor, who had been at one time ill-used by her son, but was now beginning to recover her influence in the seraglio. A Jewess, who was often with the princess, was perpetually talking of the King of Sweden's exploits, and charmed her by reciting them. The Sultana, by a secret inclination which most women feel for extraordinary men, even without having ever seen them, took the King's part openly in the seraglio and called him "her lion." "When will you," she said sometimes to the Sultan her son, "help my lion to devour this Czar?" She even went beyond the strict rules of the seraglio so far as to write several letters with her own hand to Count Poniatowski, who still possesses them.

However, the King was taken to Bender with pomp, across the desert formerly called the desert of Getæ. The Turks took care that his journey should be made as agreeable as possible; many Poles, Swedes and Cossacks, who had escaped from the Russians, came from different directions to increase his train. When he arrived at Bender he had 1,800 men with him, all fed and lodged, they and their horses, at the expense of the Grand Seignior.

The King chose to encamp near Bender rather than in the town. The Serasquier, Jussuf, had a magnificent tent pitched for him, and also furnished all his suite with tents; some time after the King built a house on this spot, and his officers followed his example. The soldiers, too, raised barracks, so that the camp became gradually a little town.

The King was not yet cured of his wound, and had to have a decayed bone removed from his leg, but as soon as he could mount a horse he renewed his usual exercises, rising at sunrise, tiring out three horses a day, and making his soldiers drill. His only amusement was an occasional game of chess. If details are typical of character, it may be remarked that he always brought out his king in the game; he used him more than his other pieces, and so always lost the game.

At Bender he found plenty of everything about him, rare good fortune for a conquered and fugitive king; for besides more than enough provisions and the 500 crowns a day he got from the Ottoman generosity, he got money also from France, and borrowed of the Constantinople merchants. Part of this money was used to carry on the intrigues in the seraglio, in buying the vizirs or procuring their downfall; the rest he distributed profusely among his officers and the janissaries who guarded him at Bender.

Grothusen, his favourite and treasurer, dispensed these bounties; he was a man who, contrary to the custom of a man of his station, was as eager to give as his master. One day he brought him an account of 60,000 crowns in two lines, "10,000 given to the Swedes and janissaries, and the rest eaten up by me." "This," said the King, "is the kind of balance-sheet that I like; Mullern makes me read whole pages for the sum of 10,000 francs, I like Grothusen's laconic style much better." One of his old officers, thought to be slightly covetous, complained to the King that he gave everything to Grothusen. "I give money," answered the King, "to none but those who know how to make use of it." This generosity often reduced him to such straits that he had nothing to give. Better economy in his liberality would have been more to his advantage and no less honourable, but it was the Prince's failing to carry all the virtues to excess.

Many strangers hurried from Constantinople to see him. The Turks and the neighbouring Tartars came in crowds; all honoured and admired him. His rigid abstinence from wine, and his regularity in attending public prayers twice a day, spread the report that he was a true Mussulman. They burned to march with him to the conquest of Russia.

During this life of leisure at Bender, which was longer than he had expected, he developed unconsciously a great taste for books. Baron Fabricius, nobleman of the duchy of Holstein, an agreeable youth who had the gaiety and the ready wit which appeals to princes, induced him to read. He had been sent to him as envoy from the Duke of Holstein, to protect the interests of the latter, and succeeded by the amiability of his manner.

He had read all the French authors, and persuaded the King to read the tragedies of Corneille, and of Racine, and the works of Despreaux; the King did not at all enjoy the latter's satires, which are by no means his best performances, but he appreciated his other writings, and when he read the passage in the eighth satire, where he calls Alexander a "frantic madman," he tore out the leaf.

Of all the French tragedies Mithradates pleased him most, because the condition of the King, conquered and breathing forth vengeance, was like his own. He pointed out to M. Fabricius the passages that struck him, but he would read nothing aloud, nor venture on a word of French. Even afterwards, when he met M. Desaleurs, the French ambassador to the Porte, a person of distinction, who only knew his mother-tongue, he answered him in Latin, and when the ambassador protested that he did not understand a word of that language he called for an interpreter, rather than express himself in French. Such were the occupations of Charles at Bender, where he was waiting till a Turkish army should come to his assistance.

His ambassador presented memoirs in his name to the Grand Vizir, Poniatowski, and supported them with his readily-acquired prestige. The intrigue succeeded entirely; he wore only Turkish dress, and he insinuated himself everywhere; the Grand Seignior had him presented with a purse containing 1,000 ducats, and the Grand Vizir said to him, "I will take your King with one hand, and a sword in the other, and I will lead him to Moscow at the head of 200,000 men." But the first minister soon changed his mind. The King could only treat, while the Czar could pay; he did pay, and it was the money that he gave that Charles used; the military chest taken at Pultawa provided new arms against the vanquished. No more mention was made of making war on Russia. The Czar's influence was all-powerful at the Porte; they granted honours and privileges to his ambassador at Constantinople such as had never been enjoyed by a previous envoy; he was allowed to have a seraglio, that is, a palace in the quarters of the Franks, and to converse with foreign ministers. The Czar even felt strong enough to demand that Mazeppa should be handed over to him, just as Charles had demanded Patkul. Chourlouli-Ali-Pasha now found it impossible to refuse anything to a Prince who made demands with millions behind him. Thus the same Grand Vizir who had solemnly promised to take the King of Sweden to Russia with 200,000 men, had the impudence to propose to him that he should consent to the betrayal of Mazeppa. Charles was enraged at the request. It is hard to say how far the Vizir would have carried the matter had not Mazeppa, who was then seventy years old, died at this juncture.

The King's grief and resentment increased when he heard that Tolstoy, who had become ambassador from the Czar to the Porte, was served in public by the Swedes who had been enslaved at Pultawa, and that these brave men were daily sold in the market-place at Constantinople. Besides, the Russian ambassador remarked aloud that the Mussulman troops at Bender were there rather as a guard to the King than for his honour.

Charles, abandoned by the Grand Vizir, and conquered by the Czar's money in Turkey, as he had been by his arms in Ukrania, found himself deluded, scorned by the Porte, and a kind of prisoner among the Tartars. His followers began to despair. He alone remained firm and did not show dejection even for a moment. He thought that the Sultan was ignorant of the intrigues of his Grand Vizir; he determined to inform him, and Poniatowski undertook this bold task. Every Friday the Grand Seignior went to the mosque, surrounded by Solacks, a kind of guard, whose turbans were so high that they hid the Sultan from the people. Any one who had a petition to present to the Sultan, must mingle with these guards, and hold the petition up in the air. Sometimes the Sultan deigned to take it himself, but generally he bade an aga take charge of it, and afterwards, on his return from the mosque, had the petitions laid before him. There was no fear that any one would importune him with unnecessary petitions, or petitions about trifling affairs, for at Constantinople they write less in a year than at Paris in a day. Much less dare any one present petitions against the ministers, to whom the Sultan hands them generally without reading them. But Poniatowski had no other means of conveying the King of Sweden's complaints to the Grand Seignior. He drew up a strong indictment of the Grand Vizir. M. de Feriol, then Turkish ambassador from France, got it translated into Turkish. A Greek was hired to present it; he mingled himself with the King's guards, and held up the paper so high, and so persistently, that the Sultan saw it and took it himself.

Some days after, the Sultan sent the King of Sweden, as the only answer to his complaints, twenty-five Arabian horses, one of which had carried his Highness, and was covered with a saddle enriched with precious stones, and with massive gold stirrups. With this present he sent a polite letter, couched in general terms, and such as seemed to show that the Vizir had acted with the Sultan's orders. Chourlouli, too, who knew how to dissemble, sent five fine horses to the King.

Charles said haughtily to the man who brought them, "Return to your master and say that I do not receive presents from my enemies." M. Poniatowski, who had already had the courage to get a petition against the Grand Vizir presented, had formed the bold plan of having him deposed; he knew that the Vizir was no favourite of the Sultan's mother, and that he was hated both by Kislar-aga, the chief of the black eunuchs, and by the aga of the janissaries. So he urged them all three to speak against him. It was a strange sight to see a Christian, a Pole, an unaccredited agent of the King of Sweden who had refuged with the Turks, caballing almost openly at the Porte, against a Viceroy of the Ottoman Empire, and one who was, too, both a useful minister and a favourite of his master.

Poniatowski would never have succeeded, and the mere notion of his design would have cost him his life, had not a stronger power than those on his side given the last blow to the Grand Vizir Chourlouli's fortune. The Sultan had a young favourite, who has since governed the Ottoman Empire and been killed in Hungary in 1716, at the battle of Petervaradin, gained over the Turks by Prince Eugene of Savoy. His name was Coumourgi-Ali-Pasha; his birth much the same as that of Chourlouli; he was the son of a coal-heaver—as the name signified—for Coumir is Turkish for coal. The Emperor Achmet II, uncle of Achmet III, meeting Coumourgi as a child in a wood near

Adrianople, was so struck by his great beauty that he had him taken to the seraglio. Mustapha, Mahomet's eldest son and successor, was taken with him, and Achmet III made him his favourite; he was then only selic-tar-aga, sword-bearer to the crown. His extreme youth did not allow him to stand for the office of Grand Vizir, but his ambition was to make it. The Swedish faction could never gain this favourite; he was never a friend of King Charles, or of any other Christian prince, or their ministers, but on this occasion he was unconsciously of service to the King. He united with the Sultana Valida, and the leading officer of the Porte, to bring about the fall of Chourlouli, whom they all hated. This old minister, who had served his master long and well, was the victim of the caprice of a boy and the intrigues of a stranger. He was deprived of his dignity and his wealth, his wife, daughter of the last Sultan, taken from him, and he himself banished to Cassa in Crimean-Tartary. The bul, i.e. the seal of the Empire, was given to Numan Couprougli, grandson of the great Couprougli who took Candia. This new Vizir was what misinformed Christians hardly believe a Turk can be, a man of incorruptible virtue and a scrupulous observer of the law, which he often set up in opposition to the will of the Sultan.

He would not hear of a war against Russia, which he thought unjust and unnecessary, but the same respect for the law which prevented him from waging war against the Czar, made him punctilious in the duty of hospitality to the King of Sweden. "The law," he said to his master, "forbids you to attack the Czar, who has done you no harm, but it commands you to help the King of Sweden, who is an unfortunate Prince in your dominions."

He sent his Majesty 800 purses (a purse being worth 500 crowns), and advised him to return peaceably into his own country, through the territories of the Emperor of Germany, or in some French vessels that were then lying in the harbour at Constantinople, and which M. de Feriol, the French ambassador, offered to Charles to take him to Marseilles. Count Poniatowski continued negotiations with the minister, and gained in the negotiations an ascendancy of which Russian gold could no longer deprive him in dealing with an incorruptible minister. The Russian faction thought that the best plan was to poison such a dangerous diplomat. They bribed one of his servants, who was to give him poison in his coffee; the crime was discovered in time; they found the poison in a little vial which they took to the Grand Seignior; the poisoner was judged in full divan, and condemned to the galleys, because, by Turkish law, crimes that have failed of execution are never punished by death.

Charles, still persuaded that sooner or later he would succeed in making the Turkish Empire declare against that of Russia, would agree to none of the proposals for his return in peace to his own dominions; he persisted in pointing out to the Turks as dangerous the very Czar whom he had long despised; his emissaries kept up their insinuations that Peter the Great was aiming at gaining control of shipping in the Black Sea; that, after having beaten the Cossacks, he had designs on the Crimea. Sometimes his representations roused the Porte, sometimes the Russian minister nullified their effect.

While he was thus letting his fate depend on the caprice of a vizir, and was forced to put up with the affronts as well as accept the favours of a foreign power—while he was presenting petitions to the Sultan, and living on hospitality in a desert—his enemies roused themselves to attack his kingdom.

The battle of Pultawa was at once the signal for a revolution in Poland. King Augustus returned thither, protesting against his abdication and the Peace of Altranstadt, and openly accusing Charles, whom he now no longer feared, of robbery and cruelty. He imprisoned Finsten and Imof, his plenipotentiaries, who had signed the abdication, as if in so doing they had exceeded their orders and betrayed their master. His Saxon troops, which had been the excuse for his dethronement, brought him back to Warsaw with most of the Polish counts who had formerly sworn fidelity to him, had afterwards done the same to Stanislas, and were about to renew their oath to Augustus. Siniawski himself joined his party, forgetting the idea he had had of making himself King, and was content as Grand General of the crown. Fleming, his first minister, who had been obliged to leave Saxony for a time, for fear of being given up as Patkul had been, managed matters at that time so as to bring over a great part of the Polish nobility to his master.

The Pope released his people from the oath of allegiance they had sworn to Stanislas. This step of the Holy Father, taken at the right time, and supported by Augustus's forces, had no small weight in establishing the interests of the Court of Rome in Poland, where they then had no wish to dispute with the sovereign pontiff the chimerical right of meddling with the temporalities of kings.

Every one was ready to submit to Augustus's authority again, and received without the least opposition a useless absolution which the Nuncio did not fail to represent as necessary.

Charles's power and the greatness of Sweden were now drawing to their last phase. For some time more than ten crowned heads had viewed the extension of Sweden beyond her natural boundaries, to the other side of the Baltic, and from the Duna to the Elbe, with fear and envy. Charles's fall and absence awakened the interests and jealousy of all these princes, after they had lain dormant for a long time through treaties and inability to break them.

The Czar, who was more powerful than them all together, making the best use of his victory, took Wibourg, and all Carelia, inundated Finland with troops, besieged Riga, and sent a corps into Poland to help Augustus to recover the throne. The Emperor was then what Charles had once been— the arbiter of Poland and the North; but he consulted only his own interests, whereas Charles's ambitions were always of glory or vengeance. The Swedish monarch had helped his friends, and overcome his enemies, without exacting the smallest reward for his victories; but the Czar, rather a prince than a hero, would not help the King of Poland except on condition that Livonia should be given up to him, and that this province, for the sake of which Augustus had begun war, should belong to the Russians for ever.

The King of Denmark, forgetting the treaty of Travendal as Augustus had that of Altranstadt, had from that time thoughts of making himself master of the Duchies of Holstein and Bremen, to which he renewed his claim. The King of Prussia had long-standing claims to Swedish Pomerania which he wished to revive; the Duke of Mecklenburg was provoked at seeing Sweden still in possession of Wismar, the finest city in his duchy. This Prince had married the Emperor of Russia's niece, and his uncle was only looking for an excuse to establish himself in Germany, after the example of the Swedes. George, Elector of Hanover, also wanted to enrich himself from the spoiling of Charles. This Bishop of Munster, too, would have been glad to have made some claims had he possessed the means to do so.

There were about 12,000 or 13,000 Swedes defending Pomerania, and the other districts which Charles held in Germany; here was the seat of war. But this storm alarmed the Emperor and his allies. It is a law of the Empire that whoever invades one of the provinces should be considered an enemy to the whole Germanic body.

But there was still greater difficulty involved, for all these princes, except the Czar, were then leagued against Louis XIV, whose power had for some time been as formidable to the Empire as that of Charles himself.

At the beginning of the century Germany found herself hard pressed between the French on the south and the Swedes on the north. The French had crossed the Danube, and the Swedes the Oder; if their victorious forces had united, the Empire would have been lost. But the same fatality that had ruined Sweden had also humbled France; yet some resources still remained to Sweden, and Louis carried on the war with vigour, though unsuccessfully. If Pomerania and the Duchy of Bremen became the seat of war, it was to be feared that the Empire would suffer, and being weakened on that side would be the less able to withstand Louis. To prevent this, the Princes of Germany, Queen Anne of England, and the States of Holland, concluded at the Hague, in 1709, one of the most extraordinary treaties ever signed.

It was stipulated by these powers that the seat of the war should not be in Pomerania, nor any other German State, but that Charles might be attacked by his enemies anywhere else. The King of Poland and the Czar themselves agreed to this treaty, and had a clause inserted which was as strange as the treaty itself, to the effect that the 12,000 Swedes in Pomerania should not leave it to defend their other provinces.

To safeguard the treaty it was proposed to raise an army, which was to encamp on the Oder, to maintain this imaginary neutrality. It was an unheard-of thing, to levy an army to prevent war! Those who were paying the forces were, for the most part, very much concerned to bring about the war they were pretending to prevent. The army was, by the treaty, to consist of the troops of the Emperor, the King of Prussia, the Elector of Hanover, the Landgrave of Hesse, and the Bishop of Munster.

This project was, as might be expected, not carried through. The princes who were to furnish their quota for the army contributed nothing; not two regiments were formed. There was much talk of neutrality, but no one observed it; and all the Northern princes who had any controversy with the King of Sweden were left at full liberty to dispute who should have his spoils.

At this point the Czar, having stationed his forces in Lithuania and left orders for carrying on the siege of Riga, returned to Moscow, to show his people a sight as new as anything he had yet done in his kingdom. It was a triumph little inferior to that of the ancient Romans. He made his entry into Moscow under seven triumphal arches, erected in the streets, and adorned with all that could be produced in that climate, and that the flourishing trade which his energy had nourished could supply. The procession began with a regiment of guards, followed by the artillery taken from the Swedes at Lesnow and Pultawa, each piece being drawn by eight horses with scarlet trappings hanging to the ground. Then came the standards, kettle-drums, and the colours won at these two battles, and carried by the officers who had won them; all the spoils were followed by the Czar's picked troops. After they had filed past, the litter of Charles XII, in a chariot made for the purpose, appeared as it had been found on the battle-field, all shattered by cannon-shot. Behind this litter marched the prisoners two by two, and among them Count Piper, Prime Minister of Sweden, the famous Marshal Renschild, Count Levenhaupt, Generals Slipenbak, Hamilton, and Stackelburg, and all the officers and soldiers who were later scattered through Russia. Immediately behind them came the Czar, riding the same horse he had used at Pultawa; just behind him were the generals who had their share in the success of this battle; after them came another regiment of guards, and the wagons loaded with Swedish ammunition brought up the rear.

This procession was accompanied by the ringing of all the bells in Moscow, by the sound of drums, kettle-drums and trumpets, and an infinite number of musical instruments, echoing each other. Volleys were discharged from

200 cannon, to the acclamations of 5,000,000 men, who at every halt of the Czar in his entry cried, "God save the Emperor our father!"

This imposing procession increased the people's veneration for his person, and gave him greater prestige in their eyes than all the good he had really done them. In the meantime he continued the blockade of Riga, and the generals subdued the rest of Livonia and part of Finland. At the same time the King of Denmark came with his entire fleet to attack Sweden, where he landed with 1,700 men, whom he left under the command of Count Reventlau.

At that time Sweden was governed by a regency, composed of some Senators appointed by the King at his departure from Sweden. The Senatorial body, which regarded the right of governing as their prerogative, were jealous of the regency. The State suffered from these divisions, but directly they received news at Stockholm after Pultawa, that the King was at Bender in the hands of the Turks and Tartars, and that the Danes had made an attack on Schoner and had taken the town of Elsingburg, all jealousy disappeared, and they concentrated on saving Sweden. There were now very few regulars left, for though Charles had always made his great expeditions with small armies, yet his innumerable battles for nine years, the continual necessity for recruits, the maintenance of his garrisons, and the standing army he was obliged to maintain in Finland, Livonia, Pomerania, Bremen, and Verden, had cost Sweden, during the course of the war, more than 250,000 men; there were not as many as 8,000 of the veterans who, with raw forces, were now Sweden's only resource.

The nation is born with a passion for war, and every people unconsciously imitate their King. Nothing was discussed from one end of the country to the other but the great exploits of Charles and his generals, and of the old regiment which fought under them at Narva, Duna, Crassau, Pultask, and Hollosin. Thus the humblest of the Swedes were filled with a spirit of emulation and thirst for glory. Besides this, they loved their King, were sorry for him, and hated the Danes thoroughly. In many other countries the peasants are slaves or are treated as such; here they form part of the body politic, consider themselves citizens, and think worthy thoughts. So that in a short time these forces became the best in the North.

By order of the regency, General Steinbock put himself at the head of 8,000 veteran troops and 12,000 recruits, to pursue the Danes, who were ravaging all the country round Elsingburg, and had already put some places far inland under contribution.

There was neither time nor money to get uniforms for the soldiers; most of the country labourers came dressed in their linen smocks, with pistols tied to their girdles by cords. Steinbock, at the head of this extraordinary army, came up with the Danes three leagues from Elsingburg, on the 10th March, 1710. He intended to rest his troops some days, to entrench, and to give his raw recruits time to get accustomed to the enemy; but the peasants clamoured to fight directly they arrived.

Some officers who were there told me that they saw them almost all foaming with rage, so great is the Swede's hatred of the Dane. Steinbock took advantage of this disposition, which is almost as effective in war as military discipline. The Danes were attacked, and the strange sight was seen—of which there are, perhaps, no two other instances—of raw forces equalling in bravery a veteran corps at the first attack. Two regiments of these undisciplined peasants cut the Danish army to pieces, and left only ten survivors.

The Danes, entirely routed, retreated under the cannon of Elsingburg. The passage from Sweden to Zeeland is so short that the King of Denmark heard of the defeat of his army in Sweden the same day at Copenhagen, and sent his fleet to bring off the remnant of his army. The Danes hastily left Sweden five days after the battle, but, being unable to bring away their horses, and not wishing to leave them to the enemy, they killed them all and fired their provisions, burning their corn and baggage, and leaving 4,000 wounded in Elsingburg. The majority of these died from the infection from the large number of dead horses, and from lack of food, which even their own countrymen deprived them of, lest they should fall into Swedish hands.

At the same time the peasants of Delecarlia, having heard in the depths of their forests that the King was prisoner in Turkey, sent a deputation to the Regency at Stockholm, offering to go, at their own expense, to rescue their master from the enemy's hands with a force of 20,000 men. This proposal, useless as it was, was heard with pleasure, because it proved the courage and loyalty of the proposers, though it was rejected; and they gave the King an account of it, when they sent him word about Elsingburg. King Charles received this cheering news in his camp near Bender, in July 1710, just after another event which confirmed him in his hopes.

The Grand Vizir Couprougli, who was opposed to his plans, was turned out of office after he had been in the ministry two months. Charles XII's little Court, and his adherents in Poland, boasted that he made and removed vizirs, and was governing Turkey from his retreat at Bender. But he had no hand in the ruin of this favourite.

The rigid justice of the Vizir, it was said, was the only cause of his fall; his predecessor had been accustomed to pay the janissaries, not out of the Imperial treasury, but from the money he got by extortion. Couprougli, on the other hand, paid them from the treasury. For this Achmet accused him of putting the subjects' interest before that of the Emperor. "Your predecessor, Chourlouli," he said, "managed to find other ways of paying my troops." The Grand Vizir replied, "If he had the art of enriching your Highness by theft, it is an art of which I am proud to be ignorant."

The great secrecy observed in the seraglio rarely lets such stories leak out, but this got known at the time of Couprougli's fall. The Vizir's courage did not cost him his head, because real goodness often forces even those whom it offends to respect. He had leave to retire to the island of Negropont.

After this the Sultan sent for Baltagi Mahomet Pasha of Syria, who had been Grand Vizir before Chourlouli. The Baltagis of the seraglio, so called from balta, meaning an axe, are slaves employed to cut wood for the use of princes of the blood and the Sultana. This Vizir had been baltagi in his youth, and had always retained the name, according to the custom of the Turks, who are not ashamed to bear the name of their first profession, their father, or their birthplace. While Baltagi was a servant in the seraglio he was fortunate enough to do Prince Achmet some trifling service, that Prince being then a prisoner of State in the reign of his brother Mustapha. Achmet gave one of his female slaves, of whom he had been very fond, to Baltagi Mahomet, when he became Sultan. This woman made her husband Grand Vizir by her intrigues; another intrigue deposed him, while a third made him Grand Vizir again. Baltagi had no sooner received the seal of the Turkish empire than he found the party of the King of Sweden dominant in the seraglio. The Sultana Valida, the Sultan's favourite, the chief of the black eunuchs, and the aga of the janissaries, were all in favour of war against the Czar. The Sultan had decided on it, and the very first order he gave the Grand Vizir was to go and attack the Russians with 200,000 men. Baltagi had never been in the field, but was no idiot, as the Swedes, out of pure malice, have represented him to be. When he received from the Sultan a sabre set with precious stones, "Your Highness knows," he said, "that I have been brought up to use an axe and fell wood, and not to wield a sword, or to command armies. I will do my best to serve you; but if I fail, remember that I have begged you not to lay it to my charge." The Sultan assured him of his favour, and the Vizir prepared to carry out his orders. The Ottoman Porte's first step was to imprison the Russian ambassador in the castle of seven towers.

It is the custom of the Turks to begin by seizing those ministers against whom they declare war. Strict observers of hospitality in every other respect, in this they violate the most sacred of international laws. They act thus unfairly under the pretext of fairness, persuading themselves and trying to persuade others that they never undertake any but a just war, because it is consecrated by the approbation of their Muphti. Thus they look upon themselves as armed to chastise the violation of treaties (which they often break themselves), and argue that the ambassadors of kings at variance with them are to be punished as accomplices of their masters' treachery. Besides this, they affect a ridiculous contempt towards Christian princes and their ambassadors, whom they regard as only consuls and merchants.

The Kan of Crimean-Tartary had orders to be ready with 400,000 Tartars. This Prince rules over Nagai, Bulziac, part of Circassia and all the Crimean district called by the ancients the Tauric Chersonese, whither the Greeks carried their commerce and their arms, building large cities there; and whither the Genoese afterwards penetrated, when they were masters of the trade of Europe.

In this country there are the ruins of Grecian cities, and some Genoese monuments still subsisting in the midst of desolation and savagery. The Kan is called Emperor by his own subjects, but in spite of this grand title he is a mere slave to the Porte. The fact that they have Ottoman blood in their veins, and the right they have to the Turkish Empire on the extinction of the race of the Sultan, make their family respected and their persons formidable even to the Sultan himself: that is why the Sultan dare not destroy the race of the Kans of Tartary; but he hardly ever allows them to continue on the throne to an advanced age. The neighbouring pashas spy on their conduct, their territories are surrounded by janissaries, their wishes thwarted by the Grand Vizir, and their designs always suspected. If the Tartars complain of the Kan, this is an excuse for the Porte to depose him; if he is popular among them it is regarded as a crime, for which he will be even more readily punished. Thus all of them leave the throne for exile, and finish their days at Rhodes, which is generally both their place of exile and their grave.

The Tartars, their subjects, are the most dishonest folk in the world; yet, at the same time (inconceivable as it seems), the most hospitable. They go a fifty leagues' journey to fall upon a caravan and to destroy towns, but if any stranger happens to pass through their country, he is not only received and lodged everywhere, and his expenses paid, but everywhere the inhabitants strive for the honour of having him as guest.

The master of the house, his wife and daughters vie with one another in his service. Their ancestors, the Scythians, transmitted to them this inviolable regard for hospitality; and they still retain it, because the scarcity of strangers in their country, and the cheapness of provisions, makes this duty in no way burdensome to them. When the Tartars go to war with the Ottoman army they are maintained by the Sultan, but receive no other pay but their booty; this makes them more ardent at pillage than at regular warfare.

The Kan, bribed by the presents and intrigues of the King of Sweden, got permission to have the general rendezvous of troops at Bender, under the King's eye, that he might realize that the war was being made for him. The new vizir, Baltagi, not being bound in the same way, would not flatter a foreign prince so far. He countermanded the order, and the great army was collected at Adrianople.

The Turkish troops are not so formidable now as they were when they conquered so many kingdoms in Asia, Africa and Europe. Then they triumphed over enemies less strong and worse disciplined than themselves by physical strength, courage and the force of numbers. But now that Christians understand the art of war better, they seldom failed to beat the Turks in a drawn battle, even when their forces are inferior in number. If the Ottoman empire has lately gained some success, it is only in a contest with the Republic of Venice, reputed more wise than warlike, defended by strangers, and ill supported by Christian princes, who are always divided among themselves.

The janissaries and spahis attack in disorder, and are incapable of action under command, or of a rally; their cavalry, which should be excellent, considering the good breed and agility of their horses, is unable to sustain the shock of German cavalry; their infantry were not yet able to use the fixed bayonet; besides this, the Turks have had no great general since Couprougli, who conquered Candia. A slave brought up in the idleness and the silence of the seraglio, made a vizir through favouritism, and a general against his own inclinations, headed a raw army, without experience and without discipline, against Russian troops, with twelve years' experience in war, and proud of having conquered the Swedes.

The Czar, according to all appearances, must have vanquished Baltagi, but he made the same mistake with regard to the Turks as the King of Sweden was guilty of in his own case; that is, he had too poor an opinion of his enemy. Upon the news of the Turkish preparations he left Moscow; and having given orders to change the siege of Riga into a blockade, he drew up his army of 24,000 men on the Polish frontier. With this army he marched to Moldavia and Wallachia, formerly the country of the Daci, but now inhabited by Greek Christians, tributary to the Sultan.

Moldavia was then governed by Prince Cantemir, a Greek by birth, who had the talents of the ancient Greeks together with a knowledge of letters and of arms. He was reputedly descended from the famous Timur, famous under the name of Tamberlain: this genealogy seemed more distinguished than a Greek one. They proved it from the name of the conqueror; Timur, they said, is like Temir: the title Kan, which Timur had before his conquest of Asia, appears again in the name Cantemir: thus Prince Cantemir is a descendant of Tamberlain; that is the sort of basis on which most genealogies are built.

To whatever house Cantemir belonged, he owed all to the Ottoman Porte. Scarcely had he been invested with his principality than he betrayed the Emperor his benefactor for the Czar, from whom he had greater expectations. He believed that the conqueror of Charles XII would easily triumph over an obscure vizir, with no military experience, who had appointed as his lieutenant the chief customs officer of Turkey; he reckoned on all Greece joining his faction, and the Greek priests encouraged him in his treachery. The Czar made a secret treaty with him, and having received him into his army, marched up country, and arrived in June 1711 on the northern side of the river Hierasus, now Pruth, near Jazy, the capital of Moldavia.

As soon as the Grand Vizir heard that Peter had arrived, he left his camp at once, and following the course of the Danube, was going to cross the river on a bridge of boats near Saccia, at the same spot where Darius had built the bridge that bore his name. The Turkish army marched so rapidly that they soon came in sight of the Russians, with the river Pruth between them.

The Czar, sure of the Prince of Moldavia, never expected that the subjects might fail him; but the Moldavians often oppose their interests to those of their masters. They liked the Turkish rule, which is never fatal except to the grandees, and pretends a leniency to its tributaries; they were afraid of the Christians, especially the Russians, who had always used them ill.

Those who had undertaken to furnish the Russians with provisions made with the Grand Vizir the same bargain they had made with the Czar, and brought all their provisions to the Ottoman army. The Wallachians, neighbours of the Moldavians, showed the same care for the Turks, for to such a degree the remembrance of former cruelties had alienated their minds from the Russians.

The Czar, thus frustrated of his hopes, which he had perhaps indulged too readily, found his army suddenly destitute of food and without forage.

In the meantime the Turks crossed the river, cut off the Russians, and formed an entrenched camp in front of them.

It is strange that the Czar did not dispute the passage of the river, or at least repair this fault by engaging the Turks at once, instead of giving them time to tire out his army with fatigue and famine. But that Prince seems, in this campaign, to have acted in every way for his own ruin; he was without provisions, with the river Pruth behind him, and about 4,000 Tartars continually harassing him to right and left. In these extremities he said publicly, "I am at least in as bad a case as my brother Charles at Pultawa."

Count Poniatowski, indefatigable agent to the King of Sweden, was in the Grand Vizir's army with some Poles and Swedes, who all thought the Czar's ruin inevitable.

As soon as Poniatowski saw that the armies must inevitably meet, he sent word to the King of Sweden, who, eager for the pleasure of attacking the Russian Emperor, started that moment from Bender, with forty officers. After many losses, and several destructive marches, the Czar was driven back on Pruth, and had no cover left but some *chevaux de frise* and some wagons. A party of the janissaries and spahis fell immediately on his army in that defenceless condition, but they attacked in disorder, and the Russians defended themselves with an energy inspired by the presence of their Prince and despair.

The Turks were twice driven back. Next day M. Poniatowski advised the Grand Vizir to starve out the Russians, for they lacked all necessaries, and would be obliged to surrender at discretion in one day.

The Czar has since then repeatedly acknowledged that he never felt anything so acutely as the difficulties of his position that night: he turned over in his mind all that he had been doing for so many years for the glory and good of his people, so many great plans, always interrupted by war, were perhaps about to perish with him, before having reached completion. He must either die of hunger or attack nearly 200,000 men with feeble troops, reduced by half from their original number, a cavalry with scarcely a horse between them, and infantry worn out by hunger and fatigue.

He called General Czeremetoff at nightfall, and ordered him peremptorily to have all ready by daybreak for an attack on the Turks with fixed bayonets.

He gave strict orders also that all baggage should be burned, and that no officer should keep more than one wagon, so that in case of defeat the enemy might not have the booty they expected.

Having made all arrangements with the general for the battle, he withdrew into his tent overcome by grief, and seized with convulsions, to which he was subject, and which worry brought on with redoubled violence. He forbade any one to enter his tent during the night on any pretext whatever, not wanting to receive remonstrances against a desperate but necessary resolve, and much less that any should witness the wretched state he was in. In the meantime they burned the greater part of the baggage as he had ordered; all the army followed this example with much regret, and some buried their most cherished treasures. The generals had already given orders for the march, and were trying to give the army the confidence which they did not feel themselves; the men, exhausted by fatigue, and starving, marched without spirit or hope. The women, of whom there were too many in the army, uttered cries which further unnerved the men; every one expected that death or slavery would be their portion next morning. This is no exaggeration, it is the exact account of officers who served in the army.

There was at that time in the Russian camp a woman as extraordinary as the Czar himself. She was then known only by the name of Catherine. Her mother was an unfortunate country woman called Erb-Magden, of the village of Ringen in Estonia, a province held in villeinage, which was at that time under the rule of Sweden. She had never known her father, but was baptized by the name of Martha. The priest of the parish brought her up out of pure charity till she was fourteen, then she went into service at Mariemburg, in the house of a Lutheran minister whose name was Gluk.

In 1702, at the age of eighteen, she married a Swedish dragoon. The day after her marriage part of the Swedish troops were beaten by the Russians, and the dragoon was in the action. But he never returned to his wife, and she could never learn whether he had been taken prisoner, nor later could she get any news of him.

Some days after she was taken prisoner herself, and was servant to General Czeremetoff, who gave her to Menzikoff, a man who had known fortune's extremes, for he had become a general and a prince from being a pastry-cook's boy, and then was deprived of everything and banished to Siberia, where he died in misery and despair. The Czar was at supper with this prince when he first saw her and fell in love with her. He married her secretly in 1707, not fascinated by womanly charms, but because he found that she had the strength of mind to second his designs, and even to continue them after him. He had long since put away his first wife Ottokefa, daughter of a boyard, on a charge of opposition to certain political reforms he had made.

This was the greatest of all crimes in the Czar's eyes. He would have none in his family who differed from him. In this foreign slave he expected all the qualities of a sovereign, though she had none of the virtues of womanhood. For her sake he scorned the petty prejudices which would have hampered an ordinary man, and had her crowned Empress. The same capacity which made her Peter's wife gave her the empire after her husband's death. Europe was amazed to see a bold woman, who could neither read nor write, supply her lack of education and her weakness by spirit and courage, and fill the throne of a legislator gloriously.

When she married the Czar she left the Lutheran faith for that of the Russian Church; she was baptized again according to the Russian rite, and instead of the name of Martha she took that of Catherine, by which she has been known ever since. This woman was in the camp at Pruth, and held a private council with the generals and the Vice-Chancellor while the Czar was in his tent.

They agreed that it was necessary to sue for peace, and that the Czar must be persuaded to this course. The Vice-Chancellor wrote a letter to the Grand Vizir in his master's name, which the Czarina, in spite of the Emperor's prohibition, carried into the tent to him, and after many prayers, tears and argument, she prevailed on him to sign it; she then took all her money, all her jewels and valuables, and what she could borrow from the generals, and having collected by this means a considerable present, she sent it with the Czar's letter to Osman Aga, lieutenant to the Grand Vizir.

Mahomet Baltagi answered proudly, with the air of a vizir and a conqueror, "Let the Czar send me his first minister, and I will see what can be done." The Vice-Chancellor came at once, loaded with presents, which he offered publicly to the Grand Vizir; they were large enough to show they needed his help, but too small for a bribe. The Vizir's first condition was that the Czar, with all his army, should surrender at discretion. The Vice-Chancellor answered that the Czar was going to attack him in a quarter of an hour, and that the Russians would perish to a man, rather than submit to such shameful conditions. Osman seconded him by remonstrances.

Baltagi was no soldier. He knew that the janissaries had been repulsed the day before, and was easily persuaded by Osman not to risk certain advantages by the hazard of a battle. He therefore granted a suspension of hostilities for six hours, during which the treaty could be arranged.

During the discussion an incident occurred, proving that the word of a Turk is often more reliable than we think.

Two Italian noblemen, related to a M. Brillo, colonel of a regiment of grenadiers in the service of the Czar, going to look for forage, were taken by the Tartars, who carried them off to their camp, and offered to sell them to an officer of the janissaries. The Turk, enraged at such a breach of the truce, seized the Tartars and carried them before the Grand Vizir, together with the two prisoners. The Vizir sent them back at once to the Czar's camp, and had the two Tartars who had carried them off beheaded. In the meantime the Kan of Tartary opposed the conclusion of a treaty which robbed him of all hopes of pillage. Poniatowski seconded him with urgent and pressing reasons. But Osman carried his point, notwithstanding the impatience of the Tartar and the insinuations of Poniatowski.

The Vizir thought it enough for his master the Sultan to make an advantageous peace; he insisted that the Russians should give up Asoph, burn the galleys that lay in that port, and demolish the important citadels on the Palus-Mæotis; that all the cannon and ammunition of those forts should be handed over to the Sultan; that the Czar should withdraw his troops from Poland; that he should not further disturb the few Cossacks who were under Polish protection, nor those that were subject to Turkey, and that for the future he should pay the Tartars a subsidy of 40,000 sequins per annum—an irksome tribute which had been imposed long before, but from which the Czar had delivered his country.

At last the treaty was going to be signed, without so much as a mention of the King of Sweden; all that Poniatowski could obtain from the Vizir was the insertion of an article by which the Russians should promise not to hinder the return of Charles XII, and, strangely enough, that a peace should be made between the King and the Czar if they wished it, and could come to terms.

On these terms the Czar got liberty to retreat with his army, cannon, artillery, colours and baggage. The Turks gave him provisions, and there was plenty of everything in his camp within two hours of the signing of the treaty, which was begun on the 21st July, 1711, and signed on the 1st of August.

Just as the Czar, rescued from his dangerous position, was drawing off with drums beating and colours flying, the King of Sweden, eager to fight, and to see the enemy in his hands, came up; he had ridden post haste about fifty leagues from Bender to Jazy, and alighting at Count Poniatowski's tent, the Count came up to him sadly and told him how he had lost a chance which would perhaps never recur.

The King, beside himself with rage, went straight to the tent of the Grand Vizir, and with flushed face reproached him for the treaty he had just made.

"I have authority," said the Grand Vizir, calmly, "to make peace and to wage war."

"But," answered the King, "had you not the whole Russian army in your power?"

"Our law," said the Vizir solemnly, "commands us to grant peace to our enemies when they implore our mercy."

"Ah," replied the King, in a rage, "does it order you to make a bad treaty, when you can impose the terms you please? Was it not your duty to take the Czar prisoner to Constantinople?"

The Turk, thus nonplussed, answered slyly, "And who would govern his empire in his absence? It is not fitting that all kings should be away from home."

Charles replied with an indignant smile, and then threw himself down on a cushion, and, looking at the Vizir with resentment mingled with contempt, he stretched out his leg towards him, and, entangling his spur with his robe, tore it; then jumped up, mounted, and rode to Bender full of despair.

Poniatowski stayed some time longer with the Grand Vizir, to see if he could prevail on him by gentler means to make some better terms with the Czar, but it was prayer-time, and the Turk, without one word in answer, went to wash and attend to his devotions.

BOOK VI

Intrigues at the Porte—The Kan of Tartary and the Pasha of Bender try to force Charles to depart—He defends himself with forty servants against their whole army.

THE fortune of the King of Sweden, greatly changed as it was, now failed him in the smallest details. On his return he found his little camp at Bender, and his whole quarters, under water, flooded by the waters of the Neister. He withdrew to a distance of some miles, near a village called Varnitza; and, as if he had a secret suspicion of what was going to happen to him, he had a large stone house built there, capable, in an emergency, of sustaining some hours' siege; he furnished it magnificently, contrary to his usual custom, and in order to impress the Turks. Besides this he built two more, one for his Chancery, and the other for his favourite, Grothusen, whom he supported. While the King was thus building at Bender, as if it was his intention to stay always in Turkey, Baltagi, being more than ever fearful of his intrigues and complaints at the Porte, had sent the resident consul of the German Emperor to Vienna to gain for the King of Sweden a passage through the hereditary dominions of the house of Austria. This envoy returned in three weeks with a promise from the Imperial Regency that they would give Charles all due honour, and conduct him safely to Pomerania.

The application had been made to the Regency because Charles, the successor of Joseph, who was then Emperor, was in Spain as a rival with Philip V for the crown. While the German envoy was carrying out his mission to Vienna, the Vizir sent three pashas to the King of Sweden bidding him begone from Turkish territory. The King, who knew their mission, sent them a message, that if they were venturing on any dishonourable or disrespectful proposal to him he would have them hanged forthwith. The pasha who delivered the message cloaked the harshness of his message in the most respectful language. Charles dismissed the audience without deigning a word of reply; but his chancellor, who remained with the three pashas, signified in few words his master's refusal, which they had already concluded from his silence.

But the Grand Vizir was not discouraged. He ordered Ishmael Pasha, the new serasquier of Bender, to threaten the King with the Sultan's displeasure if he did not haste to come to some conclusion. The serasquier was of an agreeable and tactful disposition, and had therefore gained Charles's good-will and the friendship of the Swedes.

The King held a conference with him, and informed him that he would only depart from Turkey when the Sultan granted him two things: the punishment of his Vizir, and 100,000 men with which to return to Poland.

Baltagi was aware of the fact that Charles's presence in Turkey meant his ruin, so he placed guards on all the roads from Bender to Constantinople, with orders to intercept the King's letters; he also cut off his "thaim," the allowance that the Porte makes to exiled princes in her dominions. The King of Sweden's was immense, 500 crowns a day in money, besides all that contributed to the maintenance of a court in pomp and abundance. As soon as the King heard that the Vizir had dared to cut off his allowance he turned to his steward, remarking, "So far you have had only two tables, for tomorrow prepare four."

Charles XII's officers had never found any order of their master's impossible, but having neither money nor provision they were forced to borrow at twenty, thirty, and forty per cent. of the officers' servants and janissaries, who had grown rich by the King's liberality. M. Fabricius, ambassador from Holstein, Jeffreys, English minister, their secretaries and their friends, gave what they had; the King, with his usual pride, and without a thought for the morrow, lived on these gifts, which would not have long sufficed. They had to go through the Turkish guard, and send secretly to Constantinople to borrow from European money-lenders. All refused to lend to a king who seemed to be powerless to pay; but one English merchant, named Cook, at last ventured to lend 40,000 crowns, taking the risk of losing them if the King of Sweden was killed. They took the money to the King's camp, just as they were feeling actual want, and were beginning to despair of supplies.

In the meantime M. Poniatowski wrote actually from the Grand Vizir's camp an account of the Pruth campaign, accusing the Vizir of cowardice and treachery. An old janissary, enraged at the weakness of the Vizir, and bribed by Poniatowski, undertook the delivery of the letter, and, having got his discharge, presented it with his own hands to the Sultan. Some days later Poniatowski set out from the camp and went to the Ottoman Porte to form intrigues against the Grand Vizir as usual.

All seemed to favour the design. The Czar, now at liberty, was in no hurry to carry out his promises; the keys of Azov did not come, and the Grand Vizir, who was responsible for them, justly fearing his master's resentment, dare not appear in his presence.

The seraglio was then more full of intrigues and factions than ever. These cabals, which exist at all courts, and which, in our case, generally end in the removal of a minister from office, or at most by a banishment, always meant more than one execution in Constantinople.

It ended in the execution of the former Vizir Chourlouli, and of Osman, the lieutenant of Baltagi, who was the chief author of the Peace of Pruth, and who since the peace had held a prominent office at the Porte. Among the treasures of Osman they found the Czarina's ring and 20,000 gold pieces, in

Saxon, Polish and Russian coin; this was a proof that it was money alone which had rescued the Czar from his perilous position, and had ruined the chances of Charles XII. The Vizir, Baltagi, was exiled to the isle of Lemnos, where he died three years later. The Sultan did not confiscate his property either at his exile or at his death; he was not rich, and his poverty protects his memory.

This Grand Vizir was succeeded by Joseph, whose fortune was as singular as that of his predecessors. He was a Russian by birth, and had been taken prisoner by the Turks at six years of age with his family, and had been sold to a janissary. He was long a valet in the seraglio, then became the second person in the empire where he had been a slave. But he was only the shadow of a minister.

The young Ali-Coumourgi had placed him in the slippery post until he could seize it himself, and Joseph, his creature, had nothing else to do but affix the Imperial seals to the favourite's desires. The policy of the Ottoman Court seemed to be revolutionized from the very beginning of this Vizir's ministry. The Czar's plenipotentiaries, who lived at Constantinople both as ministers and hostages, were better treated than ever; the Grand Vizir countersigned the Peace of Pruth with them. But that which annoyed the King of Sweden more than all else was the news that the secret alliance made at Constantinople with the Czar was brought about by the mediation of the English and Dutch ambassadors.

Since Charles's retreat to Bender, Constantinople was occupying the position that Rome had so often held, as the centre of the business of Christendom. Count Desaleurs, the French ambassador at the Porte, was supporting the interests of Charles and of Stanislas; the Emperor of Germany's minister was opposing them. The Swedish and Russian factions were falling foul of each other, as those of France and Spain have long done at the Court of Rome.

England and Holland posed as neutrals, but were not really such; the new trade of Saint Petersburg attracted the attention of those two trading powers.

The English and the Dutch are always on the side of the prince who most favours their trade, and there was just then much to be gained from the Czar, so that it is no wonder that the English and Dutch ministers should work secretly in his interest at the Porte. One of the conditions of this new alliance was that Charles should at once be driven from the Turkish dominions.

Perhaps the Czar thought him less formidable at home than in Turkey, where he was always on the spot ready to raise the Ottoman arms against the Russian empire, or perhaps he hoped to seize him *en route*. The King of Sweden continued his petitions to the Porte to send him home through Poland with a large army. The Divan resolved to send him back, but only with a guard of 7,000 or 8,000 men, not like a King they wished to help, but as a guest they were anxious to be rid of. With this object in view the Sultan Achmet wrote him the following letter:

"Most powerful of the Princes that worship Jesus, redressor of wrongs and injuries, and protector of justice in the ports and republics of South and North, shining in Majesty, lover of Honour and Glory, and of our sublime Porte, Charles, King of Sweden, whose enterprises may God crown with success.

"As soon as the most illustrious Achmet, formerly Chiaoux-Pasha, shall have the honour to present this letter to you, adorned with our Imperial seal, be persuaded and convinced of the truth of our intentions expressed therein, namely, that, although we had planned to march again against the Czar, yet that Prince, to avoid our just resentment at his delay in the execution of the treaty concluded on the banks of the Pruth, and renewed again at our sublime Porte, having surrendered to us the castle and city of Azov, and having endeavoured by the mediation of the English and Dutch ambassadors, our ancient allies, to form a lasting peace with us, we have granted his request, and given up his plenipotentiaries, who remain with us as hostages, our Imperial ratification, after having received his from their hands.

"We have given our inviolable and salutary orders to the right honourable Delvet Gharai, Khan of Budziac, of Crimea, Nagai, and Circassia, and to our wise counsellor and noble serasquier of Bender, Ishmael (whom God preserve and increase in magnificence and wisdom), for your return through Poland, according to your first plan which has been again laid before us from you. You must, therefore, prepare to set out next winter under the guidance of Providence and with an honourable guard, that you may return to your own territories, taking care to pass through Poland in a peaceable and friendly manner.

"You will be provided by my sublime Porte with all that is needed for your journey, both money, men, horses and wagons. But above all else we advise and exhort you to give the most express and detailed orders to the Swedes and other soldiers in your retinue not to commit any act of disorder, nor be guilty of any action which may either directly or indirectly tend to the breach of this peace. By that means you will preserve our good-will, of which we shall endeavour to give great and frequent proofs as we shall find opportunity. The troops to attend you shall receive orders to that effect, according to our Imperial will and pleasure.

"Given at our sublime Porte of Constantinople on the 14th of the month Rebyul Eureb, 1214. Which corresponds to the 19th April, 1712."

This letter did not, however, entirely destroy the hopes of the King of Sweden. He wrote to the Sultan that he was ready to go, and would never forget the favour he had shown him; but he added that he believed the Sultan was too just to send him away with nothing but a flying camp through a country already overrun with the Czar's troops. Indeed, the Emperor of Russia, in spite of the fact that the first article of the Treaty of Pruth obliged him to withdraw his forces from Poland, had sent recruits thither, and it seemed strange that the Sultan was ignorant of the fact. The bad policy and vanity of the Porte in suffering the Christian princes to maintain their ambassadors at Constantinople, and not keeping one single agent in any Christian court, gives the former an opportunity of probing and sometimes of directing the Sultan's most secret resolutions, while the Divan is always ignorant of the most public transactions of Christendom. The Sultan, shut up in the seraglio among his women and his eunuchs, sees only through the Grand Vizir's eyes; the latter is as inaccessible as his master, taken up with the intrigues of the seraglio, and without any communication with the world outside. He is therefore generally imposed on himself, or imposes on the Sultan, who deposes him or has him strangled for his first mistake, in order to choose another as ignorant or as treacherous as the former, who behaves in the same way as his predecessors and falls as soon as they.

Such is, for the most part, the negligence and profound security of this Court, that if the Christian princes leagued against the Porte their fleets would be at the Dardanelles and their army at the gates of Adrianople before the Turks could think of taking the defensive. But the different interests which divide Christendom will protect that people from a fate for which they at present seem ripe in their want of policy and their ignorance in war and naval matters.

Achmet was so little acquainted with what was happening in Poland that he sent an aga to see if the Czar's forces were there or not. Two of the King of Sweden's secretaries, who understood Turkish, went with him, to keep a check on him in the event of a false report. The aga saw the forces with his own eyes and gave the Sultan a true account of the matter. Achmet, in a rage, was going to strangle the Grand Vizir, but the favourite, who protected him, and thought he might prove useful, got him pardoned and kept him some time in the ministry.

The Russians were openly protected by the Vizir, and secretly by Ali-Coumourgi, who had changed sides; but the Sultan was so angry, the infraction of the Treaty was so palpable, and the janissaries, who often make the ministers, favourites and Sultans themselves tremble, clamoured so loudly for war that no one in the seraglio dare counsel moderation.

The Sultan at once put the Russian ambassadors, who were already as accustomed to go to prison as to a concert, in the seven towers. War was declared again against the Czar, the horse-tails hoisted, and orders issued to all the pashas to raise an army of 200,000 fighting men. The Sultan left Constantinople for Adrianople in order to be nearer the seat of war.

In the meantime a solemn embassy from Augustus and the republics of Poland to the Sultan was on the road to Adrianople. At the head of this embassy was the Prince of Massovia with a retinue of 300 persons. They were all seized and imprisoned in the suburbs of the city. Never was the Swedish party more hopeful than on this occasion; but these great preparations came to nothing, and all their hopes were dashed. If a minister of great wisdom and foresight, who was then living at Constantinople, is to be credited, young Coumourgi had other plans in his head than hazarding a war with the Czar to gain a desert. He wanted to take Peloponnesus, now called Morea, from the Venetians, and to make himself master of Hungary.

To carry out his great designs he wanted nothing but the office of Grand Vizir, for which he was thought too young. With this in view the friendship of the Czar was more important to him than his enmity. It was neither to his interest nor to his inclination to keep the King of Sweden any longer, much less to raise a Turkish army for him. He not only advocated sending the Prince away, but declared openly that henceforth no Christian minister ought to be tolerated at Constantinople; that the ordinary ambassadors were only honourable spies, who corrupted or betrayed the vizirs, and had too long interfered in the affairs of the seraglio; that the Franks settled at Pera, and in the commercial ports on the Levant, were merchants, who needed no ambassador, but only a consul. The Grand Vizir, who owed both his position and his life to the favourite, and who feared him besides, complied with his plans the more readily that he had sold himself to the Russians, and hoped to be avenged on the King of Sweden, who would have ruined him.

The Mufti, Ali-Coumourgi's creature, was also completely under his thumb: he had given the vote for war against the Czar when the favourite was on that side, but he declared it to be unjust as soon as the youth had changed his mind. Thus the army was scarcely collected before they began to listen to proposals for a reconciliation. After several negotiations the vice-chancellor Shaffiroff and young Czeremetoff, the Czar's plenipotentiaries and hostages at the Porte, promised that the troops should be withdrawn from Poland. The Grand Vizir, who knew that the Czar would not carry out this treaty, decided to sign it for all that; and the Sultan, content with the semblance of laying down the law to the Russians, remained at Adrianople. Thus, in less than six months, peace was made with the Czar, then war was declared, then peace was renewed.

The main article of all the treaties was that the King of Sweden should be forced to depart. The Sultan would not imperil his own honour and that of the Porte to the extent of exposing the King to the risk of being captured *en route* by his enemies. It was stipulated that he should be sent away, but on condition that the ambassadors of Poland and Russia should be responsible for the safety of his person; these ambassadors swore, in their masters' names, that neither the Czar nor Augustus should molest him on his journey. On the other hand, Charles was not to endeavour to make any disturbance in Poland. The Divan, having thus determined the fate of Charles, Ishmael, serasquier of Bender, repaired to Varnitsa, where the King was encamped, and acquainted him with the Porte's resolve, explaining civilly enough that there was no time for delay, but that he must go. Charles's only answer was that the Sultan had promised him an army and not a guard, and that kings ought to keep their word.

In the meantime General Fleming, King Augustus's minister and favourite, maintained a private correspondence with the Kan of Tartary and the serasquier of Bender. A German colonel, whose name was La Mare, had made more than one journey from Bender to Dresden, and these were an object of suspicion.

Just at this time the King of Sweden caused a courier sent from Fleming to the Tartar prince to be seized on the Wallachian frontier. The letters were brought to him and deciphered; there was obviously a correspondence going on between the Tartars and Dresden, but the references were so general and ambiguous that it was hard to say whether King Augustus's plan was to detach the Turks from the Swedish alliance, or to persuade the Kan to hand over Charles to his Saxons as he attended him on the road to Poland.

It is hard to imagine that so generous a prince as Augustus would, for the sake of seizing the King of Sweden, risk the lives of his ambassadors and 300 Poles, detained at Adrianople as hostages for Charles's safety.

On the other hand, Fleming was absolute, very shrewd, and quite unscrupulous. The outrageous treatment of the Elector by King Charles might be thought an excuse for any method of revenge, and if the Court of Dresden could buy Charles of the Kan of Tartary they may have thought that it would be no difficult matter to purchase the liberty of the Polish hostages of the Ottoman Porte.

These reasons were argued between the King, Mullern, his private chancellor, and his favourite Grothusen. They read the letters over and over again, and, their wretched plight increasing their suspicions, they resolved to believe the worst.

Some days later the King was confirmed in his suspicions by the sudden departure of Count Sapieha, who had sought refuge with him, and now left him suddenly to go to Poland and throw himself into the arms of Augustus. On any other occasion he would have regarded Sapieha as a malcontent, but in the critical state of affairs he felt certain that he was a traitor; the repeated requests to him to begone made his suspicions a certainty. His own positiveness, together with all these probabilities, made him continue in the certainty that there had been a plot to betray him and deliver him up to his enemies, although the plot had never been proved.

He might be wrong in thinking King Augustus had made a bargain with the Tartars for his person, but he was much more so in depending on the Ottoman Porte. But in any case he resolved to gain time. He told the Pasha of Bender that he could not go till he had the wherewithal to pay his debts, for though his thaim had been regularly paid his liberality had always forced him to borrow. The Pasha asked how much he needed. The King answered at hazard 1,000 purses, that is, about 1,500,000 francs French money full weight. The Pasha wrote to his master about it; the Sultan, instead of the 1,000 purses which he demanded, sent him 1,200 with the following letter to the Pasha—

"The object of this Imperial letter is to inform you that, upon your representation and request, and that of the right noble Delvet Gherai Kan to our sublime Porte, our Imperial munificence has granted the King of Sweden 1,000 purses, which shall be sent to Bender in the custody of the most illustrious Mahomet Pasha, to remain in your hands till such time as the King of Sweden departs, whose steps may God direct, and then to be given him with 200 purses more, as an overplus of our Imperial liberality beyond what he desires. As to the route through Poland, which he has decided on, you and the Kan, who are to accompany him, must be careful to take such prudent and wise measures as shall prevent, during the whole journey, the troops under your command and those of the King of Sweden from any disorderly conduct or anything which may be reckoned a breach of the peace between our sublime Porte and the realm and republic of Poland, so that the King of Sweden may travel as a friend under our protection.

"By so doing (and you are to desire it of him in set terms) he will receive all the honour and respect due to his Majesty from the Poles, as we have been assured by the ambassadors of King Augustus and the republic, who have offered themselves and certain other of the Polish nobility, if required, as hostages for his safe passage. At the time which you and the right noble Delvet shall agree on for the march you shall put yourselves at the head of your brave soldiers, among whom shall be the Tartars, led by the Kan, and go with the King and his men.

"May it please the only God, the Almighty, to direct your steps and theirs. The Pasha of Aulis shall continue at Bender, with a regiment of spahis and another of janissaries, to defend it in your absence. Now, by following our Imperial orders and wishes in all these points and details, you will earn the continuance of our royal favour, as well as the praise and rewards due to all such as observe them.

"Given at our Imperial residence of Constantinople, the 2nd day of the month Cheval, 1124 of the Hegira."

While they were waiting for the Sultan's answer the King had written to the Porte, to complain of the supposed treachery of the Kan. But the passages were well guarded, and the ministry against him, so that his letters never reached the Sultan. The Vizir would not allow M. Desaleurs to go to Adrianople, where the Porte then was, lest he, as the King of Sweden's agent, tried to thwart their design of driving him away. Charles, indignant at seeing himself hunted, as it were, from the Sultan's territory, resolved not to stir a step. He might have asked to return through German territory, or to take ship at the Black Sea, in order to reach Marseilles by the Mediterranean, but he preferred to ask no favour and see what happened.

When the 1,200 purses arrived, his treasurer, Grothusen, who from long residence in Turkey had learned to speak the language, went to the Pasha without an interpreter, hoping to get the money from him, and then to form some new intrigue at the Porte, on the false supposition that the Swedish party would at last arm the Ottoman Empire against the Czar.

Grothusen told the Pasha that the King's equipage could not be prepared without money. "But," said the Pasha, "we are going to defray all the expense of departure; your master will have no expenses while he continues under the protection of mine." Grothusen replied that the difference between the Turkish equipages and those of the Franks was so great that they must apply to the Swedish and Polish workmen at Varnitsa.

He assured him that his master was ready to go and that this money would facilitate and hasten his departure. The too credulous Pasha gave him the 1,200 purses, and in a few days came and respectfully asked the King to give orders for his departure.

He was most surprised when the King told him he was not ready to go and that he wanted 1,000 purses more. The Pasha was overcome by this, and remained speechless for some time; then he walked to a window, where he was seen to shed some tears. Then, turning to the King, he said, "I shall lose my head for having obliged your Majesty. I have given you the 1,200 purses contrary to the express orders of my sovereign." With these words he took leave and was going away full of grief.

The King stopped him and told him he would excuse him to the Sultan. "Ah!" replied the Turk, "my master can punish mistakes, but not excuse them."

Ishmael Pasha went to tell the news to the Kan of Tartary. The Kan, having received the same order as the Pasha, not to let the 1,200 purses be delivered before the King's departure, and having agreed to their delivery, was as apprehensive of the Sultan's resentment as the Pasha himself. They both wrote to the Porte to clear themselves, and explained that they had only parted with the 1,200 purses on a solemn promise made by the King's minister that they would go at once, and they entreated his Highness not to attribute the King's refusal to their disobedience.

Charles, quite convinced that the Kan and the Pasha intended to hand him over to his enemies, ordered M. Funk, his envoy at the Ottoman Court, to lay his complaints against them before the Sultan and to ask for 1,000 purses more. His great generosity, and his indifference to money, hindered him from seeing the baseness of this proposal. He only did it to get a refusal so that then he might have a fresh pretext for failing to depart; but a man must be reduced to great straits when he has recourse to such tricks. Savari, his interpreter, a crafty and enterprising character, carried the letter to Adrianople in spite of the Grand Vizir's care to have the roads guarded. Funk was forced to go and deliver this dangerous message, and all the answer he got was imprisonment.

Thoroughly angry, the Sultan called an extraordinary Divan and made a speech at it himself. His speech, according to the translation then made of it, was as follows—

"I hardly knew the King of Sweden, but from his defeat at Pultawa and the request he made to me to grant him sanctuary in my empire. I am under no obligation to him, nor have I any reason either to love or fear him; yet, thinking only of the hospitality of a Mussulman and my own generosity, which sheds the dew of its favour on small and great alike, I received and aided him, his ministers, officers and soldiers, in every respect, and for three years and a half have continually loaded him with presents.

"I have granted him a considerable guard to take him to his own country. He has asked for 1,000 purses to defray expenses, though I am paying them all, and instead of 1,000 I have granted him 1,200. After getting these from the serasquier of Bender he wants 1,000 more, and refuses to go under the pretext that the guard is too small, whereas it is too large to pass through the country of a friend and ally. I ask you, then, is it any breach of the laws of hospitality to send this prince away, and whether foreign princes would have any ground for accusing me of cruelty and injustice if I used force to make him go?"

All the Divan answered that the Sultan might lawfully do as he said.

The Mufti declared that Mussulmans are not bound to offer hospitality to infidels, much less to the ungrateful, and he granted his festa, a kind of mandate, which generally accompanies the Sultan's important orders. These festas are revered as oracles, though the persons who issue them are as much the Sultan's slaves as any others.

The order and the festa were taken to Bender by the Master of the Horse and the first Usher. The Pasha of Bender received the order at the Kan's, whence he went at once to the Varnitsa to ask if the King would go away in a friendly way, or would force him to carry out the Sultan's orders.

Charles XII, not being used to this threatening language, could not command his temper. "Obey your master if you dare," he said, "and begone." The Pasha in indignation set off at a gallop, an unusual thing with a Turk. On the return journey he met M. Fabricius, and called out to him without stopping, "The King won't listen to reason; you'll see strange doings presently." The same day he cut off the King's supplies and removed the guard of janissaries. He also sent to the Poles and Cossacks to let them know that if they wanted to get any provisions they must leave the King of Sweden's camp and come and put themselves under the protection of the Porte at Bender.

They all obeyed and left the King, with only the officers of his household and 300 Swedes, to cope with 2,000 Tartars and 6,000 Turks. There was now no more provision in the camp for man or beast. The King at once gave orders that the twenty fine Arabian horses they had given him should be shot, saying, "I will have neither their food nor their horses." This made a great feast for the Tartars, who, as every one knows, think that horse-flesh is delicious. In the meantime the Turks and Tartars invested the little camp on all sides.

The King, with no signs of panic, appointed his 300 Swedes to make regular fortifications, and worked at them himself. His chancellor, treasurer, secretaries, valets, and all his servants, lent a hand to the work. Some barricaded the windows, others took the bars behind the doors and placed them like buttresses.

When the house was well barricaded, and the King had reviewed his pretences at fortifications, he began to play chess unconcernedly with his favourite Grothusen, as if everything had been perfectly safe and secure. It happened very luckily that Fabricius, the envoy of Holstein, did not lodge at Varnitsa, but at a small village between Varnitsa and Bender, where Mr. Jeffreys, the English envoy to the King of Sweden, lived also. These two ministers, seeing that the storm was about to break, undertook to mediate between the Turks and the King. The Kan, and especially the Pasha of

Bender, who had no intention of hurting the monarch, were glad of the offers of their services. They had two conferences together at Bender, at which the Usher of the seraglio, and the Grand Master of the Horse, who had brought the order from the Sultan, were present.

M. Fabricius owned to them that the Swedish King had good reason to believe that they intended to give him up to his enemies in Poland. The Kan, the Pasha, and the rest, swore on their heads, calling God to witness, that they detested the thought of such a horrible piece of treachery, and would shed the last drop of their blood rather than show the least lack of respect to the King in Poland.

They added that they had the Russian and Polish ambassadors in their power, and that their lives should answer for the least affront offered to the King of Sweden. In a word, they complained bitterly of the outrageous suspicions which the King was harbouring about people who had received and treated him so well. And though oaths are often the language of treachery, M. Fabricius allowed himself to be persuaded by these barbarians. He thought he saw that air of truth in their protests which falsehood imitates but lamely; he knew that there was a secret correspondence between the Tartar Kan and Augustus, but he remained convinced that the object of this negotiation was only to force Charles to retire from the territories of the Sultan.

But whether Fabricius was mistaken or not he assured them that he would represent to the King the unreasonableness of his jealousies. "But do you intend to force him to go?" he added. "Yes," answered the Pasha, "such are our master's orders." Then he desired them to consider again whether that order was to spill the blood of a crowned head. "Yes," answered the Kan with warmth, "if that head disobeys the Sultan in his own dominions."

In the meantime everything was ready for the assault, and Charles's death seemed inevitable; but as the Sultan's command was not positively to kill him in case of resistance, the Pasha prevailed on the Kan to send a messenger that moment to Adrianople, to receive his Highness's final orders.

Mr. Jeffreys and M. Fabricius, having got this respite, hurried to acquaint the King with it. They hastened like bearers of good news, and were received very coldly; he called them forward, meddling mediators, and still insisted that the Sultan's order and the Mufti's festa were forged, because they had sent for fresh orders to the Porte. The English minister withdrew, resolving to trouble himself no further with the affairs of so obstinate a prince. M. Fabricius, a favourite of the King, and more accustomed to his whims than the English minister, stayed with him, to exhort him not to risk so valuable a life on so futile an occasion.

The only reply the King made was to show him his fortifications and to beg him to mediate so far as to obtain provisions for him. Leave was easily obtained from the Turks to let provisions pass into the King's camp till the couriers should return from Adrianople. The Kan himself had forbidden the Tartars to make any attempt on the Swedes till a new order came; so that Charles went out of his camp sometimes with forty horse, and rode through the midst of the Tartar troops, who respectfully left him a free passage; he even marched right up to their lines, and they did not resist, but opened to him.

At last the Sultan's order arrived with command to put to the sword all the Swedes who made the least resistance, and not to spare the King's life; the Pasha had the civility to show the order to M. Fabricius, that he might make a last effort with Charles. Fabricius went at once to tell him his bad news. "Have you seen the order you refer to?" said the King. "I have," replied Fabricius. "Tell them," said the King, "from me that this order is a second forgery of theirs, and that I will not go." Fabricius fell at his feet in a transport of rage, and scolded him for his obstinacy. "Go back to your Turks," said the King, smiling at him; "if they attack me, I know how to defend myself."

The King's chaplains also fell on their knees before him, beseeching him not to expose the wretched remnant over from Pultawa, and above all, his own sacred person, to death; adding, besides, that resistance in this case was a most unwarrantable deed, and that it was a violation of the laws of hospitality to resolve to stay against their will with strangers who had so long and generously supported him. The King, who had showed no resentment with Fabricius, became angry on this occasion, and told his priests that he employed them to pray for him, and not to give him advice.

General Hoord and General Dardoff, who had always been against venturing a battle which in the result must prove fatal, showed the King their breasts, covered with wounds received in his service, and assured him that they were ready to die for him, and begged him that it might be on a more worthy occasion.

"I know," said the King, "by my wounds and yours that we have fought valiantly together. You have hitherto done your duty; do it again now."

The only thing remaining was to obey; they were all ashamed not to seek death with their King. He prepared for the assault, secretly gloating over the pleasure and honour of resisting with 300 Swedes the efforts of a whole army. He gave every man his place; his chancellor, Mullern, his secretary, Empreus, and the clerks were to defend the Chancery house; Baron Fief, at the head of the officers of the kitchen, was to defend another post; the grooms of the stables and the cooks had another place to guard, for with him every man was a soldier. He rode from his fortifications to his house, promising rewards to every one, creating officers, and declaring that he would make his humblest servant captain if he behaved with valour in the engagement.

It was not long before they saw the Turks and Tartars advancing to attack the little fortress with ten cannon and two mortars. The horse-tails waved in the air, the clarions brayed, and cries of "Alla, Alla," were heard on all sides. Baron Grothusen remarked that they were not abusing the King as they shouted, but only calling him "demirbash," *i.e.* iron-head; so he resolved to go alone and unarmed out of the fort. He advanced to the line of the janissaries, who had almost all of them received money from him. "What, my friends," he said in their own language, "have you come to massacre 300 defenceless Swedes? You brave janissaries, who have pardoned 100,000 Russians, when they cried Amman (pardon) to you, have you forgotten the kindness you have received at our hands? And would you assassinate the King of Sweden whom you loved so much, and who has been so generous to you? My friends, he asks only three days, and the Sultan's orders are not so strict as they would make you believe."

These words had an effect which Grothusen himself had not expected; the janissaries swore on their beards that they would not attack the King, and would give him the three days that he demanded. In vain was the signal given for assault. The janissaries, far from obeying, threatened to turn their arms against their leaders if three days were not granted to the King of Sweden. They came to the Pasha of Bender's tent in a band, crying that the Sultan's orders were forged. To this sedition the Pasha could oppose nothing but patience.

He pretended to be pleased with the generous resolve of the janissaries, and ordered them to retreat to Bender. The Kan of Tartary, who was a passionate man, would have made the assault at once with his own troops; but the Pasha, who would not allow the Tartars alone to have the honour of taking the King while he might perhaps be punished for the disobedience of his janissaries, persuaded the Kan to wait till next day.

The Pasha returning to Bender, assembled all the officers of the janissaries, and the older soldiers; he read them and showed them the positive command of the Sultan, and the mandate of the Mufti. Sixty of the oldest of them, with venerable grey beards, who had received innumerable presents from the King, proposed to go to him in person, and entreat him to put himself into their hands, and permit them to serve him as guards.

The Pasha consented; for there was no stone he would leave unturned rather than be forced to kill the King. So these sixty old soldiers went next morning to Varnitsa, having nothing in their hands but long white staves, their only weapon when they intend not to fight; for the Turks consider it a barbarous custom of the Christians to wear swords in time of peace, and to go armed to the churches or the houses of friends.

They addressed themselves to Baron Grothusen and Chancellor Mullern; they told them that they had come with the intention of serving as faithful guards to the King, and that if he pleased they would conduct him to Adrianople, where he might speak to the Sultan in person. While they were making the proposal the King read the letters that had come from Constantinople and that Fabricius, who could not see him again, had sent to him privately by a janissary. These letters were from Count Poniatowski, who could neither serve him at Bender nor at Adrianople, having been detained at Constantinople by the Czar's order, from the time of the imprudent demand of 1,000 purses. He told the King that the Sultan's order to seize his royal person was only too true, that the Sultan was indeed imposed upon by his ministers; but that the more he was imposed upon in the matter the more he would be obeyed, that he must submit to the times and yield to necessity, and that he took the liberty of advising him to attempt all that was possible in the way of negotiation with the ministers, not to be inflexible in a case where the gentlest methods would prevail, and to trust to time and diplomacy the healing of an evil which rough handling would aggravate beyond the hope of recovery.

But neither the proposal of the old janissaries nor Poniatowski's letters could in the least convince the King that it was possible for him to give way without injuring his honour; he would rather die by the hands of the Turks than be in any sense their prisoner. He dismissed the janissaries without seeing them, sending them word that if they did not hurry he would shave their beards for them, which in the East is considered the most provoking affront that can be offered.

The old soldiers, in a rage, returned home, crying, "Down with this iron-head. Since he is resolved to die, let him." They gave the Pasha an account of their mission, and told their comrades at Bender of the strange reception they had met with. Then all swore to obey the orders of the Pasha without delay, and they were now as eager for the assault as they had been adverse to it the day before. The word was given at once; they marched up to the entrenchments, the Tartars were already waiting for them, and the ten cannon began to play. The janissaries on one side and the Tartars on the other, forced this little camp in an instant. Twenty Swedes had scarcely time to draw their swords, the 300 were surrounded and taken prisoners without resistance. The King was then on horseback between his house and his camp, with Generals Hoord, Dardoff and Sparre; seeing that all his soldiers had suffered themselves to be taken before his eyes, he said with *sangfroid* to those three officers, "Let us go and defend the house. We'll fight," he added with a smile, "pro aris et focis."

With them he immediately galloped up to the house, where he had placed about forty servants as sentinels, and which they had fortified as best they could.

These generals, though they were accustomed to the obstinate courage of their master, could not but be surprised that in cold blood and in jest he should propose that they should defend themselves against ten cannon and a whole army; they followed him with twenty guards and domestics.

But when they were at the door, they found it besieged by janissaries. Besides, nearly 200 Turks and Tartars had already got in at a window, and had seized all the rooms, except a great hall, whither the King's servants had withdrawn. Luckily this hall was near the door at which the King intended entering with his twenty men. He threw himself from his horse, pistol and sword in hand, and his followers did the same.

The janissaries fell on him from all sides, encouraged by the Pasha's promise of eight gold ducats to any who did but touch his coat, in case they could not take him. He wounded and killed all that came near him. A janissary, whom he had wounded, stuck his musket in the King's face, and if the arm of a Turk had not jostled him in the crowd the King would have been killed. The ball grazed his nose, and took off a piece of his ear, and then broke the arm of General Hoord, whose fate it was always to be wounded at his master's side.

The King stuck his sword into the janissary's breast, and at the same time his servants, who were shut up in the hall, opened the door to him. He and his little troop slipped in as swiftly as an arrow; they closed the door at once, and barricaded it with all they could find. Behold Charles shut up in this hall with all his attendants, about three-score men, officers, secretaries, valets, and servants of all kinds!

The janissaries and the Tartars pillaged the rest of the house and filled the rooms. "Come," said the King, "let us go and drive out these barbarians." Then, putting himself at the head of his men, he, with his own hands, opened the door of the hall, which opened into his bedroom, went in and fired on his plunderers.

The Turks, laden with booty, terrified at the sudden appearance of the King whom they had reverenced, threw down their arms and jumped out of the window or fled to the cellars. The King, taking advantage of their confusion, and his own men being animated with this piece of success, pursued the Turks from room to room, killed or wounded those who had not made their escape, and in a quarter of an hour cleared the house of the enemy.

In the heat of the combat the King saw two janissaries who had hidden themselves under his bed. He thrust one through, but the other asked pardon, saying "Amman." "I grant you your life," said the King, "on condition that you go and give the Pasha a faithful account of what you have seen." The Turk readily promised to do as he was told, and was then allowed to leap out of the window like the others.

The Swedes were at last masters of the house again, and shut and barricaded the windows. They did not lack arms, for a room on the ground floor, full of muskets and powder, had escaped the tumultuous search of the janissaries. This they turned to good account, firing close on the Turks through the window, and killing 200 of them in less than a quarter of an hour.

The cannon played against the house, but as the stones were very soft they only made holes in the wall, but demolished nothing.

The Kan of Tartary and the Pasha, who wanted to take the King alive, ashamed at losing time and men, and employing a whole army against sixty persons, thought it expedient to fire the house in order to force the King to surrender; they had arrows twisted with lighted matches shot on to the roof and against the door and windows; by this means the whole house was soon in flames; the roof, all in flames, was about to fall on the Swedes. The King quietly gave orders for extinguishing the fire, and finding a small barrel full of liquor he took hold of it himself, and with the help of two Swedes, threw it on the place where the fire was most violent. Then he found that it was full of brandy. The fire burned more furiously than ever, the King's room was burned, and the great hall, where the Swedes were then, was filled with terrible smoke mingled with tongues of flame, that came in through the doors of the next rooms. Half the roof fell in, and the other had fallen outside the house, cracking among the flames.

A guard called Walberg ventured, when things had got to this pass, to say that they must surrender. "What a strange man this is," said the King, "to imagine that it is not more glorious to be burned than to be taken prisoner." Another guard, called Rosen, remarked that the Chancery-house, which was only fifty paces away, had a stone roof, and was fire-proof; that they might well sally out, gain that house, and there stand on the defensive.

"A true Swede," cried the King; then he embraced him and made him a colonel on the spot. "Come on, my friends," he said, "take all the powder and ball you can carry, and let us gain Chancery, sword in hand." The Turks, who were all this while round the house, were struck with fear and admiration at seeing that the Swedes were staying inside in spite of the flames. But they were much more astonished when they saw them open the doors, and the King and his men fall on them desperately. Charles and his leading officer were armed with sword and pistol. Every one fired two pistols at a time at the instant that the door opened, and in a flash throwing away their pistols, and drawing their swords, they drove back the Turks fifty paces; but the next moment the little band was surrounded.

The King, booted according to custom, got his spurs entangled and fell. At once one-and-twenty janissaries fell on him, disarmed him, and took him away to the quarters of the Pasha, some holding his arms and others his legs, as a sick man is carried for fear of incommoding him.

As soon as the King saw himself in their hands, the violence of his rage and the fury which so long and desperate a fight had naturally inspired, gave way to gentleness and calm; not one impatient word escaped him, not one frown was to be seen. He smiled at the janissaries, and they carried him, crying "Alla," with mingled indignation and respect. His officers were taken at the same time, and stripped by the Turks and Tartars. This strange adventure happened on the 12th of February, 1713. It had extraordinary consequences.

BOOK VII

The Turks remove Charles to Demirtash—King Stanislas is seized at the same time—Bold action of M. de Villelongue—Revolutions in the seraglio—Battles in Pomerania—Altena is burnt by the Swedes—Charles returns to his kingdom—His strange method of travelling—His arrival at Stralsund—The state of Europe at that time—The losses of King Charles—The successes of Peter the Great—His triumphal entry into Petersburg.

THE Pasha of Bender waited in state in his tent, with a certain Marco for interpreter, expecting the King. He received him with great respect, and asked him to rest on a sofa; but the King disregarded his civilities and continued standing.

"Blessed be the Almighty," said the Pasha, "that your Majesty is safe. I am grieved that you have forced me to execute the Sultan's orders." The King, on the other hand, was only vexed that his 300 men had allowed themselves to be taken in their entrenchments, and said, "Ah! if they had fought like men we should have held out these ten days." "Alas," said the Pasha, "what a pity that so much courage should be misapplied." Then the King was taken on a fine horse with magnificent trappings to Bender. All the Swedes were either killed or taken prisoners. The King's equipage, furniture and papers, and the most needful of his clothes were pillaged or burned; on the roads the Swedish officers, almost naked and chained in pairs, followed the horses of the Tartars and janissaries. The Chancellor and the general officers were in the same condition, becoming slaves to those of the soldiers to whose share they fell.

The Pasha Ishmael, having brought the King to his seraglio at Bender, gave him his own room, where he was served in state, but not without a guard of janissaries at the room door. They prepared a bed for him, but he threw himself down on a sofa in his boots, and fell fast asleep. An officer in waiting near by put a cap on his head; the King threw it off directly he awaked, and the Turk was amazed to see a king sleeping on a sofa in his boots and bare-headed. In the morning Ishmael brought Fabricius to the King, and when he saw his Prince's clothes all rent, his boots, his hands, and his whole person covered with blood and dust, his eyebrows scorched, yet even in this state smiling, he threw himself on his knees unable to speak; but, soon reassured by the natural and gentle manner of the King, he resumed his ordinary familiarity, and they began to make sport of the battle.

"They tell me," said Fabricius, "that your Majesty killed no fewer than twenty janissaries." "No, no," said the King, "you know a story always grows in the telling." In the midst of the conversation the Pasha brought to the King his favourite Grothusen and Colonel Ribbins, whom he had generously ransomed at his own expense. Fabricius undertook to ransom all the other prisoners.

Jeffreys, the English ambassador, helped him with money, and La Mottraye, the French noble who had come to Bender from curiosity to see him, and who has written some account of these matters, gave all he had. These strangers, assisted by the Czar's advice and money, redeemed all the officers and their clothes from the Tartars and Turks.

Next morning they took the King in a chariot decked with scarlet to Adrianople, and his treasurer Grothusen was with him; the Chancellor Mullern and some officers followed in another carriage. Many others were on horseback, and could not restrain tears at the sight of the King's chariot. The Pasha commanded the escort. Fabricius remarked that it was a shame that the King had no sword. "God forbid," said the Pasha; "he would soon be at our throats if he had a sword." But some hours after he had one given to him.

While they were carrying, disarmed and a captive, the King who had shortly before dictated to so many countries, and been arbiter of the North and the terror of all Europe, there occurred in the same neighbourhood another instance of the frailty of human greatness. King Stanislas, seized in the Turkish dominions, was being taken prisoner to Bender at the same time as Charles was being taken to Adrianople. Stanislas, without support from the hand that had made him king, having no money, and so no friends in Poland, retired to Pomerania, and as he was not able to keep his own kingdom had done his best to defend his benefactor's.

He even went to Sweden to hasten the recruits needed in Livonia and Poland; he did all that could be expected of him as friend to the King of Sweden. At this time the first King of Prussia, a very wise prince, justly uneasy at the near neighbourhood of the Russians, planned to league with Augustus and the Polish republic to dismiss the Russians to their own country, and to get Charles himself to share in the project. There would be three great results from such a course: the peace of the North, the restoration of Charles to his estates, and a barrier erected against the Russians, who were becoming formidable to Europe. The preliminary of this treaty, on which the tranquillity of the republic depended, was the abdication of Stanislas; Stanislas not only agreed, but he undertook to carry through a peace which deprived him of the throne: necessity, the public good, the glory of sacrifice, and the interests of Charles, to whom he owed so much, decided him.

He wrote to Bender, explaining to the King the position of affairs, the evils and their remedies. He besought him not to oppose an abdication which was necessary under the circumstances, and which was to take place from honourable motives; he begged him not to sacrifice the interests of Sweden to those of an unhappy friend, who would rather sacrifice himself for the public good.

Charles XII received the letters at Varnitsa, and said, in a rage, to the courier, before many people, "Well, if he will not be a king I shall find some one else." Stanislas insisted on the sacrifice that Charles refused to accept; he wished to go himself to persuade Charles, and he risked more in the losing of a throne than he had done to gain it. He stole away at nine one night from the Swedish army, which he was commanding in Pomerania, and started with Baron Sparre, who was afterwards the Swedish ambassador to England and France, and another colonel. He took the name of a Frenchman called Haran, then major in the King of Sweden's army and since killed at Dantzig. He passed round the whole of the hostile army, stopped several times, but released under a passport in the name of Haran; at last he arrived after many risks at the Turkish frontier.

When he reached Moldavia he sent Baron Sparre back to his army, believing himself safe in a country where the King of Sweden had been so honoured; he was far from suspecting what had happened since.

They inquired who he was, and he said a major in Charles's service. They stopped him at the bare mention of his name; he was brought before the hospodar of Moldavia, who, already informed from the newspapers that Stanislas had stolen away, had some inkling of the truth. They had described the King's appearance to him, and it was very easy to recognize his pleasant face with its extraordinary look of sweetness. The hospodar questioned him pointedly, and at last asked what had been his work in the Swedish army. Stanislas and the hospodar were speaking in Latin. "Major," said Stanislas. "*Imo maximus est*," replied the Moldavian, and at once offering him an armchair he treated him like a king, but like a captive king, and they kept a strict watch outside the Greek convent where he was forced to stay till they got the Sultan's orders. The order came to take him to Bender, whence they had just removed Charles.

The news was brought to the Pasha as he was travelling with the King of Sweden, and he told Fabricius who, coming up in a chariot, told Charles that he was not the only king prisoner in Turkey, and that Stanislas was prisoner a few miles away. "Hasten to him, my dear Fabricius," said the King, "and tell him never to make peace with King Augustus, for we shall certainly have a change of affairs soon."

Fabricius had permission to go with the message attended by a janissary. After some miles' journey he met the body of soldiers who were bringing Stanislas, and addressed one who rode in the midst, in a Frankish dress and indifferently mounted. He asked him in German where the King of Poland was. It proved to be Stanislas, whom he had not recognized in that disguise.

"What," said the King, "have you forgotten me?" Fabricius then told him of the King of Sweden's sad condition, and of his unshaken but unsuccessful resolution.

When Stanislas came to Bender, the Pasha, who was returning from accompanying Charles, sent the King an Arabian horse with elegant trappings. He was received in Bender with a volley of artillery, and, except that he was a prisoner, had no cause to complain of his treatment there. Charles was on the way to Adrianople and the town was full of gossip about his battle. The Turks both admired him and thought him blame-worthy; but the Divan was so exasperated that they threatened to confine him in one of the islands of the Archipelago.

Stanislas, who did me the honour of informing me on most of these details, assured me also that it was proposed in the Divan that he too should be kept prisoner in one of the Greek islands, but some months later the Sultan softened and let him go.

M. Desaleurs, who could have championed him and prevented this affront to all Christian kings, was at Constantinople, as well as Poniatowski, whose resourcefulness was always feared. Most of the Swedes were at Adrianople in prison, and the Sultan's throne seemed inaccessible to any complaints from the King of Sweden.

The Marquis of Fierville, a private envoy to Charles at Bender, from France, was then at Adrianople, and undertook a service to the Prince at a time when he was either deserted or ill-used by all. He was luckily helped in this design by a French noble of good family, a certain Villelongue, a man of great courage and small fortune, who, fascinated by reports of the King of Sweden, had come on purpose to join his service.

With the help of this youth M. de Fierville wrote a memorial from the King of Sweden, demanding justice of the Sultan for the wrong offered in his person to all crowned heads, and against the treachery of the Kan and the Pasha of Bender.

It accused the Vizir and other ministers of having been corrupted by the Russians, of having deceived the Sultan, intercepted letters, and of having employed trickery to get from the Sultan an order contrary to the hospitality of the Mussulmans, in violation of the laws of nations, and this in a manner so unworthy of a great Emperor, that a king who had none but his retinue to defend him, and who had trusted the sacred word of the Sultan, was attacked by 20,000 men.

When this memorial had been drawn up it had to be translated into Turkish, and written upon the special paper used for the Sultan's petitions.

They tried to get it done by several interpreters, but the King's affairs were at such a pass, and the Vizir so openly his enemy, that none of them at all would undertake it. At last they found a stranger whose hand was not known, so for a considerable fee, and a promise of profound secrecy, he translated the memorial and copied it on to the right sort of paper. Baron Ardidson counterfeited the King's hand and Fierville sealed it with the arms of Sweden. Villelongue undertook to deliver it to the Sultan as he went to the mosque. This had been done before by people with grievances against the ministers, but that made it now the more dangerous and difficult.

The Vizir was certain that the Swedes would seek justice from his master, and knew from the fate of his predecessors what the probable sequel was. So he forbade any one to approach the Sultan, and ordered that any one seen in the neighbourhood of the Mosque with petitions should be seized.

Villelongue knew the order, and that he was risking his life; but he dressed as a Greek, and, hiding the letter in his breast, went early to the place. He feigned madness, and danced into the midst of the two lines of janissaries, where the Sultan was to pass, and now and then dropped some money to amuse the guards.

When the Sultan was coming they wanted to push Villelongue aside; he fell on his knees and struggled with the soldiers. At last his cap blew off, and showed that he was a Frank, from his long hair: he received several blows and was ill-used.

The Sultan heard the scuffle, and asked what was the matter; Villelongue cried with all his might, "Amman, Amman" (mercy), and pulled out the letter. The Sultan commanded that he should be brought before him. Villelongue hastened forward, and embracing his stirrup gave him the paper, saying, "Sued call dan" (the King of Sweden gives it to thee). The Sultan put the letter in his breast, went on to the mosque, and Villelongue was secured in one of the out-houses of the seraglio.

The Sultan read the letter on his return from the mosque, and resolved to examine the prisoner himself. He changed the Imperial coat and turban, and, as he often does, took the disguise of an officer of janissaries, and took an old Maltese with him as interpreter. Thanks to his disguise Villelongue had a private talk of a quarter of an hour with the Turkish Emperor, an honour that was never done to any other Christian ambassador. He did not fail to detail all the King of Sweden's hardships, accusing the minister and demanding vengeance with the greater freedom, because he was throughout the conversation talking to the Sultan as to an equal. He had recognized the Sultan, although the prison was very dark, and this made him the bolder in his discourse. The seeming officer of the janissaries said to him, "Christian, be assured that the Sultan my master has the soul of an Emperor, and that if the King of Sweden is in the right he will do him justice." Villelongue was soon released, and some weeks after there was a sudden change in the seraglio, which the Swedes attribute to this conference. The mufti were deprived, the Kan of Tartary banished to the Rhodes, and the serasquier Pasha of Bender to an island in the Archipelago.

The Ottoman Porte is so subject to such storms that it is hard to say whether this was an attempt to appease the King of Sweden or not; his subsequent treatment by the Porte showed little anxiety to please him.

Ali-Coumourgi, the favourite, was suspected of having made all these changes for some private ends of his own; the pretext for the banishment of the Kan and the serasquier of Bender was that they had given the King 1,200 purses against the express orders of the Sultan. He put on the Tartar throne the son of the deposed Kan of Tartary, a young man who cared little for his father and on whom Ali counted for military help. Some weeks after this the Grand Vizir Joseph was deposed, and the Pasha Soliman was declared Prime Vizir.

I must say that M. de Villelongue, and many Swedes, have assured me that the letter he gave was the cause of these changes, but M. de Fierville denies this, and I have in other cases met with contradictory accounts. Now, an historian's duty is to tell plain matter of fact, without entering into motives, and he must relate just what he knows, without guessing at what he does not know.

In the meantime, Charles was taken to a little castle called Demirtash, near Adrianople. Crowds of Turks had collected there to see him alight. He was carried on a sofa from his chariot to the castle; but to avoid being seen by this mob he covered his face with a cushion.

It was several days before the Porte would consent to his residence at Demotica, a little town six leagues from Adrianople, near the river Hebrus, now called Marizza. Coumourgi said to the Grand Vizir, "Go and tell the King of Sweden he can stay at Demotica all his life. I warrant he will ask to move of his own accord before the year is over, and be sure you do not let him have a penny of money."

So the King was moved to the little town of Demotica, where the Porte allowed him sufficient supplies for himself and his retinue.

They allowed him twenty-five crowns a day to buy pork and wine, a sort of provisions that the Turks do not supply, but as to the allowance of five hundred crowns a day, which he had had at Bender, it was quite withdrawn. Scarcely had he arrived at Demotica with his small court than the Grand Vizir

Soliman was deposed; his place was given to Ibrahim Molla, a haughty, bold and rough man.

He had been a common sailor till the accession of Achmet III. This Emperor often disguised himself as a private citizen, a priest, or a dervish; he would then slip in the evening into the cafés and other public places of Constantinople to listen to what was said of him, and to hear the people's opinions with his own ears. One day he heard this Molla finding fault with the Turkish ships because they never brought home any prizes, and swore that were he a captain he would never return home without some infidel ship. The next morning the Sultan gave him a ship and sent him out on a cruise. A few days later the Captain brought back a Maltese boat and a Genoese galley, and in another two years he was Admiral, and then Grand Vizir. He was no sooner appointed than he began to think that he could dispense with the favourite, and to make himself indispensable he planned to make war on the Russians; in order to do so he set up a tent near the castle where the King of Sweden was living.

He invited the King to meet him there with the new Kan of Tartary and the French ambassador. The King's misfortunes made him feel the indignity of being sent for by a subject the more; he ordered the Chancellor Mollern to go in his place, and because he feared that the Turks might be disrespectful, and force him to compromise his dignity, he resolved to stay in bed during his stay at Demotica. This he did for ten months, just as if he had been ill. The Chancellor, Grothusen, and Colonel Dubens were his only table-companions. They had none of the conveniences of the Franks, all had been carried off at Bender, so that their meals lacked pomp and elegance. They waited on themselves, and Chancellor Mullern did all the cooking during that time.

While Charles was thus staying in bed, he heard news of the wreck of all his foreign dominions.

General Steinbock, famous for having driven the Danes out of Scandinavia, and for having defeated their picked troops with a band of peasants, was still maintaining the credit of the Swedish arms. He defended Pomerania, Bremen, and the King's possessions in Germany as long as he could, but could not prevent the Saxons and Danes united from passing the Elbe and besieging Stade, a strong town near that river, and in the Duchy of Bremen. It was bombarded and burnt to ashes, and the garrison was obliged to surrender at discretion, before Steinbock could come to their assistance.

He had about 10,000 men, and half of them were cavalry, with which he pursued the enemy, though they were twice his number, and forced them to recross the Elbe. He caught them at a place called Gadebesck, on a small river of the same name, on the 20th December, 1712. The Saxons and Danes were posted with a marsh in front and a wood in the rear; they had all the advantage both in number and position, for there was no getting at them but across the marsh, through the fire of their artillery.

Steinbock led on his men, and, advancing in battle order, began one of the most bloody engagements that had ever taken place between those rival nations. After a sharp fight of three hours' duration, the Danes and the Saxons were forced back and had to leave the field.

After this victory Steinbock could not but remember how the Danes had reduced Stade to ashes, and resolved to avenge himself on Altena, a town belonging to the King of Denmark. Altena is above Hamburg, on the river Elbe, which brings up large vessels thither. The King of Denmark had granted it great privileges, in the hope of making it a place of considerable trade. Hamburg therefore got jealous, and wished nothing but their destruction. When Steinbock came within sight of the place, he sent a herald to bid them begone at once with their possessions, for he intended to destroy their town immediately.

The magistrates came and threw themselves at his feet and offered him a ransom of 100,000 crowns. Steinbock said he must have 200,000. They begged for time to send to their correspondent at Hamburg, and promised that he should have it by the next day. The General told them that if they did not pay at once he would burn their town about their ears.

His soldiers were in the suburbs ready with their torches in their hands. The town had no defence but a poor wooden gate and a dry ditch; so that the poor wretches were forced to flee at midnight. It was on the 9th of January, 1713; the weather was severely cold, and a great north wind helped to spread the flames, and to increase the sufferings of the people exposed in the open fields.

Men and women, loaded with their property, went weeping and lamenting towards the neighbouring ice-clad hills. Paralytic old folk were carried by the young on their shoulders, women just delivered were carrying their children, and died of cold on the hillside, in sight of their burning homes. The people had not all left the town when the Swedes fired it. It burned from midnight to about ten the next morning; the houses, being mostly of wood, were easily burnt, so that by morning there was scarcely any trace of a town left. The aged, the sick, and the women of delicate health, who had refuged on the frozen ground while their houses were burning, dragged themselves to the gates of Hamburg, and begged that they would let them in and save their lives, but they were refused on the ground that there had been infectious disease among them. So that most of these poor wretches died under the walls, calling Heaven to witness the cruelty of the Swedes, and of the still more inhuman Hamburgers.

All Germany was scandalized by this violence. The ministers and generals of Poland and Denmark wrote to Steinbock, complaining of his cruelty, which was inexcusable because it was uncalled for, and must set God and man against him.

He replied that he never would have gone to these extremities were it not to show his master's enemies how war ought to be made—not like barbarians, but in consideration of the laws of nations; that they had committed atrocities in Pomerania to ruin that beautiful country, and sell 100,000 people to the Turks; that his torches at Altena were only a fitting return for the red-hot bullets they had used at Stade; that it was with such violence that the Swedes and their enemies made war on each other. If Charles could have appeared then in Poland, he might possibly have retrieved his former fortune. His armies, though they needed his presence among them, were yet actuated by his spirit; but when the master is away success is seldom turned to good account. Steinbock gradually lost all that he had gained in those great actions, which might have been decisive at a more fortunate time.

With all his success it was not in his power to prevent the Russians, the Saxons, and the Danes from uniting. They seized his quarters, and he lost several of his men in little skirmishes; 2,000 of them were drowned in the Oder as they were going to their winter quarters in Holstein; these were losses which could not be repaired in a country where the enemy was strong in all directions. He intended to defend the country of Holstein against Denmark, but in spite of his ruses and efforts the country was lost, the whole army destroyed, and Steinbock taken prisoner. To complete the misfortunes of the Swedes, the King persisted in his resolve of staying at Demotica, and fed his mind with vain expectations of help from Turkey.

The Vizir, Ibrahim Molla, who had been so bent on war with the Russians in opposition to the favourite, was pressed to death between two doors. The post of Vizir was now so dangerous that none dare take the office; but after it had been vacant for about six months, the favourite Ali-Coumourgi took it. Then the King of Sweden abandoned all hope. He really knew Coumourgi, because he had been of service to him when the favourite's interest had corresponded with his own.

He had spent eleven months buried in idleness and oblivion at Demotica; this extreme idleness, following the most violent exercise, made the illness which he had before assumed a fact. All Europe believed he was dead, and the Regency which he had settled when he left Stockholm, getting no word from him, the Senate went to the Princess Ulrica Eleanora to ask her to take the Regency during the absence of her brother. She accepted it; but when she found that the Senate were trying to force her to peace with the King of Denmark, who was attacking Sweden from all sides, and with the Czar, she resigned the Regency in the certainty that her brother would never ratify the peace, and sent a long account of the affair to him in Turkey.

The King received the dispatches at Demotica, and the despotic theories which he had inherited made him forget that Sweden had once been free, and that the Senate had formerly governed the kingdom together with the Kings. He looked on them as servants, who were usurping the government in the absence of their master; he wrote to them that if they wanted to govern he would send them one of his boots, to whom they might apply for orders. Then, to prevent any attempt to overthrow his authority in Sweden, and to defend his country, hoping for nothing further from the Ottomans, he depended on himself, and told the Grand Vizir that he would go through Germany.

Desaleurs, the French ambassador who transacted all the affairs of Sweden, made the proposal to the Vizir. "Well," said the Vizir, "didn't I say that the year would not pass without the King's asking to go? Tell him that he is free to go or stay, but that he must fix his day, that we may not have a repetition of the trouble we had with him at Bender."

Count Desaleurs softened the form of this message to the King. The day was fixed, but Charles wished, in spite of his wretched position, to show the pomp of a grand king before leaving. He made Grothusen his ambassador extraordinary, and sent him to make a formal leave at Constantinople, with a suite of fourscore persons in rich attire. But the splendour of the Embassy was not so great as the mean shifts to which he descended to provide it were disgraceful. M. Desaleurs lent the King 40,000 crowns, Grothusen borrowed, through his agents at Constantinople, 1,000 from a Jew, at the rate of fifty per cent., besides 200 pistoles of an English merchant, and 1,000 of a Turk.

They amassed this money solely to act before the Divan the comedy of a Swedish embassy. At the Porte, Grothusen received all the honour paid to ambassadors extraordinary on their day of audience. The object of the whole thing was to get money from the Vizir, but the scheme failed. Grothusen proposed that the Porte should lend him a million. But the Vizir answered that his master could be generous when he wished, but that lending was beneath his dignity; that the King should have all necessary for his journey, and in a degree becoming to the giver; and that possibly the Porte might send him a present of uncoined gold, but that he was not to count on that.

The King began his journey on the 1st of October, 1714. A capigi-pasha, with six chiaoux, went to accompany him from Demirtash, whither he had removed a few days before. The presents they brought him from the Sultan were a large scarlet tent embroidered with gold, a sabre set with jewels, eight beautiful Arab horses, with fine saddles and stirrups set with massive silver. It is not beneath the dignity of history to tell that the Arabian groom, who had charge of the horses, gave the King an account of their genealogy; it is the custom there to think more of the family of a horse than of a man; which is not unreasonable, for if we are careful of the breed these animals never degenerate.

The convoy consisted of sixty chariots, laden with all sorts of provisions, and three hundred horses. The Pasha, knowing that many Turks had advanced money to the King's suite at high rate of interest, told him that, as usury was forbidden by the law of Mahomet, he desired his Majesty to settle the debts, so that his resident at Constantinople should only pay the principal. "No," said the King, "if my servants have given bills for a hundred crowns it shall be paid, even if they have only received ten for it." He proposed to the creditors to go with him, and promised payment of all their debts; and many did go to Sweden, and Grothusen was responsible for seeing that they were paid.

The Turks, to show more respect for their guest, made very short stages in the journey; this respectful delay bored the King; he got up as usual about three in the morning; as soon as he was dressed he himself called the capigi and the chiaoux, and ordered them to march in the midst of pitch darkness. The Turkish solemnity was not pleased by this novel way of travelling, and the King was glad to find it was so, and said that he would avenge Bender a little.

When he arrived at the Turkish frontier, Stanislas was leaving it by another road, intending to withdraw into Germany to the Duchy of Deux Ponts, a country bordering on the Rhine Palatinate and Alsace, which had belonged to the King of Sweden ever since it had been united to the crown by Christina, successor to Charles XI.

Charles assigned the revenue of this Duchy to Stanislas; it was then reckoned at about 70,000 crowns. And this was the end of so many wars and so many hopes. Stanislas both would and could have made an advantageous treaty with Augustus, if Charles had not been so obstinate as to make him lose his actual estates in Poland only that he might keep the title King.

The Prince stayed at Deux Ponts, till Charles's death, then this Duchy falling to the Palatine family, he retired to Weissemburg in French Alsace. When M. Sum, King Augustus' ambassador, complained to the Duke of Orleans, Regent of France, he received this strange answer: "Sir, tell the King, your master, that France has ever been a refuge for kings in misfortune."

The King of Sweden, having arrived on the German frontier, found that the Emperor had given orders for his reception with proper state throughout his dominions. The towns and villages where harbingers had fixed his route were making great preparations to entertain him; and every one was looking forward to see the passing of this extraordinary man, whose conquests and misfortunes, whose least actions and whose very times of rest had made so much talk in Europe. But Charles disliked so much pomp, nor did he, as the prisoner of Bender, care to go on show; he had even resolved to never reenter Stockholm till he had repaired his misfortunes.

So dismissing his Turkish attendants at Tergowitz, on the border of Transylvania, he called his people together in a yard, and bade them not to be anxious about him, but make the best of their way to Stralsund, in Pomerania, about 300 leagues from that spot, on the Baltic. He took no one with him, but a certain During, and parted cheerfully with all his officers, leaving them in astonishment, fear and grief. As a disguise he wore a black wig, a gold-laced hat, and a blue cloak, passing for a German officer. Then he rode post-haste with his travelling companion.

On the road he kept clear of places belonging to his real or secret enemies, and so, through Hungary, Moravia, Austria, Bavaria, Wirtemburg, the Palatinate, Westphalia and Mecklenburg, he made the tour of Germany, and doubled his route. At the end of the first day, During, who was not used to such fatigues, fainted when he alighted. The King would not wait a moment, but asked him how much money he had. He said about a thousand crowns. "Give me half," said the King; "I see you can go no further; I will go without you." During begged him to rest for at least three hours, assuring him that then he would be able to go on, and desired him to consider the risk of travelling alone. The King would not be persuaded, but made him hand over the five hundred crowns, and called for horses. During, fearing the consequences, bethought himself of a plan.

He drew the post-master to one side, and, pointing to the King, "Friend," he said, "this is my cousin; we are travelling on the same business, and you see he won't wait three hours for me; pray give him the worst horse you have, and procure me a chaise or coach." He put a couple of ducats in the man's hand, and was obeyed punctually; so that the King had a horse which was both lame and restive. He started at about ten at night, through wind, snow, and rain. His fellow-traveller, after a few hours' rest, set out again in a chaise with very good horses. At about daybreak he overtook the King, with his horse in a state of exhaustion, and walking to the next stage. Then he was obliged to get in with During, and slept on the straw; then they continued their journey, on horseback during the day and sleeping in the coach at night. They did not make any halts, and so, after sixteen days' riding, and often at the risk of being taken, they arrived at last at the gates of the town of Stralsund, at one o'clock in the morning. The King shouted to the sentinel that he was a messenger from the King of Sweden in Turkey, that he must speak that very moment to General Ducker, the governor of the place; the sentinel answered that it was late, that the governor was in bed, and that they must wait till daybreak. The King answered that he was on important business, and declared that if they did not wake the governor without delay he would have them all hanged. The next morning a sergeant went and called the governor; Ducker imagined that he was perhaps one of the King of Sweden's generals; the gates were opened, and the courier was brought into the room. Ducker, half asleep, asked the news. The King seized him by the arm. "What," he said, "my most faithful subjects have forgotten me!" The General recognized the King; he could hardly believe his eyes. He threw himself from his bed, and embraced his master's feet, shedding tears of joy. The news was all over the town in a minute; every one got up, the soldiers collected round the governor's house; the streets were full of people asking if the news were true; the windows were illuminated, the conduits ran with wine, and the artillery fired a volley.

In the meantime they put the King to bed, as he had not rested for sixteen days. They had to cut his boots from his legs, so much were they swollen from excessive fatigue. He had neither linen nor clothes. They hastily manufactured a wardrobe from whatever would fit him best that was in the town. When he had had some hours' sleep, he got up to go and review his troops, and visit the fortifications. That very day he sent his orders to all parts for renewing the war against his enemies with more vigour than ever.

Europe was now in a very different condition from that she had been in when Charles went away in 1709. The war in the South, between England, Holland, France, Spain, Portugal and Italy, was over; this general peace was due to some private quarrels in the English Court. The Earl of Oxford, a clever minister, and Lord Bolingbroke, one of the greatest geniuses and most eloquent men of his century, were in the ascendant against the famous Duke of Marlborough, and persuaded Queen Anne to make peace with Louis XIV. France having made peace with England, soon forced the other Powers to terms. Philip IV, grandson of Louis XIV, was beginning a peaceful rule over the ruins of the Spanish monarchy. The Emperor, master of Naples and Flanders, was firmly settled in his vast dominions. The only thing that Louis asked was to finish his long career in peace. Queen Anne of England died in August 1714, hated by half the nation for having given peace to so many States. Her brother James Stewart, an unfortunate prince excluded from the throne almost from his birth, failing to appear in England to try to recover a succession which new laws would have settled on him, had his party prevailed, George I, Elector of Hanover, was unanimously chosen King of Great Britain. The throne came to him not by right of descent, but by Act of Parliament.

Called at an advanced age to rule a people whose language he did not understand, and where everything was strange, George considered himself rather Elector of Hanover than King of England; his whole ambition was for the improvement of his German States; nearly every year he crossed the seas to visit the subjects who adored him. In other ways he preferred a private to public life; the pomp of majesty was burdensome to him, and what he liked was a familiar talk with a few old courtiers. He was not the most dazzling king of Europe, but he was one of the wisest of the kings, and perhaps the only one who could, as king, taste the pleasures of friendship and a private life. These were the chief princes, and this was the position of affairs in South Europe. The changes that had occurred in the North were of another kind: the kings there were at war, but all united against the King of Sweden.

Augustus had been long restored to the crown of Poland, by the help of the Czar, and with the consent of the Emperor, Queen Anne, and the States-General, who, though guarantors of the Peace of Altranstadt, in Charles's better days, forgot their obligations when they found there was no longer anything to fear from him. But Augustus was not at peace in his kingdom. His people's fears of arbitrary power returned with the return of their King; they had taken up arms to make him submit to the Pacta Conventa, a solemn compact they had with their King.

They seemed to have summoned him home only to make war on him. At the beginning of these troubles not a word was said of Stanislas, his party seemed to have disappeared, and the King of Sweden was no more remembered than as a kind of torrent, which had for a time borne down all before it.

Pultawa and Charles's absence, which caused the fall of Stanislas, was also the cause of the fall of the Duke of Holstein, Charles's nephew, who was dispossessed of his dominions by the King of Denmark. The King of Sweden had a great regard for the father, and was moved and humiliated by the son's losses. Besides, as he only acted for the sake of glory, the fall of princes which he had himself set up was as vexing to him as his own losses. His enemies vied with each other in profiting by his ruin. Frederic William, the new King of Prussia, who seemed as anxious for war as his father had been for peace, took Stetin and a part of Pomerania for four hundred thousand crowns, which he advanced to the King of Denmark and the Czar. George, Elector of Hanover, now King of England, had the Duchy of Bremen and Verden for three-score thousand pistoles which he had lent to the King of Denmark. Thus was Charles spoiled, and those who had gained these territories as pledges were from their interests as much opposed to him as those who had taken them from him. The Czar was indeed most of all to be feared. His former losses, his victories, and his very mistakes, combined with his diligence to learn, and care to teach his subjects in their turn, and his hard work, made him a remarkable man.

Riga, Livonia, Ingria, Carelia, part of Finland, and all the countries that had been won by Charles's ancestors, were now subject to Russia. Peter, who had only twenty years before not so much as one ship on the Baltic, had gained control of those seas with a fleet of no fewer than thirty ships of the line. He built one of these ships with his own hands; he was the best carpenter, admiral and pilot in the North. From the Gulf of Bothnia to the ocean he had sounded every league of the way. He had united the labour of a common sailor to the experiments of a theorist, and having become admiral gradually, and by dint of victories, as he had before when he aimed at land command. While Prince Gallitsin, a general made by him, and the best at seconding his plans, was completing the conquest of Poland, by taking Vasa and beating the Swedes, this Emperor put to sea to make a descent on Alan, on the Baltic, about twelve leagues from Stockholm.

He went on the expedition in the beginning of July 1714, while his rival Charles was in bed at Demotica.

He embarked at Cronslot, a harbour he had built four miles from St. Petersburg. The harbour, the fleet, the officers and sailors were all the work of his own hands, and he could see nothing that he had not made himself.

The Russian fleet found itself off Aland on the 15th of July; it consisted of thirty ships of the line, fourscore galleys, and a hundred half-galleys; it carried twenty thousand men, and was commanded by Admiral Apraxin, the Russian Emperor being Rear-Admiral.

The Swedish fleet came up on the 16th, under the command of Vice-Admiral Erinschild, and was weaker by two-thirds; yet they fought for three hours, the Czar himself attacking the flag-ship, and taking it after an obstinate fight.

The day of the victory he landed 16,000 men at Aland, and took many of the Swedish soldiers who could not board their own fleet prisoners. Then he returned to his port of Cronslot, with the flag-ship and three smaller ones, a frigate, and six galleys, which he had taken.

From Cronslot he went to St. Petersburg, followed by his victorious fleet and the ships he had taken. He was greeted by a salute of 150 guns. Then he made his triumphal entry, which gave him more pleasure than that at Moscow, as it was in his favourite town, where ten years before there was not so much as a shed, and which now possessed 34,000 fine houses. Then, too, he was at the head of a victorious army, and of the first Russian fleet ever seen in the Baltic; and among a people who, before his time, had never known what a fleet was.

At Petersburg the ceremonies were much the same as at Moscow. The Swedish Vice-Admiral was the *pièce de résistance*. Peter appeared as Rear-Admiral, and a Russian, who represented the Czar on these occasions, was set upon a throne surrounded by twelve senators. The Rear-Admiral presented him with an account of his victories, and was then made Vice-Admiral in consideration of his services. It was an odd ceremony, but suited to a country where the Czar had introduced military distinctions as a novelty.

The Russian Emperor, having thus got the better of the Swedes by land and by sea, and having helped to expel them from Poland, was master there himself; he made himself mediator between the King and the people, an honour perhaps equal to that of setting up a King. The pomp and fortune of Charles had passed to the Czar; he made a better use of it than his rival, for he used all his successes for his country's good. If he took a town the chief artisans were transferred to Petersburg. The manners, arts and sciences of any place he took were carried home to enrich and refine his own country. So that of all conquerors he had the best excuse for his conquest.

Sweden, on the other hand, had lost all her foreign possessions, and had neither trade, money, nor credit; her veterans were either killed or had died of want. More than a hundred thousand Swedes were slaves in the vast Russian Empire, and as many more had been sold to the Turks and the Tartars. The male population was visibly becoming scarce; but in spite of all this, their hopes revived when they heard that their King had arrived at Stralsund.

The sentiment of respect and admiration for him was still so strong that the rustic youth crowded to enlist, leaving the land without cultivators.

BOOK VIII

Charles marries his sister to the Prince of Hesse—He is besieged in Stralsund and escapes to Sweden—The enterprise of Baron Gortz his premier—Plans of reconciliation with the Czar—An attack on England—Charles besieges Frederickshal in Norway—He is killed—His character—Gortz is beheaded.

DURING these preparations the King gave his only surviving sister in marriage to Frederic, Prince of Hesse-Cassel. The Queen Dowager, his grandmother, aged fourscore years, did the honours of the *fête* on the 4th of April, 1715, and died shortly afterwards. The King could not attend the ceremony, as he was so busy finishing the fortifications of Stralsund, which was in danger from the Kings of Denmark and Prussia. But he made his brother-in-law generalissimo of all the forces of Sweden. This Prince had served the States-General in the French war, and was considered a good soldier, a qualification for his sister's hand in the eyes of Charles XII.

Misfortunes now followed as fast as victories had once done. In June 1715 the English King's German forces and those of Denmark invested the strong town of Wismar; the Danes, Saxons and Prussians, 36,000 of them, marched in a body to Stralsund to form a siege. Not far from Stralsund, five Swedish ships were sunk by the Danes and Prussians. The Czar held the Baltic with two large men-of-war, and 150 transports, which had 30,000 men on board. He threatened a descent on Sweden, appearing alternately on the coast of Elsingburg and Stockholm. All Sweden was in arms, expecting an invasion; his land forces were chasing the Swedes from the places they held in Finland towards the Gulf of Bothnia, but he attempted nothing further. At the mouth of the Oder, a river that divides Pomerania, and, passing Stetin, falls into the Baltic, there is a little island called Usedom. Its position makes it a place of considerable importance, for it commands the Oder both on the right and the left, and whoever holds it is master of the navigation of that river. The King of Prussia had dislodged the Swedes, and was holding the place as well as Stetin, saying that he did so purely for the sake of peace. But the Swedes had retaken Usedom in May 1715, and held two forts there, one called Suine, on a branch of the Oder of that name, the other called Penamonder, of greater importance, on another branch of the river. The forts were manned with only 250 Pomeranians, commanded by an old Swedish officer called Kuze-Slerp, a man who deserves to be remembered. On the 4th of April the King of Prussia sent 1,500 foot and 800 dragoons into the island. They arrived and landed on the side of Suine without opposition. The Swedish commander had left them this fort, as being the least important, and, not being able to divide his small force, he withdrew to the castle of Penamonder, resolving to await the worst.

So they were forced to make a formal siege. They shipped artillery at Stetin, and sent in a reinforcement of 1,000 Prussian foot and 400 horse. On the 18th, they opened the trenches in two places, and a brisk battery was played by cannon and mortars. During the siege a Swedish soldier, sent privately with a letter to Charles, found means to land on the island and slip into the place. He gave the letter to the commander. It was as follows: "Do not fire till the enemy come to the edge of the ditch; defend yourselves to the last drop of your blood.—CHARLES."

Slerp read the note, resolved to obey, and die as he was bid in his master's service. On the 22nd, at daybreak, the assault was made. The besieged did as they were told, and killed many, but the ditch was full, the breach large, and the besiegers too numerous. They entered at two different places at once.

The commander now thought that he had no further duty but to obey orders and sell his life dear, so he abandoned the breaches, entrenched his few troops, who all had honour and courage enough to go with him, and placed them so that they should not be surrounded.

The enemy hastened up, surprised that he did not ask for quarter; but he fought a whole hour, and when he had lost half his soldiers, was killed at last with his lieutenant and major. There were then left 100 men and one officer; these asked that their lives might be spared, and were taken prisoners. In the commander's pocket they found his master's letter, which was taken to the King of Prussia.

Just as Charles had lost Usedom, and the neighbouring islands which were quickly taken, while Wismar was on the point of surrender, with no fleet to lend aid, and Sweden in great danger, he himself was at Stralsund, besieged by 36,000 men. Stralsund, famous throughout Europe for the siege the King of Sweden sustained there, is one of the strongest places in Pomerania. It is built between the Baltic and the Lake of Franken, near the Straits of Gella. There is no land passage to it but across a narrow crossway defended by a citadel, and by retrenchments that were once thought inaccessible. There was in it a garrison of 9,000 men, and, more than all, the King of Sweden himself. The Kings of Denmark and Prussia besieged it with an army of 36,000 men, consisting of Saxons, Prussians and Danes. The honour of besieging Charles was too great an incitement to them to make any task difficult, so the trenches were opened on the night between the 19th and 20th of October, 1715.

The King of Sweden said at first that he wondered how any place well manned and fortified could be taken. True, he had taken many towns himself in the course of his victories, but none by regular attack. It was the fame of his exploits that gained them; besides, he never judged others by his own standard, and always underrated his enemies. The besiegers carried on their work with great alacrity, and they were assisted by a curious chance.

It is well known that the Baltic has no flux and reflux. The entrenchments of the town were thought impregnable, as there was an impassable marsh on the west and the sea on the east.

No one had remarked before that in a strong westerly wind the waves of the Baltic roll back so as to leave only three feet of water under the entrenchment. They had always thought it deep. A soldier, happening to fall from the top of the entrenchment, was surprised to find a bottom; but having made that discovery, he concluded that it might make his fortune. So he deserted, and going to the quarters of Count Wakerbath, General of the Saxon forces, he told him that the sea was fordable, and that it would be easy to carry the Swedes' entrenchments. The King of Prussia was not slow to take the hint.

The next day the west wind was still blowing; Lieutenant-Colonel Kepel entered the water with 1,800 men, and 2,000 advanced at the same time on the causeway; all the Prussian artillery fired, and the Prussians and Danes gave an alarm on the other side. The Swedes were sure they could deal with those who were advancing with such rashness by the causeway; but Kepel, coming in behind them from the sea, enclosed them so that they could make no headway, and the position was carried after terrible slaughter on both sides. Some of the Swedes retired into the town, but they were pursued by the besiegers, and some entered pell-mell with those that were fleeing. Two officers and four Saxon soldiers were already on the drawbridge, but they had just time to shut it, and took the men, and so for that time the town was saved. They found four-and-twenty pieces of cannon on the entrenchments, which they turned against the town. After this success the siege was carried on eagerly, the town being cannonaded and bombarded without remission.

Opposite Stralsund on the Baltic is the island of Ruegen, which is a rampart of the place, whither the garrison and people could retire if they only had boats. This island was of the first importance to Charles, for he knew that if the enemy were masters of it he would soon be invested both by sea and land, and probably buried in the ruins of Stralsund, or else taken prisoner by those whom he had formerly despised so much and used so harshly.

However, the wretched state of his affairs had prevented him from sending a sufficient garrison to Ruegen, and there were not more than 2,000 regular troops altogether on the island. For three months the enemy had been making all the preparations for an attack on it, but having built boats for the purpose, the Prince of Anhalt, favoured by good weather, made a landing at last with 12,000 men on the 15th of November.

The King, who was everywhere, was in this island; he joined 2,000 men who were entrenched near a little haven, about three leagues from where the enemy had landed. He marched with them at midnight, with great silence. The Prince of Anhalt had used what seemed unnecessary caution to entrench his cannon. His officers expected no attack by night, and had no idea but that Charles was safe at Stralsund. But the Prince, who knew Charles much better, ordered a deep ditch, with *chevaux de frise* on the edge, and took as much care as if he had to do with a superior force.

At two in the morning Charles came to the enemy's camp, without the slightest noise. His soldiers said to one another, "Come, let us pull up the *chevaux de frise.*" These words were overheard by the sentinels; the alarm was quickly given, and the enemy stood to arms. The King, raising the *chevaux de frise,* saw a great ditch. "Ah," he said, "impossible; this is more than I expected." Not at all discouraged, and knowing nothing of their numbers, nor they of his, for the night favoured him in that, he decided at once, leaped into the ditch, followed by some of the boldest. The *chevaux de frise* was removed, the earth levelled with any trunks and branches they could find, and the bodies of the dead for *fascines.* The King, generals, and boldest of the officers and soldiers got on one another's shoulders as in assaults.

The fight began in the enemy's camp; the vigour of the Swedes threw the Danes and Prussians into disorder, but their numbers being too disparate, the Swedes were repulsed in about a quarter of an hour, and repaired to the ditch.

The unfortunate King rallied his troops in the field, and the fight was renewed with equal warmth on both sides. He saw his favourite Grothusen fall, and General Dardoff, and as he fought passed over the body of the latter while he was still breathing. During, his companion from Turkey to Stralsund, was killed before his face. The King himself was shot near the left breast; Count Poniatowski, who had been so lucky as to save his life before at Pultawa, had the good fortune to do the same again, and gave him a new mount. The Swedes retired to a part of the island named Alteferre, where they still held a fort; from thence the King returned to Stralsund, obliged to leave those brave troops who had served him so well in that expedition; they were all prisoners of war two days later.

Among the prisoners was that unfortunate French regiment, the *débris* of the battle of Hochstet, which had first served Augustus, and afterwards Charles. Most of the soldiers were drafted into a new regiment belonging to the son of the Prince of Anhalt, and he was their fourth master. In Ruegen the commander of this vagrant regiment was then the famous Count Villelongue, who had so nobly risked his life at Adrianople to save Charles. He was taken with all his men, and was ill rewarded for all his services, fatigues and sufferings.

The King, having only weakened himself by all these prodigies of valour, pent up in Stralsund and expecting to be taken, was yet the same as he had been at Bender. Nothing could surprise him. All day he was making ditches and entrenchments behind the walls, and at night he sallied out against the enemy. The town was badly damaged, bombs fell thick and fast, and half the town was in ashes. The townsfolk, far from complaining, were full of admiration for their master, whose temperance, courage and fatigues were astonishing; they acted as soldiers under him, following to the attack, and were now as good as another garrison.

One day, as the King was dictating to a secretary some dispatches for Sweden, a bomb fell into the house, came through the roof, and burst very near his room. Part of the floor fell in, but the ante-room where he was at work, being attached to a thick wall, was undisturbed, and by a lucky chance none of the splinters came in at the door, though it was open. In this noise and confusion the secretary dropped his pen, thinking that the house was coming down. "What is the matter?" said the King calmly; "why are you not writing?" The man could only stammer out, "The bomb, Sire!" "Well," said the King, "what has that to do with our writing? Go on."

An ambassador of France, a M. de Croissy, was then shut up with the King in Stralsund. To send a man on an embassy to Charles was like sending him to the trenches. The King would talk with Croissy for hours together, in the most exposed places, where people were falling on all sides, killed by the bombs and cannon; the King was unconscious of the danger, and the ambassador did not care to say anything to make him chose a safer place for business. Before the siege this minister tried his best to make a treaty between the Kings of Sweden and Prussia; but the one expected too much, and the other would not make any concessions. So that the only satisfaction that Croissy got out of his embassy was the familiarity he enjoyed with this remarkable man. He often slept on the same cloak with him, and, as they shared so many dangers and fatigues, he was outspoken with him. Charles encouraged this in the case of those he liked, and would sometimes say to Croissy, "Veni, maledicamus de rege." "Come, let us talk scandal of Charles."

Croissy stayed in the town till the 13th of November. Then, with the permission of the enemy to pass with his baggage, he took leave of Charles, whom he left among the ruins of Stralsund with only a third of his garrison left, and fully resolved to stand an assault.

In fact, the assault on the horn-work was made in four days. The enemy took it twice, and were twice beaten off.

At last numbers prevailed, and they became masters of it. Charles stayed two days longer in the town, expecting every moment a general assault; on the 16th he stayed till midnight in a little ravelin quite destroyed by bombs and cannon; the day after the principal officers begged him to stay no longer in this untenable situation, but retreat was now as dangerous as to stay there. The Baltic was full of Russian and Danish ships; in the port at Stralsund there was only one boat with sails and oars. So many dangers made retreat glorious, and determined Charles to go; he embarked on the evening of December 20th, with ten persons aboard. They were obliged to break the ice, and it was several hours before they could get away. The enemy's admiral had strict orders not to let Charles escape from Stralsund. Happily they were to leeward of him, and could not approach. He ran the most risk in passing a place called the Barbette, in Ruegen, where the Danes had fixed a battery of twelve cannon. They fired, and he made all the sail he could to get clear of their range. Two men were killed close by him, and at another shot the mast was shattered. In the midst of these dangers the King met two of his ships that were cruising in the Baltic, and the next day Stralsund was surrendered, and the garrison made prisoners of war. The King landed at Isted in Scania, and came to Carlscrona, in a very different state from that in which he had left it, ten years before, when he started in a ship of twelve guns, to dictate to the North.

As he was so near his capital, it was concluded he would go there after so long an absence. But he could not bear the thought of it till he had gained some great victories. Nor did he want to see his people who loved him, and to whose burdens he had perforce to add to defend himself against his enemies. He only wanted to see his sister, and he sent for her to meet him near Lake Wetter, in Ostrogothia. He rode post-haste with one attendant, spent a day with her, and returned.

At Carlscrona, where he passed the winter, he levied new forces everywhere. He thought his subjects were only born to follow him to war, and he had accustomed them to think so too. He enlisted many of but fifteen years old. In many villages there were only old men, women and children left; in some places the women ploughed unaided. It was still more difficult to get a fleet. But to bring that about commissions were given to privateers, who enjoyed great privileges to the ruin of the country, but who provided him with some ships. This was the last effort of Sweden to meet the great expense; all the houses were searched, and half their provisions carried into the King's warehouses. All the iron in the country was bought up for his use and paid for in paper, which he sold for ready money. Whoever wore silk, or wigs, or gilded swords was taxed, and there was a heavy hearth-rate.

A people thus loaded with taxation would have revolted under any other King, but here the most miserable peasant knew that his master was faring harder than he himself. So they quietly bore what their King was always the first to bear. In the public danger, private misfortunes were not thought of. They expected hourly an attack from the Russians, Danes, Prussians, Saxons, and the English. Their fear was so strong, and so well justified, that those who possessed valuables buried them.

It was a surprise to all Europe, who had still an eye on Charles, when, instead of defending his country about to be attacked by so many princes, he invaded Norway at the head of 20,000 men. Since the time of Hannibal there had been no instance of a general who, unable to hold his own against his enemies at home, had gone to attack them in their own dominions. His brother-in-law, the Prince of Hesse, accompanied him. There is no way from Sweden to Norway except by dangerous by-ways, where at every turn one meets with pools of water, formed by the sea between the rocks; bridges have to be made every day. A very few Danes might have stopped the Swedish army, but they were not ready for such a rapid invasion.

Europe was still more surprised to find the Czar so quiet, without descending on Sweden as he had intended.

The reason was that he had a plan, which was one of the greatest, and one of the most difficult to carry out, that has ever been conceived.

Baron Gortz, a Franconian by birth, and Baron of the empire, having done the King of Sweden important services during his sojourn at Bender, was now his favourite and Prime Minister. He was the boldest and the most diplomatic of men: full of resource in adversity, ambitious in his plans, and active in his policy, no project was too ambitious for him, no means too dear for his end; he was prodigal with presents, oaths, truth and falsehood. From Sweden he went to England, France, Holland, to himself lay the train which he meant to use; he was able to inflame all Europe, and that was his idea. What his master was at the head of an army, he was in the cabinet, and this gave him more influence over Charles than any minister had ever had before. This King, who from the age of twenty had given orders to Court Piper, was now willing to receive them from Baron Gortz, and was the more submissive because his misfortunes had made it necessary for him to ask advice, and because Gortz's advice suited with his courageous disposition. He found that of all the princes in league against him Charles felt especially resentful to George of Hanover, King of England: because he was the only one whom Charles had never injured, and had entered into the affair only as a mediator, with intent to hold Bremen and Verden, which he bought for a trifle from the King of Denmark.

It was early that he discovered the Czar's secret discontent with the allies, who all wanted to prevent his getting any footing in Germany.

Since the year 1714 the Czar had been in a position to make a descent on Sweden, but whether he could not agree with the Kings of Poland, England, Denmark, and Prussia, allies whose suspicions were justifiable, or whether he thought his troops not seasoned enough to attack that people at home, whose very peasants had beat the pick of the Danish forces, he still took care to put it off.

The want of money was what had hitherto delayed him. For the Czar was one of the greatest monarchs in the world, but not one of the richest, his revenue not amounting to more than 18,000,000 French francs. He had discovered gold, silver, iron and copper mines, but the profit they yielded was uncertain, and the working of them expensive. He had established a great trade, yet at first it did not flourish; his new conquests increased his power and his fame, but brought him very little treasure.

Time was necessary to bind up the wounds of Livonia, a fertile country which had suffered much from a fifteen years' war, by fire, sword and plague—almost desolate of inhabitants, and a burden to the conqueror. The fleets he now maintained; and every day some new enterprise was exhausting all his treasures. He had been reduced to the bad expedient of raising the value of the coinage, a remedy which never cures the evil, and is particularly injurious to any country where the imports exceed the exports. It was upon these grounds that Gortz had laid the basis of a revolution; he was bold enough to suggest to the King of Sweden that he should make peace with the Czar, insinuating that the Czar was very angry with the Kings of Poland and England, and that Peter and Charles together might make the rest of Europe tremble.

There was no making peace with the Czar, unless he yielded a good many provinces to the east and west of the Baltic, but he called his attention to the fact that in yielding such places as the Czar possessed already, and which he could not possibly regain, he might have the honour of replacing Stanislas on the throne of Poland, and setting James II's son upon that of England, besides restoring the Duke of Holstein.

Charles was pleased with all this, and without giving the matter much consideration he gave the minister full powers to act: Gortz left Sweden with *carte blanche* for any prince he wished to treat with. His first business was to try how the Court of Moscow stood, which he did through the Czar's chief physician, a man devoted to the Pretender's interests, as most of the Scots are, where they are not in the pay of the English Court. This physician represented to Prince Menzikoff, with all the eagerness of a man much interested, the greatness and importance of such a plan. Prince Menzikoff was pleased with it, and the Czar approved it. Instead of an invasion of Sweden he sent his troops to winter in Mecklenburg, and came there himself on the pretext of settling some disputes between his nephew the Duke and his nobles: his real object was to gain a principality in Germany, for which he hoped to bargain with the Duke.

The allies were angry at this step, not caring to have so terrible and formidable a neighbour, who, should he once gain German provinces, might become Emperor and oppress the sovereigns. The greater was their resentment, the more that Gortz's plan flourished. But he negotiated with all the confederates in order to conceal his private intrigues. The Czar fed them all with vain hopes. Charles was all this while with his brother-in-law in Norway at the head of 20,000 men, the country was defended by 110,000 Danes in separate bands, which were routed by the King and Prince of Hesse. Charles advanced to Christiania, the capital, and fortune smiled on him again, but from want of provisions he was forced to retire to Sweden, there to await the result of his minister's plan.

This affair was to be carried through with profound secrecy, and elaborate preparations were necessary: these two are incompatible. Gortz planned to go as far as Asia in his quest, and though the means seemed undesirable, it would at least bring men, money and ships to Sweden, which could be used for an attack on Scotland.

For some time the pirates of all nations, and especially the English, had banded themselves together to infest the seas of Europe and America; they had received no quarter and had retired to Madagascar, a large island on the east coast of Africa; they were quite desperate, and famed for actions which would have made them heroes had they been legal. They wanted a prince to take them under his protection, but international law shut them out from every harbour.

When they heard that Charles XII was returned to Sweden they hoped that, as he was devoted to war and forced to take share in it, and needed a fleet and soldiers, he would be glad to make terms with them. So they sent a deputy, who travelled to Europe in a Dutch ship, to propose to Baron Gortz that they might be received at Gothenburg, where they promised to prepare three-score ships loaded with treasure.

The Baron persuaded the King to agree, and two Swedes were sent to negotiate with them. Then more honourable and substantial help came from Cardinal Alberoni, who directed the government of Spain long enough for his own reputation but not for the good and glory of that kingdom.

He took up the project of setting James II's son on the English throne with great enthusiasm. But as he had only just taken up the ministry, and Spain was to be settled before he could attempt to overthrow thrones, it appeared that there was no great likelihood of his undertaking the task at present. Yet in two years he had done so much for Spain, and had so raised her prestige in Europe that he had got the Turks (it is reported) to attack the Emperor. Then he took steps to remove the Duke of Orleans from the Regency and King George from the English throne. Such danger lies in the power of one single man who is absolute, and has the sense and capacity to use his power.

Gortz, having made this beginning in the Courts of Russia and Spain, went secretly to France, and thence to Holland, where he interviewed representatives of the Pretender's party. He got special information concerning the strength, number, and position of the disaffected in England, what money they could raise, and what men they could put in the field. They only wanted 10,000 men, with which they would feel assured of success. Count Gyllemburg, the Swedish ambassador in England, acting under Gortz's instructions, had several meetings with the disaffected; he encouraged them and promised them all they wanted. The Pretender's party even advanced considerable sums, which Gortz received in Holland, and with which he bought ships and ammunition.

Then he secretly sent some officers to France, especially a certain Folard, who, having served in thirty French campaigns without mending his fortune, had volunteered with Charles, not with any ulterior motive, but just to serve under a prince with such a reputation. He especially hoped to get the Prince to adopt the new discoveries he had made in the art of war, which he had studied theoretically and had published views of in a commentary of Polybius. Charles was pleased with his ideas, and, as he was never governed by convention, he intended to make use of Folard in his attack on Scotland.

The main point for Baron de Gortz was to settle a peace between Charles and the Czar, in spite of the many difficulties in the way. Baron Osterman, a man of weight in Russia, was not so ready to agree with Gortz. He was as cautious as the other was enthusiastic. One was for letting things gradually ripen, the other wanted to reap and sow together. Osterman was afraid his master, pleased with the plan, would grant too advantageous terms with Sweden, and so delayed the conclusion of the matter. Luckily for Gortz the Czar himself came to Holland at the beginning of 1717 on the way to France, for he had yet to see this nation, criticized, envied, and imitated by all Europe. He wanted to satisfy his insatiable curiosity, but also he hoped to arrange some political matters.

Gortz had two talks with the Emperor at the Hague, and did more by their means than he could have done in six months with plenipotentiaries. Everything went well, his great plans seemed quite unsuspected, and he hoped they would only be known to Europe in their execution. The first who discovered these intrigues was the Duke of Orleans, Regent of France, who had spies everywhere. The Duke, having personal obligations to the King of

England, made the discovery of the whole plot against him. At the same time the Dutch, having suspicions of Gortz's behaviour, communicated them to the English ministry. Gortz and Gyllemburg were getting on with their schemes rapidly, when one was arrested at the Hague and the other in London.

As Gyllemburg had broken international law by the conspiracy they did not scruple in England to attack his person. But it was thought exceedingly strange that the States-General imprisoned Baron Gortz out of mere friendship for the King of England. They even went so far as to appoint Count Velderen to question him. This was going very far, and as it turned out, only added to their confusion. Gortz asked Velderen if he knew him. "Yes," said the Dutchman. "Well, then," he answered, "you must then be aware that I shall only answer what I like."

All the foreign ministers protested against the wrong done to the persons of Gortz and Gyllemburg. Nothing could excuse the Dutch from breaking so sacred a law in seizing the King of Sweden's premier, who had never done anything against them, and so violating the spirit of freedom which has attracted so many strangers and has been the cause of her greatness. The King of England acted within his rights in seizing an enemy, so that the letters found among Gyllemburg's papers from him to Gortz were printed to justify the King's proceedings.

The King of Sweden was in Scania when the printed letters came with the news of his ministers having been seized. He only smiled and asked if his letters were printed too, and ordered the English ambassador and all his family to be seized. But he could not take the same vengeance on the Dutch, because they had no minister then at the Court of Sweden. He kept a disdainful silence towards England and Holland.

The Czar's behaviour was just the opposite: as he was not named but only hinted at by distant references in the letters of Gortz and Gyllemburg, he wrote a long letter full of congratulations to the King of England on the discovery, with assurances of his good-will. King George received his protestations with incredulity, but pretended to believe them. A plot laid by private men is at an end when once discovered, but where kings are concerned a discovery only makes it go further. The Czar came to Paris in 1717, and did not spend all his time in viewing the wonders of art and nature there: the academies, public libraries, cabinets of the antiquaries and royal palaces. He made a proposal to the Regent which, had it been accepted, would have put the finishing touch to the greatness of Russia. It was this: to himself ally with the King of Sweden, who would yield many countries to him, to take from the Danes their power in the Baltic, to weaken England by a civil war, and to attract to Russia all the trade of the North. He had thoughts, too, of setting up Stanislas against King Augustus, so that when the fire was kindled in all directions he could fan the flame or damp it as he saw fit. With these views he proposed to the King's Regent to mediate between Sweden and Russia, and to make an offensive and defensive alliance with them and Spain. The treaty, though so natural and so useful to the nations concerned, putting into their hands the balancing of power in Europe, was yet rejected by Orleans, for he did just the opposite and made a league with the Emperor and the King of England.

Political motives were then so powerful with all princes that the Czar was going to declare war against his old friend Augustus, and to help Charles his mortal enemy; while France, for the sake of the English and Germans, was going to declare war against a grandson of Louis XIV, after having so long supported him at great expenditure of blood and treasure against those very enemies. All that the Czar could obtain was that the Regent should interpose for the freeing of Baron Gortz and Gyllemburg. He returned to Russia about the end of June, having shown a rare example of an emperor travelling to improve his mind. But what most of the French people saw of him was a rough, unpolished exterior, the result of his education, while they were blind to the legislator and the genius who had founded a new nation. What he had sought for in Orleans he soon found in Alberoni, who governed all Spain. Alberoni wanted to restore the Pretender: first as the minister of Spain, so ill-used by the English, and secondly because he had a personal quarrel with the Duke of Orleans for his close alliance with England against Spain; besides, he was a priest of that Church for which the Pretender's father had lost his crown.

The Duke of Ormond, as unpopular in England as the Duke of Marlborough was admired, had left the country at the time of George's accession, and was now in Spain. He went with full powers from the King of Spain to meet the Czar, in Courland, accompanied by a certain D'Irnegan, an Englishman of ability and daring. The business was to ask the Princess Anna, the Czar's daughter, for marriage with James's son, in the hopes that such an alliance would bring the Czar over to the King's side. Baron Gortz, among his other schemes, had intended this lady for the Duke of Holstein, who did marry her later. As soon as he heard of the Duke of Ormond's plan he grew jealous and did what he could to defeat it.

He left prison in August with the Count Gyllemburg, without any apology from the Swedish to the English King. At the same time the English ambassador and his family were released at Stockholm, where their treatment had been a great deal worse than Gyllemburg's in London.

Gortz at liberty was an implacable enemy, for besides his other aims he now sought vengeance. He went post-haste to the Czar, who was now better pleased with him than ever, for he undertook to remove in less than three months all obstacles to a peace with Sweden. He took up a map which the Czar had drawn himself, and, drawing a line from Wibourg, by Lake Ladoga, up to the frozen ocean, promised to bring his master to part with all that lay east of that line, besides Carelia, Ingria, and Livonia. Then he mentioned the marriage of the Czar's daughter to the Duke of Holstein, holding out hopes that the Duke would readily give his country instead, and if once he became a member of the Empire the Imperial crown would, of course, come to him or some of his descendants. The Czar named the isle of Aland for the conferences between Osterman and Gortz; he asked the English Duke of Ormond to withdraw lest the English Court should take alarm. But D'Irnegan, his confidant, remained in the town with many precautions, for he only went out at night and never saw the Czar's ministers but in the disguise of either a peasant or a Tartar.

As soon as the Duke of Ormond went, the Czar impressed upon the King his courtesy in having sent away the chief partisan of the Pretender, and Baron Gortz returned to Sweden with great hopes of success.

He found his master at the head of 30,000 troops with all the coast guarded by militia. The King needed nothing but money, but he had no credit at home or abroad. France, under the Duke of Orleans, would give him none. He was promised money from Spain, but that country was not yet in a position to support him.

Baron Gortz then tried a project he had tried before. He gave copper the same value as silver, so that a copper coin whose intrinsic value was a halfpenny might, with the royal mark, pass for thirty or forty pence, just as the governors of besieged towns have sometimes paid their soldiers with leather money till they could get better. Such expedients may be useful in a free country, and have often been the salvation of a republic, but they are sure to ruin a monarchy, for the people quickly lose confidence, the minister is unable to keep faith, the money paper increases, individuals bury their specie, and the whole plan fails, often with disastrous results. This was the case in Sweden. Baron Gortz had paid out his new coin with discretion, but was soon carried beyond what he had intended by forces he could not check. Everything became excessively dear, so that he was obliged to multiply his copper coin. The more there was of it the less was its value. Sweden was inundated with this false money, and one and all complained of Gortz. So great was the veneration of the people for Charles that they could not hate him, so the weight of their displeasure fell on the minister who, as a foreigner and financier, was sure to suffer their opprobrium.

A tax that he arranged on the clergy gave the final touch to the universal hatred; priests are only too ready to plead that their cause is God's, and publicly declared him an atheist, because he asked for their money. The new coins were embossed with the figure of heathen gods, and hence they called them the gods of Gortz.

The ministry joined in the universal hatred of him, all the more ardently because they were powerless. None in the country liked him except the King, whom his unpopularity confirmed in his affection. He placed absolute confidence in him, giving him also his entire confidence at home. He trusted to him, too, all negotiations with the Czar, especially as to the conference at Aland, which of all things he wished to urge on with the greatest haste.

As soon as Gortz had completed at Stockholm the arrangements for the treasury which demanded his presence, he went away to complete with Osterman the great work he had in hand. These were the preliminaries of that alliance which was to have changed the face of affairs in Europe, as they were found among Gortz's papers.

The Czar was to keep Livonia, part of Ingria, and Carelia, leaving the rest to Sweden. He was to join Charles in restoring Stanislas, and to send to Poland 80,000 men to dethrone the very king on whose side he had been fighting for so many years before; he was to supply ships to carry 30,000 to Germany and 10,000 to England; the forces of both were to attack the King of England's German dominions, especially Bremen and Verden; the same troops were to restore the Duke of Holstein and force the King of Prussia to an agreement by parting with a good deal of his new acquisitions.

Charles acted henceforth as if his own victorious troops had done all this, and demanded of the Emperor the execution of the peace of Altranstadt. But the Court of Vienna scarcely deigned an answer to one whom they feared so little. The King of Poland was not altogether so safe, but saw the storm coming. Fleming was the most suspicious man alive and the least reliable. He suspected the designs of the Czar and the King of Sweden in favour of Stanislas, so he endeavoured to have him taken off to Deux Ponts, as James Sobieski had been in Silesia. But Stanislas was on his guard, and the design miscarried.

In the meantime Charles was making a second attempt upon Norway in October 1718. He had so arranged matters that he hoped to be master of the country in six months.

The winter is fierce enough in Sweden to kill the animals that live there, but he chose to go and conquer rocks where the climate is more severe and the snow and ice much worse than in Sweden, instead of trying to regain his beautiful provinces in Germany.

He hoped his new alliance with the Czar would soon make it possible for him to retake them, and his ambition was gratified by the thought of taking a kingdom from his victorious foe.

At the mouth of the river Tistendall, near the bay of Denmark, between Bahus and Anslo, stands Fredericshall, a place of strength and importance, which is considered the key to the kingdom. Charles began its siege in December. The cold was so extreme that the soldiers could hardly break the ground. It was like digging trenches in rock, but the Swedes were nothing daunted by fatigue which the King shared so readily. Charles had never suffered so severely. His constitution was so hardened by sixteen years' hardship that he would sleep in the open in a Norwegian mid-winter on boards or straw, wrapped only in his mantle, and yet keep his health.

Some of the soldiers fell dead at their posts, but others who were nearly dying dare not complain when they saw their King bearing it all. Just before this expedition he heard of a woman who had lived for several months on nothing but water, and he who had tried all his life to bear the hardest extremes that nature can bear resolved to try how long he could fast. He neither ate nor drank for five days, and on the sixth, in the morning, he rode two leagues to his brother's, where he ate heartily, yet neither his large meal nor his long fast incommoded him.

With such a body of iron, and a soul of so much strength and courage, there was not one of his neighbours who did not fear him.

On the 11th of December, St. Andrew's day, he went to view his trenches at about nine in the evening, and finding the parallel not advanced as much as he wished, he was a little vexed at it. But M. Megret, the French engineer who was conducting the siege, told him the place would be taken in eight days' time. "We shall see," said the King, "what can be done." Then, going on with the engineer to examine the works, he stopped at the place where the branch made an angle with the parallel; kneeling upon the inner slope, he leaned with his elbows on the parapet, to look at the men who were carrying on the entrenching by starlight.

The least details relating to the death of such a man as Charles are noted. It is therefore my duty to say that all the conversation reported by various writers, as having taken place between the King and the engineer, are absolutely false. This is what I know actually happened.

The King stood with half his body exposed to a battery of cannon directed precisely at the angle where he stood. No one was near him but two Frenchmen: one was M. Siquier, his *aide-de-camp*, a man of capacity and energy, who had entered his service in Turkey, and was particularly attached to the Prince of Hesse; the other was the engineer. The cannon fired grapeshot, and the King was more exposed than any of them. Not far behind was Count Sveren, who was commanding the trenches. At this moment Siquier and Megret saw the King fall on the parapet, with a deep sigh; they came near, but he was already dead. A ball weighing half-a-pound had struck him on the right temple, leaving a hole large enough to turn three fingers in; his head had fallen over the parapet, his left eye was driven in and his right out of its socket; death had been instantaneous, but he had had strength to put his hand to his sword, and lay in that posture.

At this sight Megret, an extraordinary and feelingless man, said, "Let us go to supper. The play is done." Siquier hastened to tell the Count Sveren, and they all agreed to keep it a secret till the Prince of Hesse could be informed. They wrapped the corpse in a grey cloak, Siquier put on his hat and wig; he was carried under the name of Captain Carlsbern through the troops, who saw their dead King pass, little thinking who it was.

The Prince at once gave orders that no one should stir out of the camp, and that all the passes to Sweden should be guarded, till he could arrange for his wife to succeed to the crown, and exclude the Duke of Holstein, who might aim at it.

Thus fell Charles XII, King of Sweden, at the age of thirty-six and a half, having experienced the extremes of prosperity and of adversity, without being softened by the one or in the least disturbed by the other. All his actions, even those of his private life, are almost incredible. Perhaps he was the only man, and certainly he was the only king who never showed weakness; he carried all the heroic virtues to that excess at which they become faults as dangerous as the opposed virtues. His resolution, which became obstinacy, caused his misfortunes in Ukrania, and kept him five years in Turkey. His liberality degenerated into prodigality, and ruined Sweden. His courage, degenerating into rashness, was the cause of his death. His justice had been sometimes cruel, and in later years his maintenance of his prerogative came not far short of tyranny. His great qualities, any one of which would immortalize another prince, were a misfortune to his country. He never began a quarrel; but he was rather implacable than wise in his anger. He was the first whose ambition it was to be a conqueror, without wishing to increase his dominions. He desired to gain kingdoms with the object of giving them away. His passion for glory, war, and vengeance made him too little of a politician, without which none has ever been a conqueror. Before a battle he was full of confidence, very modest after a victory, and undaunted in defeat. Sparing others no more than himself, he made small account of his own and his subjects' labours; he was an extraordinary rather than a great man, and rather to be imitated than admired. But his life may be a lesson to kings and teach them that a peaceful and happy reign is more desirable than so much glory.

Charles XII was tall and well shaped. He had a fine forehead, large blue eyes, full of gentleness, and a well-shaped nose, but the lower part of his face was disagreeable and not improved by his laugh, which was unbecoming. He had little beard or hair, he spoke little, and often answered only by the smile which was habitual to him.

Profound silence was preserved at his table. With all his inflexibility he was timid and bashful; he would have been embarrassed by conversation, because, as he had given up his whole life to practical warfare, he knew nothing of the ways of society. Before his long leisure in Turkey he had never read anything but Cæsar's commentaries and the history of Alexander, but he had made some observations on war, and on his own campaigns from 1700-1709; he told this to the Chevalier Folard, and said that the MSS. had been lost at the unfortunate battle of Pultawa. As to religion, though a prince's sentiments ought not to influence other men, and though the opinion of a king so ill-informed as Charles should have no weight in such matters, yet men's curiosity on this point too must be satisfied.

I have it from the person who has supplied me with most of my material for this history, that Charles was a strict Lutheran till the year 1707, when he met the famous philosopher Leibniz, who was a great freethinker, and talked freely, and had already converted more than one prince to his views. I do not believe that Charles imbibed freethought in conversation with this philosopher, since they only had a quarter of an hour together; but M. Fabricius, who lived familiarly with him seven years afterwards, told me that in his leisure in Turkey, having come in contact with diverse forms of faith, he went further still.

I cannot help noticing here a slander that is often spread concerning the death of princes, by malicious or credulous folk, viz., that when princes die they are either poisoned or assassinated. The report spread in Germany that M. Siquier had killed the King; that brave officer was long annoyed at the report, and one day he said to me, "I might have killed a King of Sweden, but for this hero I had such a respect that, had I wished to do it, I should not have dared."

I know that it was this Siquier himself who originated this fatal accusation, which some Swedes still believe, for he told me that at Stockholm, when delirious, he shouted that he had killed the King of Sweden, that he had even in his madness opened the window and publicly asked pardon for the crime; when on his recovery he learned what he had said in delirium, he was ready to die with mortification. I did not wish to reveal this story during his life; I saw him shortly before his death, and I am convinced that, far from having murdered Charles, he would willingly have laid down his life for him a thousand times over. Had he been capable of such a crime it could only have been to serve some foreign Power who would no doubt have recompensed him handsomely, yet he died in poverty at Paris, and had even to apply to his family for aid.

As soon as he was dead the siege of Fredericshall was raised. The Swedes, to whom his glory had been a burden rather than a joy, made peace with their neighbours as fast as they could, and soon put an end to that absolute power of which Baron Gortz had wearied them. The States elected Charles's sister Queen, and forced her to solemnly renounce her hereditary right to the throne, so that she held it only by the people's choice. She promised by oath on oath that she would never secure arbitrary government, and afterwards, her love of power overcome by her love for her husband, she resigned the crown in his favour and persuaded the States to choose him, which they did under the same condition. Baron Gortz was seized after Charles's death, and condemned by the Senate of Stockholm to be beheaded under the gallows, an instance rather of revenge than of justice, and a cruel insult to the memory of a king whom Sweden still admires.

Charles's hat is preserved at Stockholm, and the smallness of the hole by which it is pierced is one of the reasons for supposing he was assassinated.